Lucien Pissarro.

Lucien Pissarro by Camille Pissarro, 1900

Lucien Pissarro

UN COEUR SIMPLE

by

W. S. MEADMORE

NEW YORK: ALFRED · A · KNOPF

1963

TO

MUCH BELOVED

OROVIDA

Contents

List of Illustrations

Acknowledgements

I CANNOT SUFFICIENTLY EXPRESS MY GRATITUDE TO THE MANY FRIENDS who have helped me during the writing of this book.

I am indebted chiefly to Orovida C. Pissarro who placed at my disposal the wealth of her family's records and for her encouragement. And I would like to express thanks to John Rewald for his continued interest, his prompt responses to requests for information, his knowledge of Camille Pissarro and his family, his kindness in reading the proofs and writing the introduction: to Clifford Hall who also read the proofs and, like John Rewald, made valuable and stimulating suggestions: to A. M. Hammacher, Director of the Rijksmuseum Kröller-Müller of Otterlo, for permission to quote the extracts from his biography *Jean François van Royen (1878–1942)*: to Hans Lammere for his translations from the Dutch of these extracts: to John Bensusan-Butt for his vivid memories of Lucien and Esther Pissarro, and for permission to use letters: to Alan Fern for allowing me to see his thesis (for the degree of Doctor of Philosophy, University of Chicago) *The Wood Engravings of Lucien Pissarro*: to Simone Butrym who gave great assistance in the translation from French to English of letters and documents: to Mary Manson for memories of her father, James Bolivar Manson: to Elizabeth Manson for her help: to Sir John Rothenstein for permission to quote his father's letter to Lucien Pissarro and to Rodo Pissarro's wife, Rodette.

I would also like to thank the *New Statesman* for allowing me to reproduce the letter on p. 214, the Manchester Art Gallery for permission to reproduce their portrait of Lucien Pissarro by J. B. Manson and the Ashmolean Museum the pastel drawing of Lucien by Camille Pissarro used on the jacket, and as a frontispiece.

W. S. M.

The Pissarro Family

JACOB, called Camille. *b.* 18th July, 1830. *d.* 13th November, 1903. *m.* JULIE VELLAY. *b.* 2nd October, 1838. *d.* 16th May, 1926.

Their Children

LUCIEN. *b.* 20th February, 1863. *d.* 10th July, 1944. *m.* Esther Bensusan.

JEANNE, called *Minette*. *b.* 1865. *d.* 6th April, 1874.

GEORGES HENRI. *b.* 22nd November, 1871. *d.* January, 1961. Signed his paintings *Manzana*.

FÉLIX CAMILLE. *b.* 24th July, 1874. *d.* in England 25th November, 1897. Signed his pictures *Jean Roch*.

LUDOVIC RUDOLPHE. *b.* 21st September, 1878. *d.* 18th October, 1952. Sometimes called *Piton-fleuri* by his father. Signed his pictures *Ludovic-Rodo*.

JEANNE. *b.* 27 August, 1881. Known as *Cocotte*. *m.* Henri Bonin.

PAUL EMILE. *b.* 22nd August, 1884. Nicknamed *Guingasse*. Signs his paintings *Paulémile*.

OROVIDA CAMILLE. Lucien's daughter. *b.* 8th October, 1893. Signs her paintings *Orovida*.

The Bensusans of this Biography

ESTHER. *b.* 12th November, 1870. *d.* 28th November, 1951. *m.* Lucien Pissarro 11th August, 1892.

JACOB SAMUEL LEVI. Esther's father. *b.* 31st May, 1846. *d.* 8th July, 1917. Feather Merchant.

SAMUEL. Esther's brother. *b.* 29th September, 1872. *d.* 11th December, 1958. Author of books and novels about Essex and Essex people.

RUTH. Esther's sister. *b.* 9th May, 1877. *d.* 18th September, 1957. One of the first English woman doctors.

JOHN BENSUSAN-BUTT. Ruth's son. *b.* 6th June, 1911. Painter.

OROVIDA. "Aunt Roarer". Jacob Bensusan's sister. *d.* 1912.

"It is not possible for me, my nature being what it is, to make anything unconscientiously. To do things fast to make money is, for me, simply impossible."

Ingres raconté par lui-même.
et par ses amis
Pierre Cailler

"The thing which impressed me was the immense respect with which John and Sickert, as well as the rest, always listened to anything Lucien Pissarro had to say about painting: I felt, and I believe they felt, that he was the master of us all, the man from whom we could all of us learn."

Since I was Twenty-Five by Frank Rutter

Introduction

Introduction by John Rewald

LUCIEN AND ESTHER PISSARRO WERE QUITE ADVANCED IN AGE WHEN I met them in the middle 'thirties, but the warmth, kindness, and generosity they showed me could not have been greater had I been their son or—more likely—their grandson. Lucien, who bore a startling resemblance to the many photographs I had seen of his father, was usually silent, a magnificent patriarch with dark, beautiful eyes, and a benevolent smile half-hidden beneath an imposing beard. Whereas he spoke little and did so softly, his wife's liveliness filled their charming house with ceaseless bustle. Although she could be extremely biased and her suspicions were easily aroused, Esther knew no half-measures once she had bestowed her sympathy upon a new acquaintance. When she took somebody into her heart that person practically "belonged" to her, and her boundless energy was spent on two goals: to make the friend happy, while at the same time running his life by any means (and even little tricks) she could think of. Yet to say that she was domineering would not do her justice, for she meant well in everything she did. Her tremendous reservoir of good will simply would not allow her to draw a line between affection and possessiveness. Whenever a reluctant victim of her enthusiastic altruism gave her to understand that she had gone too far, that the intrusiveness of her overbearing propensities could lead to serious embarrassment, she was genuinely crushed and apologetic. But this did not prevent her from committing a similar blunder or indiscretion on the next occasion. Her nature, her frankness, and her zeal were such that they suffered no restraint. (Was she ever capable of controlling her impulses?) No remonstrances, failures, or unpleasant experiences could induce her to mend her ways. Her vitality and confidence in the basic goodness of human beings knew no limits; thus she was unable to understand that her own motives could ever be questioned. And her motives were *always* excellent. If she was meddlesome, she was also self-sacrificing; if she was stubborn, she was also devoted. She considered the most absurd ideas and projects to be practical in a fascinating and quite incongruous fashion. Determined to have her own way, she ignored objections as well as obstacles, and let her emotions run away with her

3

quick reactions. She had no equal when it came to creating confusion, and she was so outspoken in her opinions (without even attempting to conceal her various little schemes) that many found it difficult to get on with her. But at the same time she never hesitated to give fully of herself, knew no bounds to her loyalty, and found in friendship a sacred means to assert her compassion. Her authoritarianism was alleviated by unreserved tenderness, a sentiment she often tried to hide as if she were ashamed of it, although it was this tenderness which made her so endearing.

And Lucien? He was aware of both her shortcomings and her tremendous qualities. In the pages that follow I have read for the first time, and with great emotion, many of Lucien's letters which show his deep love for his wife as well as his open criticism of her faults. He was shy and retiring. Left to his own ingenuity—of which he had so little—he may have found it difficult to fend for himself. He had been raised by a kind-hearted father whose philosophy it had been not to interfere with the open aspirations or secret inclinations of his children. Camille Pissarro had gently preserved him from the friction and fierce opposition of which life is so full. Whereas Lucien knew only too well what it meant to be poor, he had nevertheless been shielded from the harshness and bitterness of compulsion, debasement and meanness. However, he was also the son of a mother who did not always find it easy to get along with others, who was demanding, self-righteous, austere, and frequently rude in her directness. Despite this she never spared herself for the comfort of an impractical husband and a terribly exacting brood which constantly depended on her. In this simple and outspoken peasant woman who knew nothing about art and yet so touchingly loved his work, Camille Pissarro had found a companion full of energy who generously contributed her strength, willpower, and abnegation to maintaining a household where, more often than not, sorrowfree days and affluence were unknown. Her realism, her down-to-earthness had admirably counter-balanced the painter's mildness and idealism, yet it had also led her children to count on a mother who always—once she had scolded them—was ready to assist them to the best of her abilities.

When Lucien proposed to Esther he, in turn, selected a spouse who would run his house for him, would mother him, would work with him and for him. It was not Esther's fault that she was not as well versed in the handling of a housewife's daily chores as Lucien's mother. She had been brought up differently, had been steeped in the preju-

4

dices as well as the dreams with which a thoroughly middle-class British girl of her days envisioned the "nicer things" of life. And after she had become the wife of a dedicated though chronically impecunious artist, she somehow never managed to reconcile her prejudices and dreams with cruel reality. Thus she was incapable of separating the essential from the superfluous, the important from the trifling. But she did not make up for this by heroically "sticking it out" through difficult times and tragic hours? No appeal to her devotion was ever denied. This was the only way in which she knew how to prove her love, and she proved it unhesitatingly. Lucien found in her a companion on whom he could not only depend but who—with a fervour that was unequalled—believed in him and in his mission as an artist. That her accounts were hopelessly mixed-up, that she foolishly spent (or even lost) what little money there was, that she interfered in his affairs, was exasperating in her obstinacy and quarrelled with friends and relatives was not, after all, due to ill-will or selfish interests. If there ever was a woman who was "impossible" and lovable at the same time it was Esther Bensusan Pissarro.

One of her weaknesses, however, made life especially difficult for her and her little family: she had no sense of humour and no tolerance for the foibles of others. Just as she never forgot a good turn, she never forgave anything that displeased her. She had no patience with those who did not see eye to eye with her or who behaved otherwise than she expected (and her code of conduct was a very strict one). This attitude sooner or later alienated many of those who had been attracted by Lucien's gentleness and wisdom.

It seems almost an irony of fate that this opinionated woman should have married into a family where practically everybody except her father-in-law and her husband were just as opinionated as she was. That this should lead to bitter clashes was wellnigh unavoidable. Lucien's mother, already gruff by nature, found much to be desired in her British daughter-in-law and made no bones about this. Ludovic-Rodo, the brother closest to Lucien, had a good share of their mother's temper and was also openly critical of Esther, who used to accept his rebukes with a smile so helpless, so sad, and so pathetic that it always made me feel sorry for her.

Rodo, whom I met in Paris before I knew Lucien and Esther, once told me that the children of Camille and Julie Pissarro resembled, with a strange regularity, in turn their father or their mother, both physically and in character. Lucien, the eldest, was the image of his father, whereas Georges had many of his mother's traits (he was the black sheep of the family whose many unpleasant adventures inspired Esther with an intense aversion); Félix, the next son, who died young, once more resembled his father, and Rodo, the fourth, again inherited his mother's nature; gentle Jeanne was like Camille, while Paul-Emile, the last born, took after his mother. (Only the first little Jeanne, two years younger than Lucien, who died at the age of nine, seems to have escaped this seesaw of influences.)

Disillusioned with his artistic career and more realistic than the others, Rodo put aside his brushes to devote himself to the renown of his father, to the history of the family, and also to all practical matters pertaining to the administration of their complicated inheritance. Though Camille Pissarro's widow liked to rely on the advice and help of her eldest son—obviously her favourite—Lucien was mostly far away and, it must be admitted, was not too well versed in questions of finance, negotiations, etc. So it was that Rodo usually took over, levelheaded, efficient, wasting few words but always knowing what had to be done. When I met him and he took me into his confidence with the bluff cordiality, the scowling affection that were his wont, he was in his middle fifties and was putting the finishing touches to that splendid catalogue of his father's paintings which is an indispensable reference work as well as a monument of filial devotion. It may not be superfluous to say that this catalogue was really Rodo's doing; only after it was finished did he appeal to Lionello Venturi for the contribution of an introduction. While Venturi, who had far more experience in this field, may have revised certain entries, the initiative and the bulk of the achievement should be credited to Rodo alone.

I was then a young Sorbonne student who derived great inspiration from Rodo's integrity, his industry, and his dedication to his difficult task. He was too blunt and too anxious to repress all sentimentality ever to openly show his feelings, so that, unlike his brother Lucien, he did not treat me as a son. Nevertheless I may safely say that, despite the absence of a paternal attitude, I felt as close to him as to a beloved uncle who alternates criticism with occasional, half-grudging expressions of approval. I cannot describe the emotion with which I learned, upon his death in 1952, that he had bequeathed to me his early sketchbooks besides many documents concerning his father and all the material he had assembled for a supplementary volume of the catalogue of Camille Pissarro's work. This supplement is now scheduled to be published in the foreseeable future.

It was Rodo who encouraged me to visit his brother on one of my frequent trips to London. I must confess that I find it difficult to remember my impressions of that first call on the old couple in their beautiful house, "The Brook". It was almost like love at first sight; there was so much genuine cordiality and hospitality, and there were so many, many visits after the initial one that it now seems as though I had known Lucien and Esther all my life. The house, the studio, the garden, the dinners in which Orovida cheerfully joined became part of my world, and still are, because they were unforgettable.

If Esther was possessive in her affection, it seems only fair to add that I was perfectly willing to be possessed, that I was fascinated by Lucien, his wife, and their daughter, that I felt drawn to them and reciprocated their cordial feelings from the bottom of my heart. "The Brook" became my haven to such an extent that my long-suffering mother once complained that on my holidays in London I spent more time there than with my parents. Esther, needless to say, was eager to extend her affection to my mother, father, and brother, but since they did not share my passion for art I remained the principal beneficiary of her fondness.

At first, I was of course attracted to Lucien as a venerable relic of bygone days, probably the last intimate witness of the historic times of Impressionism. Not only was he the son, pupil, collaborator, and confidant of one of the greatest among the impressionists, he had also known many of his father's now famous friends and associates. As a child and later as a young man, he had watched Cézanne at work or discussing art concepts with Camille Pissarro. He was nearly twenty when Gauguin began to paint under his father's guidance and spent his vacations with the Pissarros at Pontoise and Osny. He was twenty-three when Vincent van Gogh arrived in Paris, met Pissarro and learned to value his advice. He had joined Seurat and Signac in their first exhibitions and had ventured with his father into the exacting theories of divisionism. He had been close to Monet and had met all the great and near-great of those glorious days. But soon I also began to appreciate Lucien for the wonderful person he was, the kind and modest artist who had gone his own way according to the dictates of his conscience and his exquisite sensibility. How many hours did we not spend looking through portfolios of innumerable drawings and prints by both the father and the son! How we enjoyed contemplating together the paintings of Camille and of Lucien! And how careful I had to be not to express too much enthusiasm, for as often as not such delightful sessions ended in Lucien and Esther presenting me with a sketch or a proof that had particularly aroused my admiration.

Our splendid relationship became even more intimate when Lucien showed me the several hundred letters he had received from his father. Without further ado, he was willing to entrust them to me for the purpose of publishing essential excerpts. I do not remember what gave me a greater thrill, this touching proof of confidence or the prospect of editing such important documents. However, I was reluctant to take these letters in small packages with me to France, so that we finally agreed to have them copied in England, my work to be done subsequently on the basis of these transcripts. It was a slow process, yet the final version was well under way when the war broke out and put a temporary stop to the project. Only after unpleasant vicissitudes and after having found refuge in the United States was I able to take up once more the editorial task which was so close to my heart. While precariously earning a living in a foreign country, I worked after hours and deep into the night, for Lucien was getting on in years and I wanted so much for him to see this volume before it was too late. He found it increasingly difficult to answer my many queries concerning specific events mentioned by his father, yet there was a steady flow of letters to and fro while the work was in progress.

In homage to Lucien and Esther I must mention that they in no way interfered with the selections I made from Camille Pissarro's letters and imposed no restrictions on me, with one exception: all references to Georges, who had given his father a great deal of trouble and about whose conduct the old man repeatedly complained, were deleted for the good reason that Georges was still alive. But I was permitted to publish the highly instructive criticisms which Camille Pissarro had expressed about some of Lucien's wood engravings, as well as passages in which he gently mocked Esther's chronic absentmindedness. When at last the time came to draw up a contract, I thought that some credit should be given to Lucien's generosity in letting me publish these documents and suggested that they appear as "Edited with the assistance of Lucien Pissarro by John Rewald." A contract so worded was mailed to Lucien and was duly signed by him.* The volume appeared

* If I insist on this minor question, it is because the compiler of the Catalogue of the Courtauld Collection, whose first distortion this is not, has seen fit to refer to this publication (in *two* instances in the bibliography on p. 80) as "Edited by Lucien Pissarro with the assistance of John Rewald." It does seem a pity when a scholar permits what appears to be perverse pettiness, spite, and jealousy to obstruct his objectivity.

in 1943 and was immediately dispatched to London (where a separate edition was shortly to be issued). Lucien received the parcel in the very weeks in which the Allied invasion forces were slowly liberating his fatherland. He cabled me: "Book received safely all delighted writing air congratulations would like fiftten copies."

If Lucien had been too old and too weakened by the difficult war years to help extensively, Rodo, with a mind trained for research, might have been of invaluable assistance in compiling explanatory footnotes to his father's letters to Lucien. He had done so for a first batch, but the occupation of France of course prevented any further contact with him. After the war, however, and after the death of Lucien, he gave me the benefit of his great knowledge. The French edition of the letters, which subsequently appeared in Paris, thus features much additional information, part of which was also gathered from newspapers and periodicals which had not been available in New York. Moreover, Esther had meanwhile found among Lucien's papers a number of her husband's letters to his father, copies of which she sent me. Her only recommendation was once more: "In selecting passages from Lucien's letters, please avoid anything that may hurt people." With her permission, essential excerpts from these letters first appeared in the *Burlington Magazine* under the title: "Lucien Pissarro: Letters from London, 1883–1891" and were later incorporated with others in the French edition, published in 1950, two years before Rodo's death.

But besides the work which brought us close together, there were countless instances of happy meetings which crowd my memory: excursions with Rodo, visits from Lucien and Esther in Paris where they always stopped on their way to southern France, calls on "The Brook" after the war, when Esther lived there alone, pleasant afternoons and exquisite dinners in Orovida's lovely flat. And there are, of course, many anecdotes which I could add to those amusing, touching, or painful ones so abundantly related in this biography. A few have remained particularly vivid in my mind, such as Esther and Lucien's arrival in Paris with a generous dozen of the most impossible and cumbersome pieces of luggage, and Esther's indignant quarrel with a customs official who considered dutiable a small paraffin burner which she had owned for some twenty years but which had been polished so thoroughly that it looked like new (she could scrub hard and with determination despite her mother-in-law's deprecatory remarks on her talents). Or that evening at the hotel when Esther was going feverishly through one parcel, trunk, basket, and box after another in search of some inner-soles for Luciens tired feet. Finally a triumphant cry:

"There is one at last!"

"What do you mean by *one*?" I asked incredulously, whereupon she matter-of-factly explained that she would have to go through more parcels, trunks, baskets, and boxes, because she had not packed the two together.

If such incidents make her appear ridiculous, and there is no denying that she was impractical, eccentric, obstinate, fussy, confused, and impatient, she was also her own and most persistent victim. Devoted to Lucien, she may have made life difficult for him on many occasions, yet more often still she made it difficult for herself. Nevertheless, I do not remember her ever complaining (exhausted though she was herself from the journey, she bravely went on looking for that second—and more elusive—inner sole). She was as cheerful as she was disorganized and always stoically bore the consequences of her blunders. She was a warm, human being with more faults—possibly—than others, but also with more fine qualities.

I am happy that Lucien's and Esther's memory should live now in these pages. Those who have not had the good fortune of knowing them will find here a lively story about two extraordinary people, but the few who came close to them will mourn with me the marvellous friends whose disappearance left a sad and ever-present gap.

JOHN REWALD

Foreword

Foreword by the Author

DURING HIS FREQUENT VISITS TO PARIS LUCIEN PISSARRO WAS OFTEN AT HIS brother Rodo's studio in Montmartre. On one occasion Rodo asked him to help collate their father's letters, but in a long afternoon all Lucien was able to accomplish was to sort the contents of one small box. He told Rodo he had not the heart to go on. It was impossible to get the letters into any order; there were too many; the task was beyond him. And so it must have seemed to him when faced with the piled boxes and the taped bundles of correspondence which Camille Pissarro had received from his family and his artist and writer friends. Much of this collection came into Lucien's possession. He and Esther, his wife, added to it considerably. The Pissarros could not bring themselves to destroy correspondence, no matter how trifling. Esther was the same with one exception: she destroyed all her "nasty" letters to Lucien. (Lucien's replies make their contents apparent.) Otherwise she hoarded everything. The result was a mixed bag indeed, a vast accumulation of such ephemera as coloured postcards from friends on holiday, laconic messages of invitation to tea, sympathetic notes ("glad your cold is better"), bills, builders' estimates, gallery accounts, receipts, legal documents, bank statements, greeting cards, and so on. All these were mixed higgledy-piggledy with a leaven of letters of the greatest interest, such as, for example, the letters exchanged between Camille and Lucien, which John Rewald edited and published.

Here also are filed the letters to Lucien from his mother, whose ill-formed handwriting grew twisted and distorted as she aged, illiterate, but vivid in expression, letters in which she revealed her vexations and sorrows. Her version of the family history was balanced by letters from Lucien's other brothers, Georges, Paul Emile, and his sister Jeanne. The tale was taken up when Lucien's own daughter, Orovida, came to womanhood and wrote of her struggles to paint and of her successes. Here, instead of the flow of advice from Camille to Lucien, is Lucien's advice to Orovida. Rodo, Lucien's favourite brother, described as "the historian of the family", wrote frequently and

13

copiously, his themes invariably the catalogue of his father's pictures, which occupied him for many years, and a proposed biography of Camille. Scattered over the years are letters from J. B. Manson, which record an enduring friendship. These letters tell of Manson's persistent efforts to sell Lucien's pictures and reflect his own difficulties, their expression so buoyant in the early years, so sad at the last. There are also letters from other friends—Verhaeren the poet, Fénéon, *homme de lettres* and *critique d'art*, the painters, Ricketts and Shannon, van Rysselberghe, Signac, Hayet, Luce, the writer Lecomte, Van Royen, the amateur printer of fine books, and many others. Monet, the great friend of the family, wrote in his crabbed, upright, almost undecipherable calligraphy, until he could no longer see to write, and his stepdaughter, Blanche Hoschedé (his son's widow), wrote for him. Ethel Voynich, the musician, author of the "The Gadfly", wrote often and frequently. And Esther's friend, Diana White, wrote persistently year after year her closely written pages and pages of her views on art, gardening, books, the state of the world and of Esther's health and her own. Esther's nephew, John Bensusan-Butt, wrote to Esther in 1943: "Diana White continues to be my most voluminous correspondent. We have been arguing for months as to whether there was more taste in the Victorian era than there is now."

There it was, this vast miscellany, heaped on the shelves of the old presses. Spasmodic attempts were made to go through the letters and sort them. Rodo was all for drastic action, destruction of what he called the rubbish. He and Esther decided to see what could be done. Nothing was done. They disagreed at once. A bundle of drawings were pulled out. "This is a bad one," said Esther. "Tear it up." "No," said Rodo. "It's a Cézanne." "Well, I think it's a bad drawing," and Esther made a motion to destroy it. Rodo restrained her. Later, at a time of one of many crises in Lucien's and Esther's lives, it was sold to the Leicester Galleries for £200.

It was these letters, together with the patient help and memories of Lucien's daughter, Orovida, of his nephew John Bensusan-Butt, of John Rewald, and of Elizabeth Manson, which made this biography possible. Many of the letters were written in French, as Lucien did not write in English until he was over thirty. All his father's and mother's letters are in French, as are those of Lucien's numerous French friends and correspondents. These have been translated, the spirit of the originals being kept as far as the two languages will allow.

The Pissarros were good letter-writers, they expressed themselves well, and in their letters they live again. As one reads through them, time is abolished. One is with Camille in Eragny or with Lucien in London, and one is able to follow the fortunes not only of Lucien and Esther but of all the family. While the central character in this biography is Lucien, for many years the presence of his indomitable father and of his formidable mother, and to a lesser degree the other members of this brilliant family, was never far in the background.

Lucien loved his father deeply and held him in veneration. His praise he valued above all others. Lucien was too shy and modest ever to believe his work was really good. And throughout his life he was in doubt as to whether he could really paint or not. Early in his career shallow-minded critics considered that his painting resembled Camille's, and he suffered from being the son of a famous father. Actually his work grew less and less comparable to his father's. In Lucien's painting, as distinct from his small, rapid sketches, there is little of the immediate reaction to the *motif*, the snapshot effect characteristic of true impressionist painting—its greatest charm but in the last analysis its greatest weakness. In Lucien's finished, considered, pictures, there is an abundant evidence of a slow, absorbed search to express the structure of a landscape and the forms which are a part of it, a striving for an architectural quality. This intense interest in structure, allied to the impressionists' concern with the passing effect, was the form which his reaction to landscape took. The fact that he used the impressionist division of tones does not fundamentally affect his sense of structure, but only his colour sense. There can be no doubt that this vision was influenced by the years he spent making the engraved illustrations for his books, and learning (and how thoroughly) the craft of printing and designing his own type faces. Thus the emphasis on design and structure associates him more distinctly with the men who came after impressionism.

Lucien, in everyday life, had an extraordinary simplicity. He was quite without conceit, never sure of himself, somewhat of a pessimist, greatly worried about money, a family man devoted to his wife and daughter. He evokes no image of a Gulley Jimson or the artist of popular imagination. Apart, perhaps, from his hat and cape, he did not dress the part, and he was amused when the editor of an evening newspaper asked him to write an article: "Every Man should look his Job."

His constant preoccupation was to put on canvas his conceptions of beauty and perfection. No painter has depicted more poetically and charmingly the English and French landscape. The reader of this biography should not let the everyday Lucien and his family life intrude unduly on Lucien the artist. The real Lucien is revealed by his pictures.

Many years after his death I visited Hewood, the small village where, clouded by age and war, he spent his last years, and I spoke to old Perrott, the local haulage contractor, who had helped Lucien's wife Esther out of difficulties when, as so often happened, her car broke down. He retained a vivid recollection of Lucien, and had often stood and watched him painting. As he took an offered cigarette, he reflected: "He was a great smoker." He struck a match and added: "An' a wunnerful painter."

Lucien Pissarro.

La Ronde

CHAPTER I

Camille. *1830—1878*

RODO, CAMILLE PISSARRO'S FOURTH SON, ESTABLISHED AFTER MANY YEARS of research a remarkable genealogical chart in which he traced the family tree to ancestors living in Portugal in 1770. He also discovered that the Pissarros were already in that country in the terrible year of 1495, a year of widespread persecution of the Jews, when the Pissarros became of necessity *maranos*, Jews whose existence depended on lip service to Rome, and who rose high in the service of the state, or were successful as merchants. But when in 1769 an attempt was made on the life of the powerful Marquis de Pombal, suspicion fell on the *maranos*. Many were tortured and burnt, and the rest went in fear. Pierre Pissarro of Bragança took to flight and, with his wife and family, settled in Bordeaux. In 1771 his son, John Gabriel, married Rika Rodrigues-Alvares, a Jewish girl whose family had also fled to France from Gibraltar. Their son, Joseph Pissarro, married in 1799 Anne Félicité Petit and a few years later went to St. Thomas, accompanied by his family and his wife's brother, Isaac Petit. Joseph's son Frédéric born in Bordeaux in 1802 was taken by his parents to St. Thomas, a small, rocky island near Puerto Rico in the Danish Antilles, and prospered as a dealer in marine stores. In 1826 he married his aunt by marriage, Rachel Petit, *née* Rachel Pommié (she was called Manzana*), the widowed second wife of his maternal uncle. The youngest of their four sons, Jacob, known as Camille, was born at St. Thomas in 1830. He was to be the first of three generations of painters; himself, his five sons, Lucien, Georges Henri, Felix, Ludovic Rodolphe, and Paul Emile, and Lucien's daughter, Orovida.

There was a great influence of French tradition in the family, and in 1842, at the age of twelve, Camille was sent to France to be educated at M. Savary's school at Passy, Frédéric having already warned M. Savary in a letter that Camille had an inordinate impulse to draw. Camille returned to St. Thomas in 1847 and became a clerk in the family business. But he had neither aptitude nor inclination for clerking; his

* Georges, Camille's second son, used this name with which to sign his pictures.

mind saw only *motifs* for pictures. Frédéric noticed uneasily the errors and omissions in Camille's work. One of Camille's duties was to wait on ships docking in the harbour and tally cargoes as they were unloaded. He was not interested. Pulling out of his pocket the sketch-book he always kept there, he used to pass the hours in making drawings of the ships and the harbour. One morning a young man stood by his side and watched him as he made a sketch of dock labourers loading a boat. He confided that he also was an artist, that his name was Fritz Melbye, and that he was on his way from Copenhagen to Venezuela to fulfil a commission from the Danish Government to make drawings of the local flora. As Camille turned the pages of his sketch-book, Melbye was full of admiration, and suddenly made the suggestion that Camille should go with him to Venezuela and assist him. Camille made an instant decision. That night he slipped out of the house, leaving behind a note of explanation. Friendly letters passed between father and son, and Frédéric now realised it was useless to oppose his son's obstinate determination to become a painter. He agreed that he should go to Paris to study, making the one stipulation that this should be in one of the academic *ateliers*. Camille returned to Paris in 1855, the year of the *Exposition Universelle*.

Camille frequently visited the *Exposition*, and the five hundred paintings, frame touching frame, which covered the walls of the rooms dedicated to art, bewildered him. Repeatedly he returned to look at the Corots, six early works painted before the importunity of the dealers had turned Corot to his "silver" period. Camille knocked at his studio door. He was received with kindness, and Camille said he wished to become his pupil. Corot said no, he did not take pupils, but he would willingly help Camille with advice. And so he became a frequent visitor, Corot sparing him many fumblings and false starts. He was set to work finishing the skies of some of his landscapes. Years later, Camille, walking with his son Lucien in Paris, stopped in front of a shop window to look at a picture signed "Corot". Lucien exclaimed: "It is beautiful!" "Yes," said Camille, "I painted it!"*

On the quai des Orfèvres stood an ancient, sordid, smoke-begrimed building, with a poster at its entrance advertising the name of a dentist who extracted teeth at a franc apiece. Here also was the *Académie Suisse*, recently opened by a model, where students drew from the life

---

* Of the three thousand pictures which Corot painted, it is said five thousand are now in America.

I. Julie and Camille Pissarro, 1877

Group at Pontoise, 1877

Left to right: Martiné's (the photographer), Alphonso (medical student and amateur painter), Cézanne *seated*, Lucien, Aguiar (another student), Camille

for a small fee. Occasionally Camille appeared in the crowded room in search of companions, and here he first met Cézanne and Monet, both destined to be life-long friends. He often went with Monet to paint landscapes at Champigny-sur-Marne. Meanwhile, leaving the business at St. Thomas in the care of a manager, Camille's father and mother came to live in Paris, Rachel bringing with her a devoted housekeeper, a freed black slave.

A young woman, Julie Vellay, was engaged as a servant. She came from Burgundy, where her father, a *manouvrier*, was reputed to be a rough customer and a hard drinker. Julie had been born at Grancey-sur-Ource (Côte d'Or) in 1838 and so was now twenty-two. When Monet was called up for his military service and sent to serve in the Chasseurs d'Afrique in Algeria, Camille returned to Paris to his parents' house. Attracted by this magnificent looking girl, so handsome with her fair hair and sparkling eyes, he soon had to confess that he was responsible for her expected child. He wished to marry her, but his parents refused their consent. And as Camille was under the age of thirty, this refusal had the sanction of French law.

Notwithstanding his father's threat that he would not allow him a sou, Camille left home and set up a *ménage* with Julie. His sales were few, and he could hardly have existed without the small sums of money which, from time to time, his mother sent him. So, when the pregnancy ended with a miscarriage, Julie, to augment their precarious resources, found employment at a florist's. She had natural taste, and her arrangements of bouquets were greatly admired. In 1862 she again became pregnant and Lucien, her first child, was born on the 20th February, 1863. Soon after, the little family went to live at Varenne-Saint-Hilaire, and here a second child, Jeanne (Camille affectionately called her Minette), was born in 1865. In the following year a further move was made to Pontoise, and in 1869 to Louveciennes.

These were years of grinding poverty, Julie keeping house on a sum rarely exceeding twenty francs (barely seventeen shillings) a week. Shrewd, rough-tempered, a bully, and described as a tartar, she nevertheless bore the weight of her family with courage. She never spared herself, and only through the most careful housekeeping was she able to provide for the family on her pitiful allowance. She grumbled at Camille and his infernal painting which brought no money. And yet all the same, he could not have had a more thrifty or better wife: this staunch, self-sacrificing woman was the helpmate he needed. Except for rabbits and an occasional chicken, the family existed on vegetables.

If there were none, Julie used to pick potatoes in the fields, and, her wages being in kind, she used to trudge home in the evening with a sack of potatoes slung over a shoulder. She loved flowers. In her garden they grew in profusion, among them her great pride, pink peonies. Often she arranged a bunch of her flowers as *motifs* for Camille's still-life pictures. Any tale of want softened her heart, and if a beggar came to the door she would cut him a thick sandwich. Money she never gave: she had none to give. Indeed, in 1868, funds were so low that Camille worked with Guillaumin painting window-blinds. The pay was poor, but the few francs enabled Camille and Julie to survive. Guillaumin recorded on a canvas these days in his picture: "Pissarro Painting Blinds." Meanwhile Camille got to know Père Martin, a chorus singer of the Opera turned art dealer. Martin bought a few pictures from him, payment being by size, twenty francs for a small canvas, forty for a large. Execrable payment, but Camille could not argue with an empty stomach. Before long Camille had to resign himself to prices even more heartbreaking.

The year of Lucien's birth was the year of the *Salon des Refusés*. Here, Camille showed the three landscapes he had submitted to the *Salon*. Camille's landscapes escaped laughter; indeed they were favourably noticed, but he was admonished not to copy Corot. Excited and stimulated by what he had seen on the walls of the *Salon des Refusés*, Camille's painting now became imbued with human warmth and tenderness. At Pontoise he found congenial *motifs* in the play of light on the leaves in the orchards, the houses built of soft stone and grimed with smoke, the peasant women in their cotton gowns, the old wooden palings of gardens, and the fluttering and drying washing pegged to lines. This development of his talent became more noticeable in 1866, Corot's influence disappearing as one picture succeeded another. There was more self-reliance in his work, colours were laid on freely, and quiet tones disappeared from his palette giving place to a gamut of pure colours, yellows, viridian, lakes, vermilions. "The air blows more freely through his canvases," wrote a contemporary reviewer. A new vision was coming into painting, not only manifest in Pissarro, but also in the paintings of Sisley, Renoir and Monet, an impulse towards more sensitivity, for more colour, air and light.

In 1866, Manet held court in the *Café Guerbois*, where he met his friends, particularly on Friday evenings. When he could afford a glass of wine Camille used to come here and meet, besides Manet, Cézanne, Monet, Astruc, Zola, Duranty, Bazille, and many other painters and *littérateurs*. Occasionally Nadar and Guys appeared and sat at his table.

Camille had now reached the age of thirty-six. His looks were impressive, suggesting wisdom and tolerance. His dark hair was abundant, his eyes sad, his finely shaped aquiline nose prominent. Fierce arguments used to arise. Camille's calm temperament, which could yet be so belligerent, his unquestioned integrity and persistent adherence to his artistic aims, in which he was devoid of compromise and reckless of sacrifice, inspired a respectful hearing. More of an anarchist than a socialist, he was a convinced atheist. Lacking that showmanship which seemed essential for success, he disdained publicity and despised official recognition. He was never to accept the red ribbon. When told that someone had received a medal or that another was selling well, he would answer: "*Il n'y a que la peinture qui compte.*"

By 1869 Camille had moved to Louveciennes where his eldest son Lucien, was already making pencil drawings. Unexpected but temporary alleviation of poverty came. The banker, Arosa, shown some paintings by Camille, became his patron and bought a few pictures at moderate prices. A year later came the catastrophe of the war with Germany. Totally unprepared, inferior in strength and strategy, demoralised by lack of supplies and the incompetence of its leaders, the French army met with defeat after defeat. Camille's house at Louveciennes became exposed to the fire of enemy guns mounted in the fort Mont Valérien. Uneasy for the safety of his family, Camille fled with them across country, finding refuge at the farm of his friend Piette at Montfoucault in Brittany. In September, Sedan fell, the Emperor surrendered, and the Third Republic was proclaimed. At Le Hâvre, refugees jostled for a place on the boats going to England. Monet was there with Camille Doncieux, whom he had recently married after they had lived together for four years. Pissarro, apprehensive at the news from Paris and the rumours of the Commune, and possibly fearing his known anarchist sympathies would implicate him in trouble, also crossed the Channel. He found lodging for himself and his family at Chatham Terrace, Upper Norwood. The seven-year-old Lucien was shocked at the child crossing-sweepers and the ragged urchins running about barefoot in the snow and slush. They mocked the sabots he wore, shouting: "Look! Wooden shoes! Wooden shoes!" Camille painted at Norwood and in the streets around the Crystal Palace at Sydenham. An effect of snow of this time was considered by Sickert to be one of his masterpieces. The family lived sparsely; there was little money, and every ha'penny had to be counted. By chance Camille encountered Daubigny. Daubigny was flourishing, his pictures of the Thames finding a ready sale. Dismayed at Camille's lack of luck, he introduced him to the dealer Durand-Ruel who, the previous year, had opened an art gallery in the rue Laffitte and now had a branch in Bond Street. He was to become deeply involved in the future fortunes and misfortunes of Camille, and indeed of all the impressionists. Durand-Ruel bought two pictures from Camille for four hundred francs (£16). It was a happy beginning to a long association which was not always to be so happy. A few days later Durand-Ruel wrote: "Your friend Monet asked me for your address." Having found each other they became inseparable, going together to the museums and the National Gallery where they were impressed by the Turners and the Constables. They submitted to the Royal Academy, but their pictures were rejected. Camille, in after years, said: "Monet and I were very enthusiastic over the London landscapes. Monet worked in the parks, whilst I, living at Norwood, at that time a charming suburb, studied the effects of fog, snow and springtime. We worked from nature."[*] Perhaps it was the example of Monet and Camille Doncieux which now induced Camille to marry Julie Vellay, which he did at the Croydon Registry Office.

Béliard wrote to him on the 22nd February, 1871: "I have no news of your house at Louveciennes! Your blankets, suits, shoes, underclothes, you may go into mourning for—believe me—and your sketches, since they are generally admired, I like to think will be ornaments in Prussian drawing-rooms. The nearness of the forest will no doubt have saved your furniture." In March the owner of his house had written that he had been able "to well preserve some of the pictures" including those of Monet left with Camille for safe-keeping, but others had been spread as mats in the garden "by these Prussian gentlemen afraid to dirty their feet".

Monet left London for Holland, and Camille, deprived of his companionship, became nostalgic for France. To the critic Théodore Duret he wrote in June: "I am only here for a short time. My intention is to return to France as soon as possible. Yes, my dear Duret, I shall not stay here, and it is only when you are abroad that you realise how beautiful, great and hospitable is France. What a difference is here. You only get disdain, indifference and even rudeness; among one's

[*] Pissarro to Dewhurst, November, 1902. See W. Dewhurst, *Impressionist Painting, London–New York*, 1904, pp. 31–2.

confrères jealousy and the most selfish mistrust. Here there is no such thing as art; everything is treated as a matter of business. My painting does not catch on, not in the least, a fate that pursues me more or less everywhere. . . . Perhaps in a little while I'll be at Louveciennes. I've lost everything there. About forty pictures are left to me out of fifteen hundred."

The Prussians had used his studio as a slaughter-house, throwing his pictures into the yard outside to serve as duckboards to the well, others had been rolled to serve as butcher's aprons. One of the pictures never seen again was a large canvas of a family group; Lucien remembered it well and the discomfort he experienced when he posed for it as a child.

Sharply estranged from the life around her by her ignorance of English, which she made no attempt to overcome ("this succession of curious noises could not be a language"), Julie shared even more intensely Camille's longing for France. When news came that the Commune had been crushed and that the street fighting in Paris was at an end, the family returned to Louveciennes. Except for a cupboard, not discovered because it was hidden by wallpaper, which contained blankets and bedding, Camille and Julie found their house stripped and bare—a sad homecoming. The small middle-class suburb and the neighbouring Forest of Marly now no longer had appeal, and in 1872 a move was made to 26 rue de l'Hermitage, Pontoise, where Camille, as in 1868–1869, found *motifs* to his liking in the surrounding countryside of rivers and hills, and he remained at Pontoise for the next ten years. A second son, Georges, had been born before the family left Louveciennes. At Pontoise, Félix was born in 1874; in this same year the first Jeanne died of laryngitis at the age of nine.

At Pontoise, Camille was joined by Béliard and Guillaumin, who painted during the day and dug ditches at night to support his grandparents. "What courage!" Camille commented. Cézanne, with Hortense Fiquet, the young model who shared his life, also came to Pontoise, and he and Camille worked side by side. Camille was convinced that Cézanne had outstanding talent, but Manet and others did not think so. At this time, 1874, Lucien was ten. Many years later, his brother Paul asked him for his boyish impressions of Cézanne. Lucien replied that despite the exaggerations with which time tinged memory, and the play of childish imagination, Cézanne appeared to him quite clearly. "His portrait painted by father resembles him. He wore a cap, his long, black hair was beginning to recede from a high forehead, he had large, black eyes which rolled in their orbits when he was excited.

He walked with a stick, steel-pointed at the ferrule, which frightened the peasants. In Pontoise, one market day, some young conscripts were marching and singing through the groups of country people and townsmen in the square. Cézanne was standing on a corner, leaning on his stick, his eyes screwed up and half closed as if he was taking in the pictorial value of the scene. He must have presented a strange appearance since a gendarme walked over to him and demanded his papers. 'Have you your papers?' 'No.' 'Where do you live?' 'Auvers.' 'I don't know you.' Cézanne drawled out: 'I regret it.' The gendarme walked away, pulling a face. Of course, one must imagine, as part of the scene, the soft accent of Cézanne, so refined in contrast with his rough exterior. I think father's portrait of him was painted about 1874.* This must be right because on the studio wall at that time was the caricature of André Gill depicting France as a woman in bed, and M. Thiers, as a doctor, holding in his arms a newly born baby, that is to say the millions of francs of indemnity to be paid to Germany, and this caricature appears on the wall in the background of the Cézanne portrait. Cézanne lived in Auvers and he used to walk three kilometres to come and work with father. They discussed theories endlessly, and one day bought palette knives to paint with. Several pictures remain of the work they did at this time. They are very similar in treatment, and the *motifs* are often the same. One morning, father was painting in a field, and Cézanne was sitting on the grass watching him. A peasant came along and said to father: 'Your workman does not overtax himself!'"

When one day some amateurs came to dinner, Camille hoped they would buy pictures. Julie prepared an excellent meal and put on her best silk dress. The amateurs must be impressed. The meal had just begun when Cézanne appeared, as shabby as ever. He was, of course, asked to sit at the table. Julie was aping the perfect hostess, very lady-like and polite, and this acted as a spark to Cézanne's malicious humour. He began to scratch himself vigorously. "Don't take any notice, Madame Pissarro," he said. "It's only a flea."

Lucien concluded his letter: "They did not paint with the palette knife for long; they turned to divisionism. It is now that Cézanne began to paint with vertical divisions, and father with long brushes, putting on the canvas strokes that looked like tiny commas. To say who influenced the other is impossible. All I can say is that Cézanne

---

* It was. It is listed as number 293 in the catalogue of Camille's paintings made by Ludovic Rodo Pissarro, published in Paris, 1939.

borrowed one of father's pictures in 1870 to make a copy, probably to study the way it was painted. Cézanne's copy still exists: it is, I believe, in the collection of Dr. Gachet. It is good to say this because one day it might be said that father copied Cézanne. An amateur painter of Pontoise often came to see them and there was much talk. I remember some words which I overheard which have much meaning today: 'The form is of no importance. It is the harmony.'"

But the harmony which comes when there is sufficient money to pay the bills remained absent from Camille's household. The terrible anxieties of poverty continued, but there was fleeting alleviation in 1873 when at an auction at the *Hôtel Drouot* some of his paintings realised comparatively high prices, selling for as much as nine hundred and fifty francs (£38), and this money relieved the pressure of debts.

Cézanne stayed with Camille's friend Dr. Gachet at Auvers, Gachet having recently acquired a charming house on a hillside overlooking the Oise valley. He went to Paris two or three days in the week where he had a homeopathic practice, and he was an enthusiastic painter and later exhibited with the *Indépendants*. Camille, a fanatical believer in the virtues of homeopathy, had first met him in Gautier's* studio in the rue de Seine. Gachet was already attending Camille's mother, Rachel, and later, he looked after Camille's children, these visits beginning in 1871 when Georges, a few weeks old, was ill with convulsions. Camille, worried, asked Gachet to come and see the baby. Gachet discovered a poisoning caused by the rubber teat of the bottle. The teat was changed and the convulsions ceased "Would you be so kind," wrote Camille in a letter to Gachet, "as to render me a service if it is at all possible, and go and see a sick child in Pontoise. They are not rich people but very interesting. I offer you a little sketch for your trouble. These people have confidence in homeopathy. Here is the address: M. Henot, lamplighter at the Pontoise station."†

Despite the slump following his sales at the *Hôtel Drouot*, his inability to find purchasers of his pictures, the strain of supporting his family, and the poverty from which he was never free, Camille remained staunch in his adherence to the cause of impressionism, and faithful to his friends. He stood by Degas: "He's a terrible man, but

---

* Désirè-Amand Gautier, painter and engraver. Born Lille 1825, died in Paris 1894. Pupil of Souchon in Lille, came to Paris 1851, and studied with Leon Cogniet at the *Beaux Arts*. He and Gachet had been friends since when they were children.

† Undated. See *Lettres Impressionistes au Dr. Gachet et à Murer*. Paul Gachet. Paris, 1957. Pp. 38–9.

frank and loyal," he used to say.* Often he had to leave his painting at
Pontoise, get in a train for Paris, and there tramp the streets in search of
elusive francs. Sometimes he stayed the night with his mother Rachel
in the rue Paradis Poissonnière. The year 1878 saw no lessening of his
anxieties, and he was glad to accept twenty francs for a picture from
the pastrycook Eugéne Murer, who had made a fortune during the
siege of Paris from his cooking of *vol-aux-vent* made from rats. Then
he began to buy pictures. Murer was a school friend of Guillaumin's,
and contributed art articles to obscure journals, but despite his literary
ambitions he had opened a restaurant in the Boulevard Voltaire, a ren-
dezvous for artists, writers and musicians. Camille and Renoir decorated the dining-room, Renoir painting the friezes with garlands of
flowers, and Camille covering the walls with landscapes of Pontoise.
For payment Murer fed them, and occasionally he bought a picture. He
gave little and grumbled at the price. He lent Camille small amounts
of money. Once he advanced fifty francs (£2) on behalf of Dr. Gachet,
because Camille did not dare show himself in Pontoise without the
money in his pocket to pay the debt he owed his colourman for paints.
"For a whole week now," Camille wrote to him, "I have been rushing
about Paris vainly trying to discover the one man needed, the buyer of
impressionist pictures, and here I am, once more without a franc. Will
you once again lend me fifty francs to send to my people?" In a further
letter he showed himself as courageous and determined as ever: "I have
two most important things to see to. I have to go to Bellio's and ask
him for some medicine for my wife who is ill, and I have promised
Miss Cassatt to go and see her to find out whether she was able to sell
a picture of mine to one of her Sunday visitors. You must imagine
what a state of anxiety I am in at leaving a wife in an advanced state of
pregnancy all alone in the country, without money and with two
children to look after. Let Guillaumin think over the position a little;
let him bear in mind that when a man has only himself to trouble about,
he can weather out any storm—he has only got to keep himself. The
grandparents have too much influence over him. He would do miles
better to send his city job to blazes. Of course, you've got to have a
bit of grit in you, there mustn't be any chopping and changing about
it. I was at St. Thomas in '52 in a well-paid job, but I couldn't stick it.
Without more ado I cut the whole thing and bolted to Caracas in order
to get clear of the bondage of bourgeois life. What I have been through
you can't imagine, and what I am still suffering is terrible, very much

* See C. Pissarro's letter to Mirbeau, 10th October, 1891, Louvre, Paris.

more than when young and full of enthusiasm and ardour, convinced as I now am that I have no future to look forward to. Nevertheless, it seems to me that, if I had to begin over again, I should do precisely the same thing. Does that mean one ought to advise a friend to go and do likewise? It all depends on the temperament, the convictions of the individual."

In the hope of making sales by living nearer the centre of the dealers and collectors, in November, 1878, Camille rented a room in Paris, at 18 rue des Trois Frères, but he feared that the *amateurs* would never have the courage to climb the heights of Montmartre to see his pictures. The move brought no improvement in his affairs, and he wrote to Murer: "I am going through a frightful crisis and don't see a way to get out of it. Things are bad!" He owed money to the butcher, the baker, the grocer, to everyone. Julie, expecting her fourth child (Ludovic Rodolphe) was utterly depressed. Her strength sapped by the unvarying hardship and her condition, she vented her feelings in harsh criticisms, and continually grumbled. And now Camille began to complain of his sight: an ulcer was affecting his left eye. Haunted by a premonition that he would have to give up painting, he feared he was on the point of defeat. "My family must live," he cried, and in despair he asked: "Is art necessary? Is it edible?"

CHAPTER II

Lucien. 1863—1889

MEANWHILE CAMILLE'S ELDEST SON, LUCIEN, WAS GROWING UP IN THE shadow of his formidable father. The pictures by his father, and by Manet, Degas, Monet, Cézanne, and Berthe Morisot, hanging on the walls of his home, fascinated him. He climbed on chairs to look at them more closely. He was allowed in Camille's studio, and used to watch him at work in the fields, listening to the conversation of the artists, breathing always the smell of paint and turpentine. It was thus that his apprenticeship to painting began in his earliest years. Pencil in hand, he drew. Camille encouraged him, corrected his efforts, and gave advice. Julie was not pleased, grumbling that this was no way to educate a child. Left alone in the kitchen for a few minutes, when he was three or four years old, standing on tiptoe to see what was in a pan, he leaned too near the stove. In an instant his black pinafore caught fire, and he ran screaming outside into the road, his clothes aflame. The blacksmith opposite hurried from his forge. Wrapping his leather apron around Lucien, he smothered the flames. It was Lucien's first taste of disaster, the symbol of an anxiety which became inherent in him.

There is another early gimpse of Lucien when he was nine years of age. On the 11th December, 1872, Cézanne called on Camille to find that he had gone to Paris. Seated at the kitchen table, he wrote to him: "I am borrowing Lucien's pen at the moment when I should be in the train on my way home, in other words, I've missed it . . ." On this sheet of paper Lucien wrote: "My dear Papa, Mama asks me to say that the door is broken, and you are to come quickly because of burglars. Please will you bring me a paint box? Minette says please she would like a bath wrap. I have not written this well because I am not sitting properly. Lucien Pissarro."

In 1878 there was not a sou in the house. Camille did not know which way to turn, and Julie nagged him to take Lucien away from school. He was old enough to work, she said, and if he was at work, there would be a mouth less to feed. Camille's brother, Alfred, a man of commerce, contemptuous of Camille's penurious way of life, interferingly inflicted his advice whenever he had the opportunity. Urged by Julie, he found Lucien a job in a warehouse dealing in English fabrics. Camille, remembering well his own dislike of the days when he had been a clerk, sympathised with Lucien's desire to be a painter, yet had to listen to Julie's arguments. No one, she said, would want Lucien to undergo the hardships and penury Camille had endured—and to what end? Let him have the security of commercial employment, the prospect of a regular salary, and not be haunted by the fear of want. And if he wishes to paint, why, he can do so in his spare time. So Lucien went to Paris and was taught to string and wrap parcels. This was his only acquirement from his brief experiences of commerce. When, years later, he had to send parcels of his own press books, they were bundled neatly and efficiently.

He lived at the rue Poissonnière with his grandmother, Rachel, a bed-ridden, shrivelled old lady of eighty-three, the splendours of the social life she led in her youth at St. Thomas now an almost forgotten memory. She was looked after by Amélie Isaacson whose father, Phineas, living in London, had married Camille's half-sister. a daughter from Rachel's previous marriage to her husband's uncle, Isaac Petit, Amélie was thus both Camille's cousin and half-sister. Amélie was a milliner—she owned a small shop, and made her customers bonnets. Lucien found the fare at his grandmother's spartan and unvarying, Rachel being served with the *pot-au-feu*, Lucien and Amélie with tasteless meat soup. His work bored him, he did not concentrate, his thoughts were elsewhere, and he made appalling mistakes. He used to address packages, intended for India, to China. His employer wrote to Camille: "Your son is a good lad, but he has no head for business, and I doubt if he ever will have." This was Lucien's dismissal. He returned home. Camille had thought it would be like this.

On 24th February, 1882, Camille wrote to Théodore Duret: "I am not rolling in money. I am enjoying the results of moderate yet successful sales," but he dreaded repetition of the past. Affairs being thus favourable, he was able to keep Lucien going. Cézanne and Gauguin were painting with Camille at Pontoise. Lucien, either at home or in Paris, prepared Camille's exhibitions, looked after the negotiations and the business, saw that the village carpenter made a good job of the frames, and that the pictures were well hung in the galleries. This left him plenty of time for his own drawing and painting, and he worked hard. Worried about his eyes, Camille again feared he would not be able to see, a recurrent fear which was to continue for the rest of his life. His general health was also not good, the house near Pontoise was damp and, not caring to risk another winter in it, he moved to the Quai du Pothuit in Pontoise itself, but this was not satisfactory, and a further move was made to the village of Osny, some two miles away. The bad times returned. Durand-Ruel stopped buying, and again Camille was forced to trudge the streets of Paris hawking his pictures from one small dealer to another. Julie was worried. She did not know how to manage, since Lucien, a grown man, brought no money into the house and strained her resources. Uncle Alfred, overflowing with advice, suggested that Lucien should go to London to learn English: with this accomplishment he would have no difficulty in obtaining a commercial post in Paris. Camille consented, but only because he believed this parting, which would put a distance between him and Lucien, would remove the boy from his influence and induce him to follow his own path.

Lucien arrived in London early in January, 1883, and lodged at Holloway with his uncle Phineas Isaacson, his two sons, Rudolph and Alfred, and his two daughters, Alice and Esther. Phineas was a strange character, erratic in mood, sometimes amiable, often peevish and bad tempered. Lucien said he was quite nice to him, but at the bad times he did as the others, controlled his tongue and did not answer. He thought Phineas must be ill on such occasions. "Don't forget to send the money at the end of the month. Phineas keeps the girls short with the housekeeping money."

A few days after his arrival, Camille wrote: "We are all quite well, including the children; your mother is very busy and I continue to jog along, surrounded with my unfinished paintings and drawings, seeking the rare bird whose plumage is resplendent with all the colours of the rainbow, whose song is musical and pure; perfection, as Degas would say, why not! Don't forget to draw."

Lucien explored London, and thought the river scenery at Richmond magnificient. At the Albert Docks he saw a wonderful sunset in the mist shrouding the shipping. "Exactly what Turner did," he wrote to Camille. London fascinated him. He was delighted with the streets and the people, remote and mysterious; their speech incomprehensible to him. "During the day I see a world that I should really like to study, but how to do it? There are the people who pass by; you have to remember their clothes, their character, their movements, and draw them afterwards from memory. Too difficult for me! And that is what interests me. I think of a type, I see him perfectly in my imagination, but as soon as I take up my pencil the image disappears and I can do nothing. Such drawings would be something original; all these great English ladies, these mashers, or toffs as they are called, these street musicians. Nobody does them in England, all the artists are still looking through their classical spectacles." He went out to sketch with Esther, but so many children gathered that he was unable to do anything. "I have just been to a factory making oilcloth and ultra-marine blue to see if they would have me in their offices. I was recommended by Madame Henry, but this gentleman didn't want me, despite the fact that I was to work for nothing." Soon he wrote: "I have a job, for nothing, naturally, and I am obliged to have lunch in this quarter which costs me a shilling." Then there were the fares on top of that, so he had to spend nearly two shillings a day. His employment was with Stanley, Lucas, Webber and Co., music publishers in New Bond Street. As Lucien had written, he worked for nothing, but was given tickets for recitals and concerts, which he used. He was fond of music, and wrote of Wagner's *The Flying Dutchman*, "really wonderful music, very serious, no cooing singers or ballet".

"I so much want to draw," Lucien wrote to Camille, "but I have so little time. The other day I made a sketch of one of the employees with a typical head. The other employees were astounded; everybody had to see it; even the *patron* complimented me on the likeness. If you have no doubts I can do something artistically, I have many. Anyway I'll try and draw more. Mother tells me to kiss Alice for her. I much regret to report I have contented myself with just thanking her. I have never kissed my cousins, and wouldn't dare begin."

He continued to visit the galleries. On 26th February he wrote to Camille: "On Saturday I saw Whistler's exhibition. He has stolen our idea of using colour in the gallery. His is completely white with lemon-yellow borders, the drapery is of yellow velvet with his butterfly embroidered in a corner. The chairs are yellow with white straw seats. A yellow Indian mat is on the floor, and some kind of yellow dande-lions are in yellow earthenware vases. The attendant is dressed in white and yellow. All this gives an air of great gaiety in contrast to the ad-joining rooms where paintings belonging to a dealer are displayed. Whistler has a little room of his own at the end of the gallery which resembles Durand-Ruel's. Here there is nothing but etchings, nearly all views of Venice. They are very good. He does enchanting things with a few lines. It is ordinary etching, done, I believe, with a dry point.

33

Despite that it is very flexible. The English journalists have over-criti-
cised the room; on the day I went there were plenty of poeple there. The
exhibition is in Bond Street, a very smart place ... I think that if the
impressionists exhibit in London, it is imperative to have rooms like you
had in Paris. It will get talked about, and there will be a crowd. Novelty
is always attractive; you will be considered to be the French aesthetes."

Two days later (28th February), Camille replied: "How I regret
not seeing Whistler's exhibition, as much from the point of view of
fine drypoint work as for the décor, which, with Whistler, is very important. He even uses somewhat too much *puffisme* in my opinion.
Apart from that, it seems to me that white and yellow must make a
charming effect. We were, as you say, the first to try colour, my room
was lilac with a yellow border without a butterfly. But we, we poor
little rejected pariah painters, did not have enough money to carry out
our ideas of decoration. As for trying to make Durand-Ruel give a
similar exhibition it would be a wasted effort, you saw the struggle I
had to get white frames, only finally to have to abandon them. No!
I don't think that Durand-Ruel would follow that line. I am re-reading
what you say about aestheticism. I should not like to be aesthetic, at
least not in the way that it is understood across the Channel. Aestheticism is a sort of romanticism more or less imbued with trickery. It is
one way to make a misguided path for yourself. They wanted to make
impressionism into a similar theory, whereas impressionism should be
nothing but a theory of pure observation, without loss of imagination,
or freedom, or grandeur in fact all that makes an art great. But no
puffisme to deceive the fools."

Lucien was discouraged. He could not sell his drawings, but Camille
urged patience. He suggested drawing from the life at evening classes.
Lucien thought of studying at the Slade School with Legros, but
Camille, doubtful of Legros's theories, said it would be better to look
at the old masters in the museums.

"It's fearfully cold here," Lucien complained, and, despite the
woollen vest he wore under his shirt, he caught a chill and had to stay
indoors over the week-end, "to look after myself. Thanks to homeopathy I am completely recovered". He told his mother that, like
Georges, he was always making mistakes, twenty-one errors in his last
English dictation. "It's because English pronunciation is so difficult for
a Frenchman to understand." Indeed, although in after years, he learned
to speak English fluently, it always sounded strangely as it emerged
from his beard.

Camille wrote from Paris on the 3rd March that he was setting out for Osny, "tomorrow, Sunday, without a penny. Durand was only able to give me the money I sent you". Lucien visited the British Museum where he found some beautiful Greek and Egyptian statues. "I copy the Egyptians. When one sees for the first time the stiff lines of the limbs one does not realise how much experience they needed to attain such simplicity. As for the Greek gallery, I had always warned myself not to work there, believing that this art should be thrust aside from my path as though it were a danger. It is not synthetic, it is too detailed, whereas the Egyptians form a composition. Also, what kept me away from the Greeks were the numerous male and female students who copy the same statue for six months. It seems you have to copy a certain number to be admitted to the Academy schools. So their work is carefully shaded and they even put in the minutest cracks. I work as much as I can. I draw as much as possible. I think I can earn my living with this much more easily than by folding a length of cloth like an idiot from eight in the morning until six at night, in order to earn five pounds a month."

To be interned in some commercial establishment was terrifying to Lucien, it haunted his thoughts of the future. He dreaded the regular hours, the tedious employment, the waste of time. At the music publishers he asked for a salary: this was refused. It was an adequate excuse to leave: he went there no more, and instead worked daily copying at the British Museum.

Camille's letters reveal his pride in his children and his affection for them. "The children are all in pretty good health . . ." he wrote on the 10th April. "All of them draw, and the drawings always are to be sent to Lucien. But I deceive them about this, for otherwise my letters would be enormous and costly. However there are times when I am tempted to send you their fantastic landscapes, terrible horsemen, frightful massacres, in which warriors continue to battle even when they have lost their heads. Here is bravura pushed to the limit, people running like Hop-o'-my-Thumb. Here is an incredible Hoffmanesque world of fantasy! I should be happy if these youngsters gave as much attention to their lessons as they do to their drawings." At the beginning of May, Camille had an exhibition in Paris: there were many visitors. "Am I happy? Gracious, no," he comments. "My pictures don't get across. I have been paid many compliments, but I do not compliment myself. Apart from two or three things, the show is weak. Enough said on this subject. . . . Thursday, I am going to Manet's funeral."

At his exhibition Camille had an amusing encounter with a M. Tassin of Pontoise, a railway worker, who asked the price of two still-lifes. "He was shown the price list: one thousand two hundred francs each (about £48). He jumped out of his skin! He met me as I was leaving the exhibition, showed great surprise, gave a few criticisms of my work, and then made several observations which showed him to be a man skilful at handling figures. He said to me: 'But do you know that you have three hundred thousand francs' worth of paintings in there?' 'Really! I never calculated their value, I don't know! And how do you know?' 'Simple! They gave me the book of prices, I instantly added up the first column, it came to so much; there were five pages, I calculated the average, that gave the result.' Isn't that wonderful? And what respect!"

At the same time Durand-Ruel was showing a small exhibition of the impressionists in Bond Street. Lucien wrote to Camille: "There is not a single paper that does not express its opinion of your exhibition. Most of them dislike your painting and use the eternal argument, it's unfinished. But the papers who specialise in art are most encouraging. I met M. Duret at the exhibition, he is quite happy with the London exhibition. People talk about it, they come, they laugh, and that's something. There are lots of people there every time I go. Next year I think it will be imperative to have a well-organised exhibition, that is to say a large, well-decorated room, and the pictures sensibly hung." There was no space at this exhibition to step back from the pictures, people had to see them "too close", their noses almost on the paint, "so you can imagine the alarm that our manner of painting causes".

On Whit Monday, Lucien went for a long country walk with the Bensusan family. "We had a good time, the countryside was splendid, such charming things, little red houses set between trees with very clear green leaves. And the colour of the grass! Colours to make Degas run away. And beautiful flowers everywhere. We admired a village, small but so clean houses; fair-headed, red-cheeked children, bare arms and legs, playing in the doorways."

With the advent of spring Lucien sawed and hammered a few pieces of wood into a makeshift easel and made painting excursions to Hampstead Heath. In June, he visited the annual exhibition at the Royal Academy: "It is really quite as depressing as the Paris Salon. I could not find that this English art is less decadent than ours. The landscapes are ghastly. I saw twenty pictures looking as though they had been done by the same painter; even the subject is unchanged.

All have done tree-trunks and ferns to one side. Then there is the terrible variety which consists of some dozen pictures in blue-black with pieces of raw meat in the sky." But on the 11th June he wrote to Camille: "I have been to see Turner's water-colours, they are extraordinary, what I call clever and difficult without any of the tricks of the other English painters. I think Bastien-Lepage stole this way from the English, it seems to be fairly popular here. I saw figures painted like Carolus Duran's, and then the pseudo Grecian artists such as Alma Tadema, who lack, however, the qualities of design of Puvis de Chavannes. Finally there are really only two painters who did not make me regret the money I had paid for admission, Mark Fisher, a landscapist, who draws trees in a very knowledgeable way, and paints freely. They are like some of the things you did at Piette's, amongst others a landscape where I was posed lying under a large tree,* and Millais who only exhibited figures which, frankly speaking, I was not very taken with. But the Academy is not the last word on English art. There is the Grosvenor Gallery where those not admitted to the Academy exhibit."

Camille replied: "You speak to me of the Academy exhibition somewhat severely. Probably you are right, but you must not judge English art as here we judge French art by Bastien-Lepage and Gervex. Remember there is a Keene in England. He doesn't exhibit, he doesn't move in fashionable circles, that's the thing. England, like France, is corrupt to the marrow, and has only one art, that is the art of hoodwinking. Mark Fisher must be one of our imitators, because he has worked in France. I was told that he was stronger than us and, above all, more studied. I have wanted to understand this, I was once going to be introduced to him. Always learn design, one never knows what may happen: it is a useful accomplishment."

The flow of good advice continued from Camille. On 25th July, he wrote from Osny: "What you tell me about your activities in Regent's Park is all very well, but you have to understand that little bits of drawings are not enough. These must be made, of course, for you must accustom yourself to seeing the ensemble in a flash, to render its character at once, but you also have to grow in strength and attack seriously bigger things with firm contours, similar to those you started here. It is good to draw everything, anything. When you have trained yourself to see a tree truly, then you know how to look at the human

---

* See No. 361 *Paysage à Melleraye* (Mayenne, painted in 1876), in the Catalogue of the works of Camille Pissarro by L. R. Pissarro, Paris, 1939.

figure. Specialisation is not necessary, it is the death of art, whose requirements are exactly opposed to those of industry. Once again I say you can't waste time drawing landscapes conscientiously. The classroom is good only when you are strong enough not to be influenced."

In August Lucien went to France to stay with his family, spending the last few days at Rouen with his father who was working there and staying at the hotel which Murer had just opened. Soon after Lucien's return to England, Gauguin made his decision "to paint every day", resigned from his lucrative banking appointment, and joined Camille at Rouen, bringing with him his wife and five children. Camille found Gauguin disturbing. He wrote to Lucien on 31st October 1883: "He is so deeply commercial, at least he gives that impression. I haven't the heart to point out to him how false and unpromising is his attitude; true his needs are great, his family being used to luxury, just the same his attitude can only hurt him. Not that I think we ought not to try to sell, but I regard it as a waste of time to think *only* of selling, one forgets one's art and exaggerates one's value." In November, Camille concluded his series of paintings of Rouen. "I look at them constantly. I who made them often find them horrible. I understand them only at rare moments, when I have forgotten all about them, on days when I feel kindly disposed and indulgent to their poor maker. Sometimes I am terribly afraid to turn round canvases which I have piled against the wall. I am constantly afraid of finding monsters where I believed were precious gems! . . . Thus it does not astonish me that the critics in London relegate me to the lowest rank. Alas! I fear that they are only too justified! However, at times I come across works of mine which are soundly done and really in my style, and at such moments I find great solace. But no more of that. Painting, art in general, enchants me. It is my life. What else matters? When you put all your soul into a work, all that is noble in you, you cannot fail to find a kindred spirit who will understand you, and you do not need a host of such spirits. Is not that all an artist should wish for?"

Julie was for a while with Camille in Rouen. It was so beautiful, she said: how much she would like to live there! But Camille refused; that was because of Gauguin, she said. Gauguin begged him to stay at Osny: if Camille came to Rouen Gauguin feared he would not sell his paintings. It vexed Julie that Camille agreed. "What is Gauguin to us?" she asked, "that we have to stay away from Rouen because he is there!"

Lucien was still in London at Christmas. He thought the seasonal festivities very queer. "There were three days in which we dined very well at seven in the evening or three in the afternoon, the food was richer, plum pudding of Christmas, very difficult to digest, but that was nothing, all the time no one had colic or was sick. . . . And what weather we have had for the last eight days. It has been as dark as night—a fog the like of which we never see at home, and so cold that the gas would not burn. At the Christmas dinner we had to have lighted candles in front of our plates." He was trying to sell his drawings to newspapers. Working with pencil on a specially prepared paper, he hoped to succeed. "I would like to earn some money as I cannot tell you how the prospect of commerce bores me. I study as much as possible to establish myself and have bread on my plate."

In the dark winter days he became increasingly nostalgic for France. "It will be a great treat to be home again," he wrote on the 16th January, "and to see Cocotte again as you call my little sister." He had been told that she was charming, and that "she looks like a Persian painting and chats like a little woman. She looks at pictures and says: 'Cocotte like that one!'"

From Osny, Camille wrote on the 17th February, 1884, that Julie was in one of her bad, cantankerous moods. "She claims I encourage you to concern yourself with art, whereas you should think of earning a livelihood. I do not know whether my advice is good, but in any case, for the present, I urge you only to draw often, and to acquire strength by drawing the nude. When you are strong you can do as you like. But perhaps I am wrong." Looking for a new house, he was tempted by one in L'Isle d'Adam. Here there was a large garden, and the landlord promised to build a studio, but unhappily the house was next to the cemetery. Finally he decided on a house at Eragny on the Epte, near Gisors; here he was to live for the rest of his life. On the 1st March, he wrote: "The house is wonderful and not too dear: a thousand francs (£40) with garden and fields. It is about two hours from Paris." The country was more beautiful than Compiègne, although on the day Camille viewed the house it was "pouring torrents. But here comes the spring, the fields are green, outlines are delicate in the distance. Gisors is superb". But Georges wrote that it was a sad village, the baker had been killed by a train and the schoolmaster had died of a haemorrhage while mending the church clock. Julie went to their funerals and wept for the baker's widow and four children.

In March Lucien was a guest at a musical afternoon which was followed by a supper and a dance. The company bored him, but he noticed a curious effect of light during a dramatic recitation "about a poor little paper-boy who died". The gas had not been lit and "the Jewish profiles of many young ladies" against a background where the fading afternoon light still lingered was dark violet. He added that it was a pity he could not waltz. If he had learnt he would not have felt such a wallflower and could have danced with the girls.

Camille had suggested he should give some thought to the problem of how he was to sign his work. "My name would be risky since I have been in disfavour for so long, and then, also, people are only too ready to bracket you with someone else. For the present it might not be bad to sign yourself 'Vellay' (Lucien's mother's maiden name), later you may think of something better." Lucien hesitated. He signed two wood engravings "Vellay", a few paintings with his full name, and then compromised on the monogram which he thereafter never discarded. The rest of the family heeded Camille's advice. Georges signed his works "Manzana", Félix, "Jean Roch", Rodo, "Ludovic-Rodo", and Paul Emile, "Paulémile". Years later, Lucien's daughter, Orovida Camille, signed her paintings "Orovida".

Lucien returned to France in the spring of 1884, and the comradeship between him and his father was resumed, Lucien spending his time in Paris or at Eragny helping Camille. He concentrated on illustration, and became interested in political theories, sharing the anarchist views of Camille and the young painters, and making drawings for the anarchist paper *Père Peinard*. In 1885 he met Paul Signac and Georges Seurat in Guillaumin's studio, and adopted their method of painting in tiny dots of colour placed next to each other—the method of divisionism. In this technique he painted a portrait of his brother, Félix, and landscapes of the Eragny countryside. He introduced Camille to Signac and Seurat; and Camille, converted to their theories, changed his technique and palette, and painted with the dot. The result was disaster; his sales almost ceased. Nevertheless, he persisted; it would be some years before he retreated from a mode of expression in which he had faith. But finally, in 1890, he found that the theory "tied him down too much", preventing him reproducing "the spontaneity of sensation", and he returned to his former methods.

Throughout the summer of 1886 Lucien worked with Signac at Le Petit Andelys on the Seine. The weather was bad, the country beautiful, like Rouen, steep chalk hills in grey tones, cliffs, the shimmering river, little towns with ancient houses and red roofs. He wrote to Camille that Signac wished Camille to make himself at home and do as he pleased in his, Signac's, Paris studio. Lucien now contributed engravings to *La Revue Illustrée*, and sent landscapes of Eragny in water-colour to the second exhibition of the *Indépendants*.

In exchange for a collection of Lucien's wood engravings, van Gogh gave him a still-life painting he had made of apples,★ which he inscribed on the canvas *à l'ami Lucien Pissarro. Vincent.* When Lucien was again in Paris, he and Camille met him as they were walking along the rue Lepic. Van Gogh, dressed in a blue drill overall such as mechanics wear, explained he was returning from Asnières, the bundle he carried contained the pictures he had painted there, and he insisted on showing these to Camille, propping them, one after another, against a wall on the pavement. Passers-by, thinking it was a street show, stopped, and made derisive comments.

The eighth and last exhibition of the impressionists was held above the *Restaurant Doré*, 15th May to 15th June, 1886. The works of the divisionists were placed in a separate room, Seurat's vast canvas *La Grande Jatte* dominated the other paintings, and all were hung so low in a long and narrow gallery that George Moore had to kneel. He said the pictures were so much alike that he had to do this to identify the signature of the painter.

The next four years, 1887–1890, saw no alleviation of Camille's miseries. Turn where he would, he met only frustration. His painting was ridiculed, and dealers and collectors would have nothing to do with his dots. Now his old friends deserted him, and he felt the labour of years had come to nothing; all was lost but his courage. Even that faltered. He tried to persuade Monet of the truth of divisionism, and so angered him that the latter threatened to have nothing more to do with him. Renoir greeted him with a "*Bon jour, Seurat!*" In 1887, Lucien wrote to Camille: "You ask me urgently to find sixty francs for a bill. What can I do ? I have no idea." Camille wrote: "I have to husband my last few cents. Tell your mother I am enormously concerned about the rent, etc. I am splitting my head to find a way out." Disaster was staved off until June. Then: "Not a penny at home and the rent not paid." In this extremity, Camille considered selling everything, except his pastels and drawings, to the first private bidder. Even if the amount offered was paltry, a few thousand francs, it would bring peace of mind and, above all, allow him to work tranquilly. Julie suggested an auction sale of his pictures, but this Camille would not consider—a public sale would prejudice his future. Torn between the

★ Now in the Rijksmuseum Kröller-Möller, Otterloo, Holland.

necessity of money, and the fear of losing his prestige, Camille was confused.

To Lucien, Julie sent a distressing letter: "I wanted to get Georges to Paris, and so his trunk was packed, but your father grumbled so much that he did not go. Your poor father is really an innocent; he doesn't understand the difficulties of living. He knows that I owe three thousand francs and he sends me three hundred, and tells me to wait! Always the same tune. I don't mind waiting, but meanwhile one must eat. I have no money, and nobody will give me credit. I pay off a little of the debts here and there, but it is so little that they don't want to give me more credit. What are we to do? We are eight at home to be fed every day. When dinner-time comes I cannot say to them 'wait'. This stupid word your father repeats and repeats. I have tried all ways to manage. I am at the end of my tether. I give up. Your father has no more courage either. I had decided to send the three boys to Paris, and then to take the two little ones for a walk by the river. You can imagine the rest. Everyone would have thought it an accident. But when I was ready to go, I could not. Why am I such a coward at the last moment? But I feared to cause grief, and I was afraid of your remorse. Your dear father wrote me a letter which is a masterpiece of selfishness. The poor dear man says he has reached the top of his profession and doesn't want to prejudice his reputation by having a sale."

Was she serious in her threat of suicide? Lacking Camille's equipoise, bewildered, her mind troubled, she gave way to hysteria, threw herself on her back on the kitchen floor, her legs threshing the air, while the children looked on terrified, not knowing what to do. Frantic to find some solution to her troubles, she took Georges to Paris, where Alfred found work for him with a cabinet maker. Alfred was concerned when he heard there was no money in the house and gave her a hundred francs. This, he said, was not a gift, but a payment for one of Camille's drawings. "Here is a sale I did not expect," Camille commented. "I hope my work will be good enough for him." After seeing Alfred, Julie went to the *Exposition Internationale* at Petit's. Here she saw paintings by Renoir, Monet, Sisley, Berthe Morisot, Whistler, Puvis de Chavannes and Camille, but she declared that all the pictures were bad and Camille's "dots" the worst of all. From there she called on the shoemaker who, in exchange for one of Camille's pictures, was making a pair of boots for Lucien. Home again at Eragny, she wrote to Lucien: "Not a penny from Durand. You absolutely must find a job to earn a living, so as to take us out of this uncertainty and worry. We cannot help you any more. Your father is very worried and obliged to do anything to get money. I am sure he won't be able to manage. On top of this my poor mother is dying and asking us to lend her a few francs. The aunt is going nearly mad and does not know what she is doing. She is obliged to hide her grief; it is such a shame to see her like this. What a struggle life is, my poor Lucien! So much suffering just to feed oneself." On her return home she had found the servant drunk: she had finished nearly all the white wine, leaving only ten bottles.

Alfred urged Lucien to accept a commercial post. Lucien replied: "Don't think I am depressed. I am young and have the energy to make the struggle. If I accept this offer it will only be to get over this crisis. *I don't want to be a shopkeeper.* I am not servile enough. For the moment it is a matter of earning a little money, so I accept this post, forgetting my exhibition next year, thus allowing Signac to take my chance and compromising my future, *for there is a future.*"

Lucien had made a drawing for Murer—a book-cover for his novel *Pauline Lavinie*—and to him Julie appealed for help, but he said that he himself was in difficulties. Camille complained that it was impossible to discuss his affairs with Julie: "That is the state I am in, darkness, doubts, quarrels. Your mother accuses me of egoism, indifference, nonchalance. I make heroic attempts to preserve my calm." Lucien, in a letter to his mother, tried to restore tranquillity. He said he was surprised she worried—so unlike Camille who did not. "As for me, I admire his calm. If he was a man to get depressed easily, what would become of us? And if he was depressed he could not have the peace of mind to paint a good picture." And he warned Julie of Murer, who would take advantage of the position to persuade her to sell her pictures at a ridiculous price.

Determined to force an auction on Camille, Julie made the journey to Médan to solicit Zola's aid, but she was refused admittance. Her chagrin at this is shown in the letter she wrote him: "You must have been surprised to hear of my visit yesterday, and it was not nice for me to be despised. I went to see you as one goes to an old friend in the hope of a welcome. I called in the place of M. Pissarro who, if he knew of this, would die of shame. I had been walking three kilometres under a blazing sun and with a little girl of six (Cocotte). I was happy to have reached your home at last and hoped for some refreshment. I was told you were not at home. I asked for a glass of water and for the

maid to tell you who had called. It seemed that Madame wasn't at
home either. I inquired the time of the next train, it was in three hours,
a long time. Could I wait somewhere in the shade? but the maid said
she had orders not to let anyone in. You are very rude, I thought; you
do not know the rules of hospitality. Surely in such a heat I should
have been allowed to rest? At the same moment I saw Madame Zola
at a window, who addressed me in such an impertinent manner that I
was stunned and began to cry. But Madame Zola said it was my fault
for not making myself known, since I had not presented my card! I
was going to ask you a great favour as we are in great distress. We
are going to have a sale of Camille's pictures, and I beg your influence
to have an article published to help our project. Since we have not
a penny to pay for such an article, we offer any one of the pictures to be
auctioned. My husband does not know of this visit, and do not let
him know, for Camille, who is pride itself, would be furious."

"I consider it my duty to shake his hand warmly." So Zola had
written of Camille in his criticism of the Salon in 1866. Zola's thirty-
year friendship with Cézanne had ended in 1886 with the publication of
L'Oeuvre. He had sent a copy to Cézanne who, reading in its pages a
betrayal of friendship, wrote a sad letter of farewell. He and Zola never
met again. Now, possibly as a result of Julie's letter and Madame
Zola's ungraciousness, or out of loyalty to Cézanne, Camille and Zola
were not to shake hands again until the Dreyfus affair.

Lucien called at the Goupil Gallery, "Good news!" he wrote
in June to Camille at Eragny. "Your big picture has been sold to the
amateur who bought your pointillist fan of the geese. Theo van Gogh,
to replace it in his shop, said he would take the two pictures done in the
fields. He will send you some money in a day or so. As you have got
some money, can't you send me a little, so that I can pay my entrance
to the exhibition? The transport of my canvases I will share with
Signac, it won't cost very much, a friend will take them on a barrow.
Vincent sent three picture to the *Indépendants*. He is still in the
South."

But, in July, 1887, Lucien was at work with the publishing firm of
Manzi. Here he learned the process of printing colour blocks. Up at
six in the morning, he walked to his aunt's apartment and made himself a pot of tea. At midday he ate with one of the workmen at a
cheap restaurant, a franc sufficed to pay for all he required. After
spending the day making by hand the little colour dots for the chromos,
in the evening his eyes were so strained that he was unable to draw; the

paper in front of him swam with coloured dots. But the experience was to be invaluable when he began to make his own colour blocks. For some weeks he worked without a wage, then he was told that what he did was not difficult, but that he did not manage it well. Now his work was to be more complicated. He was asked how much he thought he was worth. Lucien did not know what to reply, the unskilled workmen earned sixty centimes an hour. He asked half of that. He was content, he said, to have enough money to pay for his food, "until I am clever enough to get my twenty sous an hour".

With his friend Hayet, Lucien attended a school of drawing. The *maître* was an oddity, a professor type, and myopic. He wore enormous spectacles and shambled. "He said to me the first day," Lucien wrote to Camille: "'One sees well you are not used to drawing.' I haven't yet done anything from the life because it is not until tomorrow that the model comes. One week drawing from nature, the next, from the antique, that's the rule. We are drawing 'The Discobolus Thrower', very boring, I can assure you, but we do it to impress that we conform, but when the next week of the antique comes, we shall go sketching. I am getting on well at the workshop and am beginning to work on the zinc the illustrations to *L'Abbé Constantin*. . . . All my time is occupied. I leave the workshop at seven in the evening, dine at one, and then go with Hayet, either to the school, or to sketch. That is why my letters are short. They are written at the workshop when the *patron's* back is turned."

Soon, Hayet had to go to serve his period of conscription.* He told Lucien: "I have just tasted something new in the army. I have had to go to prison for four days. That was a new medicine. But it was not too bad, I was quite well treated." Confined in a small room, he had to sleep in full uniform on a straw mattress thrown on the floor. But he was working again, painting a water-colour every week to keep his hand in. "I have been punished every Sunday since I returned from my leave. *Bon courage*." Lucien was also making drawings, a number of which were published in *La Vie Franco-Russe*, some of them to illustrate Turgeniev's short story *La Malheureuse*.

Camille reminded him, on the 12th August, 1889, not to forget to go to the *mont-de-piété* to pay what was owing. "Since you have said nothing about this in your letter your mother is very much afraid that you will overlook the matter, and it is urgent."

Lucien, encountering Renoir in the street, was shocked at his manner

* Lucien was not conscripted, his father being Danish by birth.

and appearance. He told Julie: "This poor Renoir has half of his face paralysed. It is very sad, he cannot work. Always so temperamental, now he is more excitable than ever." Camille now finally abandoned the "dot" after four years of experiment, and either repainted or destroyed most of the pictures he had painted during this period. His sales remained at the whim of chance, few and far between. Help came from Lucien. He had sold to Goupil twenty-five prints of his wood engravings, *Les Travaux des Champs*, at five francs each, altogether one hundred and twenty-five francs. "Since you have no money I send you immediately one hundred francs. You cannot imagine how happy I am to be able to do this when we are so hard up."

It was not until the following year, 1890, that the long-drawn-out crisis ended. Then, at an exhibition of Camille's paintings organised by Theo van Gogh, *Entrance to the Village* was sold for two thousand one hundred francs (£84), and *The Roquencourt Road* for one thousand four hundred (£56). Camille's first thought was of Lucien and his drudgery at Manzi's. He recalled him to Eragny.

For the last year Theo's brother Vincent had been confined at the Saint-Rémy asylum following his outbreak of insanity at Arles. Now, weary of his surroundings and confident that he was cured, he asked Theo to find him some quiet place near Paris where he could live and work in tranquillity. Theo sought help from Camille. Camille was willing to have him at Eragny, but Julie said no. She was afraid of the effect of an unbalanced mind on the children. She had been through so much, that she did not want to start fresh difficulties and troubles. Camille recommended Vincent to Dr. Gachet at Auvers who agreed to take charge of him. Vincent arrived in Paris in May and stayed at Theo's new apartment in the Cité Pigalle, Montmartre. Camille and Lucien went to see him. They were impressed with his healthy colour, his broad shoulders, and his look of determination. He was even gay.

One Sunday, two months later, Vincent shot himself with a revolver he had borrowed. The bullet entered his body below his heart. He stumbled back to the inn where he lodged and went to bed, his face to the wall. M. Ravoux, the innkeeper, came into the room to ask if he was coming to dinner. Vincent turned and displayed his bloody chest. "I tried to kill myself," he said, "but missed." Theo came. Early on the following Tuesday morning Vincent whispered to Theo: "I wish could go home now," and died in his brother's arms.

Many artists, Lucien among them, were at Auvers for the funeral.

Vincent's brushes were strewn on the floor, the wooden coffin was covered with flowers, among them the sunflowers he had loved to paint. His last canvases were nailed on the walls of the room. Lucien walked in the funeral cortège to the top of the hill and the little cemetery. Here, under a blue sky and overlooking the fields of wheat ready for reaping, Vincent was buried.

CHAPTER III

Lucien and Esther. 1889–1890

WHEN, IN 1883, LUCIEN WAS LIVING AT HOLLOWAY WITH HIS UNCLE, Phineas Isaacson, a young girl, aged thirteen, named Esther Bensusan, came to stay in the house for a while to be with her great friend Esther Isaacson. She lived at Norwood. She and her brother Sam bickered and so disturbed their parents that they were glad for her to go. But Lucien, engaged with his work in Bond Street during the day, and often at concerts in the evening, saw little of her. It was a time when he was shy and self-conscious. Girls made him uncomfortable, and he did not know what to say to them. But in 1889, when Esther Bensusan went to Paris on holiday with her parents, Lucien was no longer tongue-tied. Assiduous in his attentions, he escorted them to various places of interest.

Jacob, Esther's father, a Spanish Jew, exact in the observances and ritual of his religion, had wished in his youth to be a rabbi. Instead he had become an inefficient but prosperous feather merchant. Esther had matured in the atmosphere and shibboleths of a well-to-do and middle-class Jewish family. Jacob had an enthusiasm for church music, and when Esther was of age, when other children were treated to a circus or a pantomime, she sat with her father in the Crystal Palace and listened to the oratorios of Bach and Handel. Interested in art, and drawing with facility, she was a student at the Crystal Palace Art School.

In Paris she saw much of Lucien. Often they were left alone. One day they went together to the Louvre and to an exhibition of Monet and Rodin. "Monet is a *splendid* impressionist," she recorded in her diary. Another day it poured with rain and she stayed "at home" playing "head, body and legs", with Lucien. On another day, when she was "at home", Lucien "drew in this book", and on odd pages of her diary are pen and ink sketches of a girl, no doubt, herself. They made an expedition to St. Cloud together and she "played ball with him in the wood". In this young girl, attractive and intelligent, just blooming into womanhood, Lucien found an attentive and sympa-

48

thetic listener to his views on painting, music, the sad state of the world, and his belief that socialism (or was it anarchism?) was the panacea for the ills of mankind. His mother invited the Bensusans to Eragny for the day. Mrs. Bensusan thought her poor French would make the day difficult, but she allowed Esther to go alone. She travelled by an early train, the 6.10, from Paris. "Spent a most splendid day," she wrote in her diary. "Madame Pissarro gave me a picture and all were delightful." The Pissarro family liked Esther, she liked them, they made a fuss of her, and when she returned to London there began a regular exchange of letters between her and Lucien. The Pissarros made a book for her, and sent it as a birthday offering. It was inscribed: "From Eragny artists to Miss E. Bensusan"—an album of old French songs bound in cotton print cut from one of Julie's dresses. Lucien wrote in a beautiful calligraphy the words and notation of the nine songs, he also made the page decorations. Camille painted the frontispiece, and the brothers, Georges, Rodo and Félix, contributed pages of illustrative water-colours. This exquisitive and lovely book is now in the Ashmolean Museum at Oxford, part of a Bequest made by Orovida Pissarro. In December 1889, Esther wrote a thank-you letter for the gift, and the Pissarros replied: "The artists of Eragny are all delighted to hear that you are satisfied with the album and assure you that if you are pleased to receive it, we are also pleased, because so few people understand us. So it is a joy to do something for someone who does."

"The artists of Eragny"—their ages were Georges, eighteen, Félix, fifteen, Rodo, eleven, Jeanne, eight, and Paul Emile, five—delighted in making albums of school exercise-books, usually lined and with a picture of an animal on the cover, bought at the village shop. These they filled with their drawings and caricatures, tinted with chalks or water-colour, charming in colour, accomplished in execution. Their subjects at this time and in the immediate years which followed were invariably the jokes of the family, coarse, often cruel; sensibilities were not spared, features and dress exaggerated. Georges in particular displayed a malicious invention. He drew pictures of Julie physically attacking Camille, of Lucien sitting, his eyes calf-like, with Esther by the river, of Esther painting whilst Lucien did the household chores and fetched water from the well in the garden. He depicted Camille afraid of a rabbit, or stepping back from an easel and falling over a cliff. Still more cruel was a drawing of Camille and Lucien trying to persuade a bashful and astonished village girl to undress and pose in the nude. Animals were superbly and fantastically depicted. There was a series of a dog who followed the Pissarro family, always with one of their noses, shown as of excessive length, between his teeth.

Washing-day was a tumultuous affair at Eragny. Sheets, blankets, and other linen and garments, which had been thrown into the loft as they were soiled, were brought down, and the day given over to washing, drying and ironing. A washerwoman came to help Julie and the servant: tempers were lost, invectives hurled. The males hid themselves, and there was no dinner. The events of such days were recorded with zest. Even little Cocotte made her books; all were a pungent comment on the family life at Eragny in those days. It may be that the drawings were influenced by Champfleury's *Histoire de la Caricature*, illustrated by Daumier, which Camille had bought in Rouen—a great favourite with the children. Many of the books they made have been preserved, they are remarkable examples of the talents of the young Pissarros, gifted to an extreme, and it is not surprising that Julie was scared at the precocious skill of her sons. She would have preferred them to have given their time to carpentry or some other hobby which in time might earn them a living. But Camille chuckled at their jokes and encouraged.

1890

Letters between Lucien and Esther became frequent, his often had charming drawings, sometimes tinted with water-colour. He recalled the pleasant time they had together in Paris. Does she remember the street hawker they talked to and how she wanted him to make a drawing of him? He went to London in October, 1890, for a few days to try and interest editors in his drawings. Afterwards he wrote: "The time of my stay seemed so very short; we were so occupied that it went quickly. I have such a lot of things to tell and ask you." Impressed by the sensibility of her paintings, he asked the favour of something of hers to add to his collection. Esther thanked him for his letter and said her name was Esther, not Miss Bensusan. When next he wrote it was to thank her for the nice painting she had sent him. He had been to Paris, had sent two of his paintings of the Eragny countryside to the Exhibition of the *Indépendants*, and had painted a picture from a window in Monmartre; now he was invited to show at the Twenty Group in Brussels. This Group had been established in 1884 by twenty young artists, including Lucien's friend, Théo van Rysselberghe, and James Ensor. In London, Esther went from one publisher to another, trying to interest them in Lucien as an illustrator of children's books.

She was received with politeness and that was all. Esther submitted some of Lucien's drawings to *Punch,* but the treatment was considered un-English, the spirit too French. A friend of Esther's, Margaret Rust, had written a children's story: *The Queen of the Fishes.* Lucien made some illustrations for it, but Esther's attempts to get the book published also resulted in disappointment.

Lucien wrote that he had started a series of paintings which "promise well". In many letters he discussed his theories on religion and socialism. Jacob Bensusan must have read these. He would certainly consider it his right to supervise his daughter's correspondence, and he wrote (the note was ominous): "Esther thoroughly appreciated your kindness in going about with her in Paris. She will always be pleased to hear from you as letters are sure to be instructive as well as friendly." But he requests, as a great favour, that Lucien should not on any consideration write to his daughter on any subject connected with the socialists. "She, unfortunately (according to my ideas), has interested herself too much with socialism with which I have not the slightest sympathy. It is a dangerous subject."

In October, 1890. Lucien wrote: "You probably remember the young man who showed us some pictures at the Maison Goupil at the time of your journey to Paris. This poor man has just gone mad. It is all very sad for his family and for all the impressionist painters for he was more than a dealer to them. Nobody took more to heart their affairs and at this moment there is not in Paris a man able to replace him." The poor young man was Theo van Gogh, Vincent's devoted brother. He died shortly after in January of 1891, and was eventually buried alongside Vincent in the cemetery at Auvers.

Meanwhile, Georges, aged eighteen, was staying in London with his uncle Phineas Isaacson and his daughters, Esther and Alice. The Isaacsons had moved from Holloway to Colville Square, Bayswater, and here the sisters had established a boarding house. Phineas left its care to them, since he had affairs in the city, but he was much in evidence, cantankerous, ready to take offence, and to bicker with his daughters and the boarders. He greeted Georges with the laconic remark: "Your hair wants cutting," but when Georges returned from the barber's, Esther Isaacson disapproved. He had spoilt his appearance and no longer looked like an artist. "I met cousin Fanny," wrote Georges to Lucien, "that queer woman with the face of a devil. She talks, talks, talks, and if there is no one to talk to, she talks to the chairs and quarrels with herself. Uncle Phineas also talks a lot, and when they are together they talk and quarrel. We sit in the drawing-room where there are a lot of father's pictures, and Esther teaches me English. When the others are there, she tempts me to get my sketch-book. I draw uncle and he asks if I am giving him beautiful eyes, but what can I do? They are like the narrow slits of a mole."

With Esther he visited her friends, Madame Henry and her daughters. Madame moved in a coterie of rich Jews and gave music lessons to their children, and at her home these pupils give musical evenings. Georges was amused, "the Henrys look like birds. They are ridiculous but very kind. Madame is a mother to Alice and Esther". His uncle continued testy and absurd. "I have to leave the room because he says that it gets on his nerves to see me writing to you. 'I am the master of this house,' he roared at me. So I finish this letter in my bedroom". Soon after this Georges returned home.

Camille, anxious about Lucien, doubted if he would be able to make his way in Paris where he himself had only obtained a precarious foothold. But not only that, he feared his own formidable influence on his impressionable son; for Lucien to escape it, there must be a distance between them. He advised Lucien to go to London where no doubt he could make a living by giving lessons in drawing and the sale of his engravings. Lucien was of the same mind. Esther was the magnet. He would be near her. He told her of this decision, she was delighted. She would join his class and try to find him pupils. Lucien arrived in London in the November of 1890, rented a large room as a studio in Cornwall Road, and hung his pictures on the walls. He was to take his meals with the Isaacsons.

On Lucien's first Sunday in London Phineas Isaacson was charming to him. "We will go for a walk to Richmond," he announced, and Lucien commented to his father: "Here we are, walking and walking, the conceited old man wanting to prove that despite his seventy-two years he could outdo a young man of twenty-seven. The result was an enormous appetite, but all we could get in a public house was a biscuit and a small piece of cheese. We did not get back until five in the afternoon; Phineas was famished, he devoured enormous helpings of duck and olives. I thought he would never stop." Isaacson's pleasantness soon evaporated and turned to dislike. He resented the presence of another male in the house, he was like that; in the past he had driven his two sons from home. For days he was often in a bad temper and a bad mood as a result of overeating. His stomach nagged, and he sulked. "The next Sunday," reports Lucien to his father, "he sent me

III. Lucien and his cousins Frédéric Pissarro and Alfred Isaacson

IV. Eragny, 1894. *Left to right:* Paul Emile, Jeanne, Camille, Tommy Pissarro, Rodo, Alice Isaacson, Julie and *La Bonne. Lying in the foreground,* Da, the Great Dane

Va. Julie and Camille in the garden at Eragny, 1897

Vb. Julie, Paul Emile, Camille and Jeanne Pissarro in the orchard, Eragny, 1897

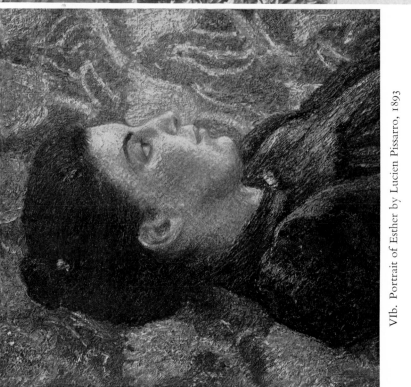

VIb. Portrait of Esther by Lucien Pissarro, 1893

VIa. The Bensusan Family, 1890
J. S. L. Bensusan, his wife, and Esther, with Ferdinand *standing at the back*

a letter, addressing me as M. Pissarro, requesting me to discontinue my visits." On this day Lucien dined in a cheap restaurant, the cheapest he could find. "A few days after he (Isaacson) inquired: 'Why is it Lucien no longer comes?' Now I only go when I am told that he will not be there. He does not like to meet me. When we do come face to face he derides artists as good-for-nothing, lazy mendicants."

Lucien paid ten shillings a week for his studio, and one pound for a bedroom and his board at the house of a French widow, a Madame de Bouvière. Degas was a good friend to her and the guardian of her son. She gave French lessons and found Lucien a pupil for his drawing class. He was amused with the people at the boarding house. At meals he sat next to an aging spinster "with teeth coming out of her mouth" who was furious when his place was moved next to a French woman who imagined he was Degas's nephew.

On the 25th December Camille, in Paris, wrote to Lucien: "Your mother made me take Titi (Félix, now seventeen) with me so that I could find a job for him. I took him along but sent him back to Eragny. She accuses me more than ever of having brought you up to do nothing; as always I let the storm pass. For, after all, what is the point of putting a boy, Titi or Georges, in a factory? . . . Wouldn't it be better to have them wait for a good opportunity, and in the meantime let them work for me? But these false notions prevent me from setting them to work with good effect."

Lucien met John Gray, "a charming young man. He took me to meet Ricketts* who lives in Chelsea in Whistler's old attic. Ricketts is a man of about thirty, he resembles Van Prag in face, but is more sickly and much more intelligent, naturally! Shannon was not there, he is in Devonshire at the moment but Savage, another artist, was. Ricketts speaks very good French; we understood each other at once. They are great admirers of Rossetti, but know little of the impressionists, share many of our ideas and—a strange thing—they all do wood engraving! And, my goodness, very well too—very simple and in the tradition of the old masters. We have the same ideas as them on this subject, only they are very clever, having learnt the trade of engraving. They also do lithography and etching. They should be coming this afternoon to see my things. I am writing to you while waiting for them. *PS.* Ricketts, Shannon and Savage have just come. They liked my wood engraving and painting very much, even though it was night and they

* Lucien's friend, Félix Fénéon, had given him letters of introduction to Ricketts and Shannon.

saw them by gaslight. I showed them some of your *gouaches* which they thought very beautiful. What would they say if they saw some really good things, for what I have are quite ordinary things for you! Ricketts told me that when I got bored on a Sunday to go and see him, that he was not at all like an Englishman, and he would always be delighted to have me. Nice! Ricketts will show me some things of Burne-Jones, and he will introduce me to Whistler, who it appears is not so ferocious as all that."

The friendship with Ricketts and Shannon was to continue for many years. Ricketts, a small man with a stoop, had a high forehead and a goatee beard, a cloud of fine tow-coloured hair surmounted his head like a dandelion puff. He dressed carelessly in blue serge. He had met Shannon when he was sixteen, for the rest of their lives they lived together, sharing all things in common, including a unique collection of old master paintings, drawings and rare museum-pieces. They recklessly spent all their ready money on a tempting find, heedless of the privations and self-denial that must follow until money was in their pockets again. Augustus John remarked: "They lived with the masters: even their w.c.s were hung to the ceiling with the stimulating productions of Titian and Giorgione." Lucien's friend, T. Sturge Moore, the poet, said of their friendship: "Between Ricketts and Shannon existed the most marvellous human relationship that has ever come within my observation, and in their prime, each was the other's complement." They had been apprenticed to Mr. Roberts, the wood engraver at the City and Guilds Institute in the Kennington Road. Shannon now, for four or five days a week, taught at the Croydon Art School, whilst Ricketts had a quarterly allowance of twenty-five pounds from a grandfather. They lived in a top flat in the Vale, Chelsea, and here Oscar Wilde shared dishes of eggs prepared by Ricketts, washed down with a cheap wine. When in prison, Wilde inquired after them, and on being told that their circumstances had improved, said: "I suppose if you go to supper now, they give you fresh eggs."

CHAPTER IV

Love in the British Museum. 1890–2

ESTHER BENSUSAN HAD PROMISED LUCIEN TO JOIN HIS CLASS WITHOUT telling her father, but he heard of it. Furious at the deceit, the blood rushed to his head, and he at once wrote : "*11th November, 1890.* M. Lucien Pissarro. Dear Sir, I have been informed that Esther intends joining a class for drawing that you are about to start. I regret to inform you that I cannot allow her to become your pupil. I am, dear Sir, Yours very truly, J. S. L. Bensusan." The same post brought a letter from Esther : "Please forgive me for causing you this unpleasantness. There is nothing that I would like more than to belong to your class. Always, your most sincere friend, Sterbee." Esther Bensusan was called Esther B. or Sterbee to distinguish her from her friend, Esther I—Esther Isaacson.

Jacob considered his daughter's friendship with Lucien dangerous and undesirable. He had written the letter to Lucien sitting at his desk in his grubby little office in Finsbury with its pervading smell of naphthalene. Now he wrote a long and astonishing letter to Esther: "I cannot possibly describe to you how deeply grieved I am at not being able to consent to the plans that you made respecting Lucien's class." He was hurt that she had not taken him into her confidence. No doubt it was difficult for her to understand his feelings, but if she reflected she would know "how distasteful it must be for me to find my daughter, who in her younger days gave such promise of being an affectionate, good and religious girl, now turning entirely aside from all the good counsel she has received from her grandparents and parents, and allowing herself to be entirely guided by people who have had no religious training, and who boast of principles that would not be tolerated in any Jewish or Christian family". Had she no gratitude? "Why am I always to be unhappy, my life to be made miserable and almost unbearable by seeing my own child who ought to be a blessing and a comfort to be perfectly indifferent as to my happiness?" She should have regard "for your dear old grandmother, now so often alone", and he insidiously suggests, "you won't have her for ever".

Turning the page, he had some very special pleading: "Can you forget—can you ever forget—your beloved grandfather—his death-bed scene that you yourself witnessed. Can you forget, about one hour before he passed away, his calling out to your grandmother in a voice of entreaty—almost his last words: 'Mother, see that the children always say their prayers.'" He begged her to let these words outweigh anything she might hear from unbelievers, and to be guided by her own flesh and blood and not by strangers. Esther replied, in writing, for at home Jacob would not talk to her, that she saw no harm in joining the art class, that she wanted tuition, and it seemed a very good way. His bugbear, socialism, would not be discussed. The idea of the class was to work, not to talk. She reminded her father of his intolerance in the past, and recollected that when she said she liked Wagner but not Gounod, "you got furious with me", and that his arguments against socialism consisted only of the words "vile" and "bosh", words she incorporated into her own vocabulary in later life.

She recorded in the November days of her diary: The 8th: "Terrible row. Papa won't receive, or let me learn with Lucien." The 9th: "Papa won't alter. Most miserable." The 10th: "Saw Lucien. Most miserable." The 12th: "My birthday, Most wretched." The 13th: "Wrote to Papa and he answered by coming and talking for two hours. No result. Most wretched." The 14th: "Most wretched." The 15th: "Still as wretched." And the entry for the last day of the year was: "No hope of anything. End of most wretched year of my life."

1891

But in the New Year, and like other lovers in such circumstances, she and Lucien began to meet furtively, their favoured venue being the British Museum, where Esther went to copy from the antique. Sometimes they met at Kew and walked in the Gardens. Lucien afterwards said that these gardens were the loveliest of all gardens to him. Esther naïvely wrote: "I have always liked you, but lately I have broken all my promises in order that I might see you. May I see you tomorrow? I shall be at the Museum." Lucien confided to Camille that he was obliged to go often to the British Museum to study the fine collection in the Print Room. "When I see Esther B. I naturally talk to her. I don't understand why her father was so cordial to me at first, and now I am forbidden the house. What has happened? If he is afraid I want to marry Esther, what does he base that on? I have never spoken of it, and in my position I cannot, unfortunately, even consider it."

Esther unwisely trusted her girl friends. One chattered. Jacob was told "in confidence" of the secret meetings, and that Esther visited Lucien's studio. Nothing could have horrified him more. He admonished her—she will be taken for a loose woman, everyone will think she is Lucien's model, and he again forbids her to see him. But Esther had no intention of not seeing Lucien. With the silent companionship of the Assyrian and Egyptian antiquities at the Museum the timid love passages were continued. One morning she wore a red rose pinned to her coat. "I remember that day at the Museum so well," wrote Esther, "When you asked for my rose. I felt very excited but could not tell why you wanted it so much, for I saw that you did." She sent him a lock of her dark brown hair which he kept throughout his life. He was not always romantic, and in one letter he wrote: "I am beginning this in a very private apartment, hence the pencil." Esther's prudery was shocked; she asked if there was nowhere else where he could write quietly. His letters to Camille were pessimistic. He missed a model, particularly the "graceful Cocotte". His pupils were few, despite the efforts of Madame Henry. They paid three guineas for twelve lessons, which was not very lucrative. He had had to borrow twenty pounds from Esther Isaacson to pay his way. She was kind and did not wish him to return it until he could afford to do so. But it worried him. Esther Bensusan's aunt, Orovida, could get him innumerable fans to paint at ten shillings a dozen, but that meant drudgery for a pittance. "I do not know what to do," he told Camille. "I am so discouraged. I must earn some money if I am to stay here."

Camille fought Lucien's pessimism; already he had written (12th December, 1890): "I'm really astonished by your expressions of discouragement. For you to write in this way means many scenes here at home. After I wrote just to warn you, you had to put your foot in it! If you are already discouraged you will not accomplish anything in London. You must understand once and for all that one must be sure of success to the very end, for without that there is no hope! He who doubts is lost beforehand! How many times have I not told you that where there's a will there's a way; but nothing comes of itself. You've hardly been gone a month, damn it, and it takes a little time to arrange one's affairs. You have good opportunities, you ought to succeed, *besides it is absolutely necessary that you do so.* The worst of it is that your discouraging letter comes to cap other troubles, such as our not having a maid, my not having heard from Durand-Ruel about my five fans, my fears that this Durand will play me some dirty trick, and the consequences of Theo van Gogh's madness. These things do not discourage me at all; I have been in such predicaments before, but your mother can't keep her grip. She is constantly discouraged, and if you continue to take the tone you have, you can imagine what the moral effect will be! So hold fast! I am writing this letter without your mother's knowledge for I don't want to add fuel to the fire. I am by no means so pessimistic as you are." Lucien could not help it, it was in his bones to be pessimistic, and pessimistic he continued to be.

Working from a pattern, Lucien completed a dozen fans; the job was tedious and laborious. The fans were said to be satisfactory, but he received no further commissions. Camille wrote on the 7th January, 1891: "My eyes have been so bad that I had to interrupt all I had in view. . . . For some time now I have been anticipating this trouble with my eyes. The intense cold to which I was exposed in my runnings around aggravated my condition to such a point that the doctor was afraid of erysipelas, which seems to be a very serious matter. By constant medication we were able to control the swelling but not to prevent an abscess from forming. I have kept to my room since Friday and I probably won't be able to get out for several days." On the 22nd January Camille was happy to note evidence in Lucien's letters of new developments: "You seem to have more self-confidence and will, these are the fruits of strict application and long experience. Result: your work has more assurance and more personality. This is a good sign."

And from Eragny on the 21st February: "The woodcut you sent me is just beautiful, your personality comes out perfectly, the work is charming in every respect, The movement is original, the values are precise, the terrain in the foreground is very delicately modelled, the background is well drawn and well cut. You are making progress, you have found yourself and that is immense; you can now go boldly in search of your own conventions."

Lucien showed his wood engravings to Walker, the editor of *The English Illustrated Magazine*. Walker admired them and said he would show them to William Morris. "He was careful to say he could not use them in his magazine. The public is not ready for this kind of work, he said. It is always the same tune!" To his mother he wrote: "You ask if I have had a new suit made. Certainly not! I do not even have my shoes repaired and I don't know if I will, my rent takes all my money. I can see that quarrels at home still exist. Instead of living as pleasantly as possible, you spend your time quarrelling. It is sad. So useless. Surely you have enough serious troubles without making them."

Lucien was often with his new friends Ricketts and Shannon, long sessions in which they discussed woodcuts and etchings, studied Goya's bullfight prints and old woodcuts. He was shown the first number of *The Dial* which they edited, and asked to contribute to the next issue. Lucien spent much of his time making woodcuts from sketches made at Eragny, or working from memory,* a better method for *la synthèse*. Besides meeting Esther at the British Museum, he also studied there in the print-room. He told his father: "In a conversation (when I go to their place we talk until long past midnight) Ricketts told me that the English are not interested in engraving! that it was only in France that one saw those ardent amateur collectors. I disillusioned him, naturally, and told him that in France we imagined that only the English still interested themselves in engraving. Astonishment on both sides! What ideas we have of ourselves!! Ricketts will soon have his typographic press and we are all going to work on prints.

"Ricketts and Shannon came to see your etchings. They were delighted, and here is word for word what Ricketts said to me of the *Place de la République*: 'You know I certainly prefer certain of your father's etchings to those of Whistler, and to find another such etcher you have to go back as far as Rembrandt.' Isn't that a delightful compliment? And he said it so sincerely and I believe he is right because it is Rembrandt who invented that free etching on beaten metal, so right that one cannot conceive how else it could be done. By not bothering yourself too much with the technical finish, you have found something similar to what Rembrandt did; a way of using the metal sympathetic to the medium. That is precious.

"I have met more and more people. I met Oscar Wilde, the famous aesthetic poet who was so talked about a dozen years ago. He has visited Paris, dined at Nitti's, and is very up-to-date with the impressionist movement. He has promised to come and see me. Then at Horne's, the editor of *The Hobby Horse*, I was present at a re-union of poets who read their own works. I understood not a word. Walter Crane was there and we made each other's acquaintance. We talked engraving. He liked my things in colour very much, and also the engravings I did from your drawings. I have also to put Horne in

* Degas suggested this to Lucien.

touch with a symbolist poet, he wishes to publish a French poem of this school in his paper. There is a whole troupe of young people here who follow this new movement ardently, Parisians have no idea of the influence abroad of certain writers they despise."

Horne took Lucien to Ford Madox Brown's studio where he met William Rossetti, Dante Gabriel's brother, but Lucien was not greatly impressed by the pictures he saw; he thought they were too much influenced by Van Eyck and Memling. He went with Shannon, Horne and Image to visit Fanny Cornforth, Rossetti's mistress and model for many years. She and her second husband, Schott, were the proprietors of The Rose Tavern in Jermyn Street, where Fanny showed Lucien the pictures she had acquired from Rossetti. Horne also took him to a river-side wharf at Limehouse to visit Ernest Dowson, the tragic, gentle-mannered poet, who "flung roses riotously", and was in love with a commonplace twelve-year-old daughter of a Polish ex-waiter, the proprietor of a Soho restaurant. Dowson played halma with "Mussie" as he called the girl. She laughed at his adoration and, when older, married a waiter. Lucien joined the socialist group at Hammersmith of which William Morris and Crane were members. In May, 1891, Horne induced him to take part in a debate at an artists' club. Of this, he wrote to his father: "This club is partly composed of more or less official painters; there are even R.A.s. I did the paper which was very well translated by Selwyn Image, a painter between Burne-Jones and Morris, who does much illustration, ornamentation, etc. At this club the speakers were young men from the New English Art Club. In other words, English impressionists. They spoke as if they did not know the first thing about impressionism, they are artists who paint flat and have black on the palette. My discourse, which I made short and purely historical, carefully avoiding any personality, stating that impressionism is not realism, and explaining the division of tone and all that can generally constitute a painter of this school, was quite successful. It will surprise you that I, so timid, undertook such a task; say what you will, you will never be so surprised as I am. After the meeting, W. Steer and Sickert and some others asked to be introduced to me. Sickert—a young man who knows Degas—asked me to lunch. I went to his place; he has Degas's little lithograph finished in pastel that we saw at Clauzel's, then I went to his studio. Deplorable!! Then Steer asked me to his place. I went this morning. He separates the tones as we do and is very intelligent; here is, at last, an artist! Only he has doubts because the others make fun of him and nobody understands him. I think we shall become quite good friends. He seems very glad to have met me and told me that he prefers your work to Monet's."

On the 30th March, Camille wrote: "Terrible news to report: Seurat died after a very brief illness. I heard the cruel news only this morning. He had been in bed for three days with a bad throat. Improperly treated, the illness developed with ruinous speed. It is my impression that the malady was the very one de Bellio told me about some time ago—diphtheria. . . . It is a great loss to art." Camille expressed his pleasure at Lucien's work: ". . . I looked for a long time at your engravings at the exhibition (that of the *Indépendants*, which Seurat had arranged), they are hung to admiration on a panel which divides the room of the impressionists into two sections. Your coloured engravings are excellent, they are real pearls and the others are very good; your lithograph has delicacy and distinction, which by the way, are your outstanding qualities. Your prints have attracted a lot of attention; several of the newspapers mentioned them. M. Paul Mantz* gave them high praise. It is obvious that from the point of view of art you have an important place at this exhibition . . ." Lucien was sad to hear of Seurat's death. "So young, so promising, such a future. Doubtless pointillism dies with him," he wrote to Camille.

The following day, 1st April, Camille wrote: "I am prepared to see you changed by England, that is inevitable, but I can assure you that you will never lose your naïve and discreet nature. Don't be anxious then about the changes taking place in you. Go forward, resolutely, and if you put your whole soul into perfecting a work it will be original. And persist *obstinately, obstinately*, in what you did at Eragny, only with greater knowledge and experience. Yesterday I went to Seurat's funeral. I saw Signac who was deeply moved by this great misfortune. I believe you are right; pointillism is finished, but I think it will have consequences which later on will be of the utmost importance for art. Seurat really added something."

In this same month, Camille was still troubled with his eyes, a new abscess broke out and he was again forced to suspend his work. On the 2nd May, he wrote: "I leave on Sunday, that is, tomorrow, for Paris. I will go to see Parenteau who will probably operate on my eyes. I was penniless and didn't know how I could leave here (Eragny). As a last resort I wrote to Monet who promptly sent me a thousand

* Art critic of the *Gazette des Beaux-Arts*.

francs (£40). I will be able to give Grancey two hundred francs (£8), pay the rent, put a little aside for the house, and make the trip to Paris. Good, but when will I sell something?"

But five days later (7th May) he sent Lucien one hundred and fifty francs (£6) "for your expenses. This money is the result of my modest show which had a certain amount of success. Isn't that amazing? Monet has opened his show, I wrote to you about it. Well, it has just opened, my dear boy, and every painting has already been sold for from three thousand to four thousand francs (£120 to £160) each! If I could only sell one-fourth that many pictures I would be only too happy to help Alice and Esther (the Isaacsons) in my turn, but no, it has been decreed that I am not to have the satisfaction of making happy those near me, even your mother who certainly deserves some rest from care. It breaks my heart." On the 9th May there was another letter: "I have to send you on behalf of Madame Seurat, in memory of her son, a drawing and a small panel."

In London, Lucien was happy and, contrary to his habitual pessimism, optimistic. He enjoyed the company of his new friends, he worked hard, the future appeared roseate, and he was in love. But he missed the countryside of Eragny. In London, to find suitable *motifs*, he had to make long and expensive journeys which he could ill-afford. He read Kropotkin and found his theories similar to his own and his father's. On the 20th May, Esther was at Bushey, staying with Diana White, a friend met at the Crystal Palace Art School. "She is strong in character and yet so fascinatingly womanly," Esther wrote. "I hope you will like her when you know her." Lucien did. She was a serious painter, and after his father's death, Lucien came to rely on her criticisms. He said he would know if the picture he was painting was good when Diana saw it. He could never see objectively what he did himself. Naughty, racy, full of spirits, Diana stimulated Lucien. Many years after, he was amused when she asked Sickert to take her niece, Regina Middleton, as a pupil, and on Sickert agreeing inquiring, with innocent round eyes: "Please, Mr. Sickert, will she need to buy an iron bedstead?"

Lucien joined his father at Eragny in August. Camille's eyes were better, the bandages off, and he worked indoors painting *motifs* seen through closed windows. Early in October, Lucien returned to London with Georges. Julie, to help out their slender resources, sent them baskets of food from Eragny. Lucien began two paintings, but progress was slow, the light fading too quickly in the afternoon. He had a letter of introduction to John Sargent, given him by Mirbeau. Sargent invited him and Georges to lunch: "He was very, very nice. I don't like his painting; he doesn't seem to me to be much of an artist. He has promised to come and see us." Camille commented (6th October): "As for his painting, that, of course, we can't approve of. He is not an enthusiast but rather an adroit performer. It was not for his painting that Mirbeau wanted you to see him. . . . Did you inform him that you give painting and drawing lessons?" Lucien had been too shy to do so. He introduced Georges to Ricketts and Shannon; Georges thought them marvellous: "They live together in complete harmony, never an unpleasant word between them. It is comic to see Ricketts, when something arouses his enthusiasm, throw his short arms with a wild gesture into the air."

The reluctant tide turned at last in Camille's favour. He began to sell at good prices, but all the same Lucien was surprised to hear in October (letter dated the 23rd) of 1891 that his father expected to make some ten or twelve thousand frances (£400 to £480) before the end of the year. "And if the money is forthcoming as quickly as I expect, we can set you up in London. What do you think of that?" In December, Camille saw with Julie and Mirbeau a representation of Maeterlinck's *Les Aveugles*. It was a miserable performance, but, said Camille, Julie was astonishing, and that Lucien would not have recognised her with her black velvet coat, stylish hat and opera glasses. It was nothing short of a resurrection: "If she knew what I was writing about her she would be angry," yet she came to Rodo's in Montmartre with her clothes for the occasion packed in two straw baskets. In the interval at the theatre, Carrière came to shake hands with Camille, and abruptly said: "You have had a great success in New York. Presently you will receive orders. Don't be taken by surprise." Bernheim said to him: "Your moment has come." It was true. In February, 1892, Lucien was in Paris for his father's exhibition at Durand-Ruel's. Despite bad weather and snow in the streets, the rooms were crowded day after day. Sales, if not phenomenal, were good, and at the close of the exhibition, Durand himself bought all the unsold paintings.

"The exhibition is a success," wrote Lucien to his mother. "Mirbeau's article in *Le Figaro* made a noise, and plenty of people came. As soon as the exhibition was opened a picture was sold for fifteen hundred francs (£60). When you come to Paris you will be surrounded with people patting you on the back and wanting to buy the pictures father has given you, but do not. Soon they will be twice the value they are today. At last the time has come when you will be happy and able to buy yourself a beautiful dress. It is time. You have been patient long enough."

Lucien was exhibiting at the Twenty Group in Brussels, he went there from Paris. His pictures were praised, they were hung near those of Mary Cassatt. "The last paintings of Seurat are changed, a disaster! Those of Signac luminous, mine are very, very gray. The group have a dinner tonight, I have not got my dress clothes, but I shall go all the same."

1892

On 20th May, Camille wrote: "It seems that M. Dallemagne is compelled to sell his house. Your mother wants me to *borrow* in order to buy it; I am opposed. The moment I am beginning to sell does not seem to me the right time to burden ourselves with a debt that will cause me anxiety, and all to the end of remaining in Eragny, which I would like to leave. It is too far from Paris, a badly constructed house which doesn't stand straight, with a garden far too large for your mother to look after, about which she has not failed to complain often enough. No, it doesn't suit me. If we have to move you can come and help us."

At some time in the spring Lucien had sent Esther a declaration of love and had asked her to marry him. His proposal was contained in a small and beautiful wooden box, carved and coloured by himself. This Esther showed to her father. Jacob was outraged. Never, he exclaimed, would he consent. "The day we are married," Esther wrote, "he declares he will go abroad and leave everybody." Religion was the root of his discontent. "He said he would consent if we were married in a synagogue and you were made a Jew." In spite of all she was extremely happy and not worried. There were violent scenes at Esther's home, or Jacob sulked and ignored her. It was agreed that the subject should not be discussed. One evening he exploded. The pretence was Esther's underclothing, he objected to their arrangement, she was flaunting herself. Esther's aunt witnessed the outburst, and the next day wrote to Esther: "My mind is too torn to pieces to talk to you, and besides I have made up my mind not to do so any more after the scene last night. I think it my duty to tell you what took place so that you may guide yourself in the future. Your grandmother was so upset by your obstinacy and the insulting way you spoke to your father that after crying for about an hour she had a heart attack and I thought she would die. Dr. Carter told me that she must be very careful to guard against anything like that as her heart is very weak. Now bear in mind what you do as I suppose you would scarcely like to have, in spite of your indifference and coldness, her death on your conscience." Esther replied that she thought a girl of her age should be allowed to have her own opinions about her underclothing.

Jacob appeared to compromise. They must be married in a synagogue. Lucien refused. Their children must be brought up in the Jewish faith. Lucien replied they would be brought up in no faith, but the principal religions would be explained to them when they were of an age to understand and make their own choice. Then the sons must be circumcised. That remained to be seen, guardedly replied Lucien. Lucien thought there was no future for him in England, and said that after the marriage he would return to Paris. Esther remained indifferent to the flow of argument, her mind made up. She would marry Lucien and did not care if this involved never seeing her parents again. Jacob wrote once more to Lucien: "As against my wish and without my consent you continue to pay your addresses to my daughter, and as I learn she accompanies you to Kew Gardens, I beg to inform you that I consider such conduct most improper and I must prohibit it in future. If you and she persist in disobeying my wish I shall take further steps to prevent it. I am informed that Mr. Isaacson has consented to allow my daughter to meet you at his house, and as you seem determined to disregard my commands it would certainly be more respectable to my mind that you should meet there and not in the public streets. You certainly seem to show very little respect for the feelings of her family."

This having no effect, Jacob played his trump card, explained by a letter Lucien wrote afterwards: "At the beginning, Esther, I was always telling myself that you were a rich girl, and that is why I did not dare to speak to you of my love. I was afraid that you would believe it was because of this money I wanted to marry you. But what your parents now have done will surely show you that it is you and you alone I love." Jacob had written, through his solicitor, that if Lucien would agree to all his stipulations and delay the marriage six months, not attempting during that time to see Esther, he would make a settlement on Esther at her marriage. Lucien said the proposal was a trap; he found the offer revolting. "Money could never have any weight on my decision in this matter." Jacob consented to see Lucien. The meeting was friendly, but Lucien said "nothing came out of it."

Jacob said a marriage unblessed by the church could have no good
result. On the contrary, said Lucien, my parents were married in an
English registry office, the results have been good, and they are both
very happy. As the marriage still hung fire, it was now that Lucien
begged Camille to come to London, confident his tact would conciliate
Jacob Bensusan. "You no doubt know," he wrote, "as mother knows,
that I love Esther Bensusan. That is why I regret so much that I am
unable to earn my living. I have talked to her, she says she loves me,
and we have made up our minds to marry one day. I think you will
approve and if this happens I look to you to help us until the day we are
able to manage. Will you help me now and write or come and see Mr.
Bensusan? To come would be better." Camille consented: "All
right. I know you love Esther B. Well, no other solution left than to
ask the father. I am quite ready to do what is necessary to help. I will
go to London as soon as I can, and when I think it will be the right
moment. I hope that we will succeed. You are a good boy and a son
of whom one can be proud. But you have one defect in your character. You are too frank. Your mother accepts your decision. We like
Esther B. What more? I will do all that is possible to help you." But
Julie had doubts about the marriage. "This girl is used to comfort
that you won't be able to give, and is not used to work, do you think
she will live in poverty for the love of you? Because you know you
must not rely too much on us, we still have three little ones to bring
up. Think well about it and be sure that you tell the young girl your
situation. I hope you haven't compromised yourself. The laws are
very strict on this matter." Lucien replied: "Don't worry, dear
mother, father Bensusan will not murder me."

Camille said he would be in England in eleven days, and bring with
him Maximilien Luce, Lucien's old friend. "I must tell you something
very sad. Our friend Luce is in great despair. His wife has left him,
and is not returning to him. The poor boy is out of his mind, I did not
know how to comfort him in his deep grief. I asked him to come to
London, so as to get him away from the surroundings which always
remind him of his wife. Could you find a modest room for him near
Leicester Square or in your district? Do your best."

Camille arrived in London on the 21st May, and on the 27th met
Jacob. They respected each other's opinions, but Camille made no
headway, Jacob reverting to his original objections to the marriage,
and insisting that he would only give his consent if Lucien became a
Jew and was circumcised. "Father discussed this with him," Lucien

wrote to Julie, "but he would not budge, he would rather, he said, see his family dead than go against his faith. He said he would never see Esther again if she married me, and would forbid the family to do so. It would kill the grandmother. The comic part is that he declared he would fast on the wedding day, and eat no food for twenty-four hours. However, we don't need his consent. Esther loves me and we shall go ahead with our plans."

Notice was given to the registrar, the day of the wedding fixed. Esther wrote to Julie: "Dear Madame Pissarro, I have so many times tried to tell you how happy I shall be to be your daughter-in-law. . . . I don't know much about housekeeping, but I hope I will learn quickly, and I hope to be a good wife and companion for our dear Lucien."

Camille and his two sons, Lucien and Georges, went to Kew to look for a lodging where they could all be together, and rooms were found over a baker's shop opposite the church and the green. Luce was with them, "it is almost impossible to comfort him".

Meanwhile Julie had been busy. As soon as Camille was away she hurried off to Monet at Giverny and asked him to lend the money to buy her house. When he learned this, Camille shrugged his shoulders and wrote to Monet backing her request. As ever, Monet did not hesitate to help his old friend, and in June Camille sent Lucien to Eragny to have the necessary deeds prepared. Lucien wrote to Esther, his letter headed Giverny: "You will be surprised at what you see at the top of this letter. I came here to see Monet, I had to explain to him about the famous house. Can you imagine this place, a small village, but very picturesque, the quarried hills dropping down to the Seine, lovely vistas of the river unfolding like a ribbon. This is a place I will have to show you when we will be at Eragny. The hotel where I write is full of Americans. There is a colony of them, men and women, all painters. After lunch they go to their landscapes with their boxes and easels. The fields look as if they are covered with mushrooms (in the margin of the letter is a drawing of a painter at his easel with an umbrella over his head, the effect like a mushroom). Monet must be much admired to attract so many people! The room in which I write is hung with the paintings of the Americans, who come to paint *à la Monet*. but the results are more *à la Julian* than Monet. They go hand in hand with the New English Art Club. There is no difference."

Lucien returned to England, but it was not until 11th August (1892) that he and Esther were married at the Richmond Registry Office. Mr. Prescott, Jacob Bensusan's confidential clerk, was there to witness that Esther was truly wed. The ceremony was delayed because he continued to talk with the Registrar on the merits of that year's Academy. Camille, Prescott, Ricketts and Shannon signed the register as witnesses to the marriage.

Lucien had been confused over the wedding date. He, Esther and the guests, including Luce, had arrived the day before, Ricketts and Shannon together, Ricketts with a bunch of yellow roses. Notwithstanding that there was no wedding, all sat down to the wedding breakfast prepared at the baker's shop. Esther returned home. Her younger sister Ruth thought Esther very silly not to have stayed with Lucien.

In the months before the wedding Camille had been at work, painting the church and a Bank Holiday fair on Kew Green, in Kew Gardens, the river by Charing Cross, and at Primrose Hill; he now returned to Eragny. Lucien and Esther set out on their honeymoon, Esther in a home-made dress, her pince-nez gripped firmly on her nose. They stayed at Rouen for two days, Lucien mindful that he must not spend too much, then, plotting their way from a map, they walked across country to Eragny where Camille and Julie awaited them. On the way Lucien wrote to Julie that he hoped her mood about his dear little Esther would change before their arrival. It was not without reason that he feared Julie's rough tongue and impatience with a girl she considered so inadequately trained to make her son a good wife.

CHAPTER V

Birth of Orovida. Epping. 1893

THE HOUSE AT ERAGNY WAS LITTLE CHANGED SINCE ESTHER'S FIRST VISIT.
The walls of the white-tiled hall had been decorated with paintings by
Georges of turkeys, cocks, hens, and other birds, and Félix had painted
on his bedroom door a ferocious black and white rat. Camille indifferent to the interior furnishing of the three-storied house and attics, had
left this to Julie's taste—mostly, heavy furniture, and an effect of rich
plush in the salon. The long garden extended to a stream, scene of the
family washing. Pollarded willows sprouted along the marge of the
stream: in the garden were flower-beds and a vegetable plot, and
apple trees and a walnut tree grew in a paddock. A *basse cour* had
hutches and hen-runs filled with rabbits and chickens. When a visitor
came, one of these was killed and cooked. The butcher called twice a
week, his conveyance a horse-drawn, blue-hooded cart. Opposite the
house was a red-bricked building where the trotting horses of M.
Charon, the farmer, were stabled. Along the one street, the main road
to Dieppe, was a café and the village shop kept by Madame Herbie,
where every kind of commodity was stocked in a pervading smell of
fusty femininity and spiced foods, and sales were wrapped in yellow-
brown paper. The Pissarro children went there to spend their sous on
sweets, barley-sugar was their favourite.

Sometimes there was a commotion in the street, and the villagers
gathered at their doors to watch a passing band of men and boys.
"Who are they?" asked Esther. "It's the sweeps, those poor boys
from Auvergne who climb the chimneys, children their parents
have given or sold away. They don't get enough to eat." And Julie
carved a large loaf into doorsteps covered with jam, ran out and fed
the boys.

Camille had a studio in the garden, now rarely used for he was
mostly in Paris painting his *rue St. Lazare* series. Esther would have
fared better had he been at home to restrain Julie, for she, convinced
that Lucien could not have married a worse wife, continually criticised
and nagged her. What sort of a helpmate was she for Lucien, when she

could not cook or sew? One morning Lucien had to leave the house early to go to Paris. He and Esther were awakened at five o'clock by thumps on their door by Julie, who insisted that Esther also got up and walked with Lucien to the station. She returned miserable at the prospect of a long day with Julie without Lucien's support. Julie was in the kitchen. She flung one of Lucien's shirts on the table. "It wants mending," she said. Esther did not know how to mend. "I'll show you," said Julie. It was the first of many lessons she gave Esther on how to patch and darn, to use her needle and to cook.

In December, Julie, in Paris with Camille, was agitated by news of Georges. To Lucien, at Eragny, she wrote: "Esther Isaacson doesn't tell me a word about the hundred francs I sent her, but oh, what a shock, she says she is married to Georges. Even Alice, her sister, did not know." It was true. The romantic Esther at the age of thirty-six who rebuked Georges when he had had a haircut that he no longer looked like an artist, had secretly married this boy fourteen years younger than herself a month after Lucien's wedding. Julie feared they would come and make their home at Eragny, but: "Oh, no," wrote Georges to Lucien, "she should not be scared like that, the poor woman. I never thought of such a thing. Certainly not. To let my wife be under her petticoats, why, I would never dream of it. Think how rude she has already been to your Esther."

1893

In March, 1893, Lucien and Esther went to Paris for Camille's exhibition, but Camille was in bed at his hotel, ill with bronchitis and yet another abscess on his eye. When he became bored Lucien read him the newspapers. Monet visited him. "Monet is working like mad on his cathedrals," Lucien reported, "painting from a window over a shop, from six in the morning until eight at night, ten pictures at the same time, turning from one to another as the effects of light change. Then he has dinner and is so tired that he goes to bed. One morning he saw in the street below someone waving an arm. He did not pay any attention, all day people are raising their arms and pointing to the effigies on the cathedral, but this unknown came across the street and knocked at his door. Monet opened, only then did he recognise Murer. 'Damn you,' said Monet, 'I have no time for you,' and slammed the door. Monet thought this a terrific joke." Monet told this anecdote to amuse Camille. He knew Camille no longer saw Murer as a good friend, but rather as a mercenary fellow who had taken advantage of his misfortunes. Camille was suspicious that Murer did not return one of his pictures because he had sold it. "I had entrusted to you two pictures that you were going to show to M. Laurent-Richard. You gave me back one, but you kept the best one, without right. This is quite clear. I have not stopped asking for it for the last fifteen years."

Julie continued to bully Esther. It made her miserable: she longed to return to London to set up a home and live alone with Lucien. But it was not until June of 1893, after nearly a year's stay at Eragny, that they were in furnished rooms in Lancaster Road, Westbourne Park, while looking for a country cottage near London.

Returning one afternoon from such a search in Essex, Lucien saw a row of mean houses reflected on the dark-green scummed water of a canal. Ragged children played on the towing path, slatternly women, arms akimbo, stood and gossiped in doorways. A cold grey sky and a creeping mist enhanced the impression of squalor and sordid poverty. Lucien, sad with pity, visualised a series of paintings, vehement protests that such poverty should be tolerated.

Finally a cottage was found in Hennell Street, Epping. The rent was twenty-one pounds a year—Lucien thought it excessive, but had seen nothing cheaper. But he liked the aspect of the surrounding landscapes, so similar to Eragny, he thought, but wider, and the oaks and the weeping willows in the forest lovely. The landscapes and the forest suggested many *motifs*, he was eager to set up his easel and get to work but, confused with the variety of subjects offered, did not know what to start on. No matter, he would get out his palette and results would come. So he wrote to Camille. The furniture came from Esther's mother; if it had not, as he had no money, they would have had none. Also her mother bought Esther's clothes and Aunt Orovida offered to pay the wages of a maid. Only her father, Jacob Bensusan, stayed "in his corner". A large room with deep windows served as a studio, a garden stretched back and front, and Lucien was in love with his new home. He named it Eragny House after the village where Camille lived. He told his mother Esther was not at all the girl she thought she was, on the contrary, she was splendid in the house, every morning she did the shopping, and she had refused the aunt's offer of a maid, as she was determined to do everything herself. And she was pregnant.

On the 26th July, Camille sent a recipe for painting with cheese. "Georges tells me that Epping is not very beautiful. Bah! One can make such beautiful things with so little. . . . Everything is beautiful, the whole secret lies in knowing how to interpret." Five weeks before, Georges' marriage to Esther Isaacson had ended tragically. Two days after giving birth to her baby Esther died. The child, a boy, survived.

The other Esther's child was born on the 8th of October, 1893, and named Orovida after Esther's aunt. Esther was disappointed, as she had wished for a boy. Lucien, true to the family tradition, said the only thing that mattered was that the child should turn out to be an artist. Julie wrote to Lucien: "How much torment you must have had to see your wife suffer like this. And how much you must have been afraid. Well, it is past, and I hope all will be well now. But what a funny name you have given your Orovida." She hoped that now Esther was a mother she would be more reasonable and not disturb him so much in his studio as she did at Eragny. "Think more of good cooking and sewing," she advised. "Georges is very unhappy and so makes us unhappy as well. Paul has made a portrait of Georges' child." Camille sent twelve hundred francs (£48) and a box of chocolates. He warned Lucien: "Beware of the after-effects of confinement. Be careful at night!"

Once each week Lucien went to London and spent the evening with Ricketts and Shannon. A dish of rice and tomatoes was kept hot for him against his return. He still spoke and understood English with difficulty. One night, at Liverpool Street station, he gathered from a cockney porter that his train was at midnight. He waited an hour, but there was no train. The last train had gone from another platform. A policeman directed him to a "respectable" hotel. Here he was told that the charge for bed and breakfast was five shillings and sixpence. He counted his money, he had only five shillings, but the matter was arranged. He paid three shillings for a room and went without breakfast. He found the bed hard. Early next morning he walked to the National Gallery, but oh, "*bon dieu!* The lazy English!" the Gallery did not open for another hour.

1894

In February of 1894, Camille wrote that he thought it would be good to go and paint at the seaside when his exhibition closed, if he could find shelter against the wind. "I saw your two pictures at Contet's. They are quite nice. But at first sight I think you are too close to my way of painting. I will come to Epping, but I must work very hard for the last few years I have left, and for as long as I can see and feel nature, so that I can end my life properly. Yes, my dear Lucien, we are all going, one after the other: our poor friends de Bellio and Caillebotte have gone, and the poor Tanguy, such a good man, so honest. If we had not made that silly mistake of buying Eragny Castle,* all of us could have been together in England. I had a feeling about this at the time: all the same we will have to do this one day."

Since he was a child Lucien had shown a passionate interest in books; he loved books, loving them as objects apart from their literary interest. One of his childish amusements had been to make books, which he wrote, illustrated and bound. Delighted with the English books for children illustrated by Randolph Caldecott (also greatly admired by Gauguin), Kate Greenaway and Walter Crane, he planned to make a book illustrating children's songs: *Il était une Bergère*. This project, however, had been refused by editors who pleaded that the costs of publication prohibited any profit. Upon this Lucien decided to learn engraving and thus be able to do the work himself. He went to Lepère for help "who, nice as he always is", gave him a few indications on tools and how to use them. His first efforts were directed at sketches drawn for him by his father. F. S. Dumas, director of the *Revue Illustrée*, commissioned him to illustrate a short story by Octave Mirbeau, *Mait' Lizéard*, but the wood engravings he made aroused criticism. "Something you will permit me *not* to appreciate," wrote one indignant reader to the editor of the *Revue*, "oh! not at all, are those would-be realist illustrations by Pissarro. I prefer the peasants of Jeanniot, at least they are drawn. How could you have drawings like this in an artistic journal when there are so many draughtsmen who would be glad to make pretty things? Aren't you going to give us something about the beaches and the seaside? The last number had a few pretty things..." There were other abusive letters and Dumas had to refuse further work from Lucien. Most of the protests came from the students at Cormon's *atelier*.

Lucien's meeting with Ricketts and Shannon in 1891 had revived his interest in bookmaking, for they were sympathetic to his ideas. It is not without significance that William Morris published the first book of his Kelmscott Press in this same year. The following decade was to see a new impulse in England towards printing and making beautiful books as exemplified in the private presses that began to be founded. In 1894, Lucien's first book was published, and in this year C. H. St.

---

* In English in the letter, a mocking reference to Camille's recently acquired house in Eragny.

John Hornby began the Ashenden Press. In 1895, the first Vale Press book appeared, and in 1896 C. R. Ashbee initiated the Essex House Press. Soon after, Emery Walker and T. J. Cobden-Sanderson began work on a type face for the Doves Press. Lucien's books and the work of these English private presses were increasingly exhibited on the continent and made a profound impact. The distinguishing characteristic of all these presses was their own individual type faces, in general conceived to provide harmony between the text and the illustrations or borders.

Ricketts, with the financial help of Hacon, established a business to produce and sell artistic books under the name of the Vale Press. The typography which he created he allowed Lucien to use, and this he did from after his first book until 1903, when Ricketts, considering he had achieved his own aim, destroyed his founts by throwing them into the Thames. Lucien had already been working on a type face since 1901 when Ricketts withdrew his type. This was the "Brook" type, named after Lucien's house at Stamford Brook. It was cast, and Lucien continued making his books with it until 1914 when increasing difficulties which came with the outbreak of war made further publications impossible. Lucien's first book, *The Queen of the Fishes*, was finished and published in 1894. Printed on Japanese handmade paper, on uncut pages, on one side only, as in Chinese books, the handwritten text was decorated with sixteen woodcuts, one printed in five colours, four in four, eight in grey resembling the text, and three in red. The title was in gold, and the frontispiece border in gold, repeated three times in green. Copies subscribed before publication were bound in soft green leather, the others in vellum. This exquisite example of craftsmanship and of wood engraving preceded the fifteen volumes printed in the Vale type. Nothing produced by private presses has ever surpassed the delicate colourings of the wood blocks Lucien made for the Eragny Press as it was called. He was a pioneer in using colour in wood engraving. Further, his engravings were always considered in their relationship to the typography, he never attempted to bring out of the wood anything foreign to the medium. He tried to express things seen or felt personally, especially in the colour engravings. His early prints depicted men and women at work in the field or home, figure studies. The style was imitative of Camille's, but Lucien had learnt from Lepère the mellow surface which could be obtained by rich contrasts of value and texture. Soon there was a significant change, and he drew "a languid type of woman, elongated and drooping, who

74

moved in a pastoral dream world. No sharper contrast could be imagined to the matter-of-fact peasants and townspeople of his earlier prints".*

After taking a course of instruction in wood engraving, Esther worked at the making of the books with Lucien and was of great help. When they began, Lucien, knowing nothing of the craft of printing, was faced with unexpected difficulties. A hand-press was purchased with money lent by Camille, and *The Queen of the Fishes* was begun, two pages at a time, the gold used being real gold powder. Tools were imperfect, registration gave trouble, and it was only after the waste of many sheets of paper that the final result was achieved.

On the 24th June, President Carnot was assassinated by an anarchist at Lyon. Towards the end of the next month Camille, at the Hotel de Bruges, Knocke, wrote: "I am afraid I shall be forced to stay abroad for some time. Since the last law passed by the French Chamber it is absolutely impossible for anyone to feel safe. Even a concierge is allowed to open your letters. A mere denunciation can land you across the frontier, or in prison, and you are powerless to defend yourself. Our friends have successively left France. Mirbeau, Paul Adam, Bernard Lazare, Steinlen, and Hamont were to be arrested, but they managed to escape in time. Poor Luce was caught; probably someone denounced him. And since I don't trust certain persons in Eragny who dislike us, I shall remain abroad." Lucien went to stay with Camille. From the ship he saw his white beard on the quayside. "Félix and Rodo were with him. We had an English tea at the Yellow House." At the hotel Lucien met a priest about to *jeter le froc aux orties,* an English painter who resembled a chick just out of its shell, but very nice! and a lady with her two young cousins, who had just finished their schooling at a convent, "ignorant as fish but as cunning as monkeys, and one is in love with the priest. The *demi-vierge* truly exists. I heard kissing on the stairs!"

When he was home again in October, Lucien received a grumbling letter from Julie: he did not tell her his news. "Your mother doesn't take much place in your life—what a lot of trouble you gave her to bring you up. How are you going to manage if your father does not give you any more? I don't know how you are going to live." She complained that not one of her sons was able to earn a living. It was Camille who managed to make them all allowances and keep them

* *Notes on the Eragny Press and a letter to J. B. Manson,* by Alan Fern. Cambridge. Privately printed. 1957.

going. He sent Lucien two hundred francs (£8) every month, enough to live on in those days, and often Lucien made further demands on him. "You all beg from your father. I wanted so much for you to have a job, but you would not take my advice, only laughed at me. God help you! I hope you won't regret it. We are ourselves without money. Your father gave me a thousand francs (£40) last June, since then I have had nothing. Do you want me to send you any food?" In a further letter she said that Durand still offered poor prices. "We shall have worries again. Your father's paintings lean against the wall, but he does not allow me to sell them." But she would let one of her own pictures go to help Lucien. "It is worth six thousand francs (£240), if I can find a buyer, I will accept four. Do not let your father or the others know." She could not let Esther alone and Lucien had to reprove her: "You seem still to have animosity against poor Esther who, however, does her best to keep the house tidy and look after the baby. You speak about her cooking. She does cook and well. She has no time for drawing."

1895

His life in 1895 was reflected in his letters. He was incessantly at work on his wood engraving and the preparations for a new book: there were problems of paper, and he fretted that his money went such a little way. He was asked to contribute illustrations to continental periodicals, "but, if so, one works for the love of art, or so I am persuaded, and that means a small payment or, more probably, nothing."

He thought it an excellent idea for Camille to paint at Rouen; sitting at a window he would do marvellous things, certainly "the effect of rain cannot be obtained otherwise."

On the 5th April, the Eighth Marquess of Queensberry was acquitted of the charge brought against him of criminal libel, and Oscar Wilde was arrested and taken to Holloway Prison. Lucien wrote to Camille: "You have probably heard of the Oscar Wilde affair. You cannot conceive of the venom and hatred there is against him. It is not so much his sodomy but the artist and the intellectual over which the storm rages. I fear he is lost." This opinion was no doubt inspired by Ricketts, whose friendship with Wilde was of long standing. Lucien was an innocent: it was only after he had known Ricketts and Shannon for many years that he remarked to Esther: "They are a couple of old aunties." Shannon began a portrait of Lucien in oils and he went to Chelsea every week to sit.

The printing of *The Queen of the Fishes* was now completed: of the hundred copies made, seventy were taken by John Lane of the Bodley Head, but when, on 15th May, Wilde was sentenced to two years imprisonment with hard labour, there was reaction against Lane's innocuous "Yellow Book",* ludicrously regarded as a symbol of decadence, and Lucien told Camille: "This Wilde affair has seriously interfered with Lane's business, which is upside down. Here in this country one lives as if it were still in the middle ages." Shannon wrote to Lucien on the 26th September from Beaufort Street: "We have heard no news of Oscar at all. The new Ministry may make it easier for him in prison, but I am afraid any idea of shortening the sentence would be impossible. We are very much frightened because Sir Edward Clarke refused to take office as Solicitor-General, and the alternative man was Carson, the lawyer who appeared in the Queensberry trial, but this I think is arranged now, and Clarke will be in office. Unfortunately it does not mean that he can do anything." On the same day Ricketts wrote: "I have just written to Oscar Wilde who complains that he cannot sleep and that they do not give him enough food."

Camille wrote on the 20th October: "Despite a great sweep of work, I am very bored in Eragny. . . . Is it anxiety about money, the feel of winter approaching, weariness with the same old *motifs*, or lack of data for the figure paintings I am doing in the studio? It is partly due to all these things, but what hurts me most is seeing, little by little, the breakup of the family. Cocotte is gone (she was at boarding school in Paris), soon it will be Rodo. Can you see us two old people alone in this great house all the winter? It is not gay. . . . They say it makes one work. I don't agree. Although I don't like anyone pestering me when I am working, isolation doesn't give me an eagerness to paint." On the 10th December, he wrote: "I am conducting a campaign here against forgers who are peddling fake paintings and *gouaches,* among others a large *gouache* by Piette signed with my name, forged of course, the name mispelled. . . . I have almost finished my large figure paintings. Finished? That is to say I leave them about the studio until the moment

---

* When Wilde was arrested he had in his hand a copy of Pierre Louÿ's *Aphrodite* bound in a yellow cover. Newspapers, the next morning, had the headline: "ARREST OF OSCAR WILDE. YELLOW BOOK UNDER HIS ARM." It was consequently widely believed that the book was "The Yellow Book". A crowd demonstrated outside the Bodley Head and smashed the windows. "It nearly killed the Yellow Book," John Lane said, "and it nearly killed me." See *A Study in Yellow*, by Katherine Lyon Mix (Constable. 1960).

77

when I find the final sensation that will give them life." The final
sensation! That was the gospel to Lucien, he reiterated his father's
words throughout his life. The Camden Town Group came to know
them well.

Lucien tried to finish two pictures started the previous year, he had
not touched a brush for months, now he began again, from this time he
abandoned the "dot", and it disappeared from his painting. "Here is
winter," he wrote to Camille, "and, of course, we are short of money."
But he had not given up hope, he was only impatient. "Frost, fog,
snow, but I have a fire and a comfortable room to work in. I am not
to be pitied." Hayet, his old school friend, had visited him in London.
"He works and decorates a room at Olympia, and he has saved four
hundred francs (£16)." "Do you remember the young Conder, a friend
of Rothenstein's, whose pictures of Algerian landscapes we saw at
Thomas's? This boy sinks lower every day with drunkenness and
debauchery. Bing★ has asked him to decorate a room and here again
English art will be represented by Julian." In his anxiety for exactitude
Lucien asked Rodo at Eragny to send him some fallen leaves from under
the cedar. He wanted to be correct in his drawing of their shapes.

1896

Camille wrote from Rouen on the 20th January of the change in
Cézanne. He had further evidence that he was unbalanced and resentful of old friends. "He said: 'Pissarro is an old fool, Monet a cunning
fellow; they have nothing in them. I am the only one who can make a
red!'" "It is strange what you say of Cézanne" Lucien replied. "Do
you remember the poor Père Tanguy said a long time ago that he was
not right in his head? We thought it was Tanguy's way of speaking, he
was such a simple man, but perhaps he was right. Is it the effect of his
parsimonious habits and excitability? It is all very strange. Esther
helps me with the book and does the wood engravings of my letters and
decorations." Lucien asked: "How have you managed to paint eleven
pictures from your window?" Julie was anxious that he was at Rouen
alone, "the cold and the fog is not good for him". "The mother has
written me such a solicitous letter about you," Lucien told Camille.

Camille continued to encourage and advise Lucien. "I sense in your
letters a great enthusiasm for your work", he wrote on the 20th Feb-

★ Bing was noted for his gallery of objects of art imported from the Far East,
particularly Japan. He also showed contemporary arts and crafts. His gallery was
the headquarters of *L'Art Nouveau*. It was Fritz Thaulow who persuaded Bing to
giver Conder this commission.

ruary, "that is the main thing, with that one can go a long way. All this gives me comfort and the encouragement I needed to finish the paintings I have so rashly begun."

Progress on a new book was laborious and slow. Lucien found it hard to print with a hand-press. After his first book, he was printing in the Vale type. Dependant on the local printer, he had to spend much time in his workshop: "I am the director and the workman, and when I come back home after a day's work there, I still have the paper to damp and prepare for the next day." When he had finished he was so exhausted that he dropped on his bed and was asleep immediately. On 17th March, Camille wrote: "I am sending you a letter from Pouget who is in prison, and on the back you will read your mother's harsh words for me because I am moved by his misfortunes. However, I am only returning to another what Caillebotte did for us when we were in trouble and glad we were to have this help. I don't understand her reproaches. I write to her all the time [Camille was still in Rouen], but she scarcely sends me a word—except of reproof!"

In April, Ricketts and Hacon opened their shop, painted in apple green with a small, white-panelled room at the back, with an exhibition of wood engravings by Ricketts and Lucien.

Orovida caused anxiety, her legs were weak and she did not walk properly, so massage was advised. To save the expense of a trained nurse, Esther undertook a course of instruction. "Her plump and short hands are just the thing," said Lucien, and she became extremely proficient; in the next year her skill was to be invaluable when Lucien was seriously ill. Already this coming illness had cast a shadow and he had had to consult his doctor about recurring attacks of dizziness. In June he joined his father in Paris; from there they travelled by boat to Rouen, Lucien drenched with the spray from the paddle-wheel. The streets of Rouen brought back memories of his honeymoon, "the most beautiful moments of my life", he wrote to Esther, and he lingered outside one shop, for it was there, he remembered so well, that he waited for her while she was inside buying a pair of gloves. In Paris he went with Camille to a Renoir exhibition. He said there were some charming things, "the series of children exquisite". Ricketts dined with them and was very gay, he and Lucien planned to write a little book on engraving.* Lucien also dined with Fénéon and Verhaeren.

* This they eventually did and it was published in Paris *en vente chez Floury* and titled *De la typographie moderne: William Morris et son influence sur les arts et métiers*. It was also sold by Hacon and Ricketts in London, 1898.

On the 14th July he wrote "the weather is superb", and during the day he watched the processions. When evening came the narrow streets off the *boulevards* were illuminated with Chinese lanterns, and everyone danced to the music of bands perched on rough and ready platforms of planks. "It was all very gay and jolly, but I felt very much alone."

In August, Julie came to London for a holiday, bringing with her Rodo and Paul Emile. She rented a flat of four rooms for fifty shillings a week. "Far too expensive!" she wrote to Camille. "It is a waste of money, so we shall only stay a day or two and go to Lucien's. Tell the maid to water my flowers and not forget the birds." She made an excursion to the Crystal Palace, and visited the church at Sydenham which Camille painted in 1870. She went to Kew Gardens and was amazed at the profusion of flowers, but most of her afternoon was spent in the hot-houses. When she returned to Eragny she abused Esther and Lucien to Camille. She complained they were living beyond their means and Esther was the worst of housekeepers. Lucien, angry when he heard of this, said that more than usual was spent to make Julie welcome. "She thinks we should live in poverty as she did. I do my best to earn some money. Nevertheless it has only been twenty pounds this year. This lack of money paralyses my efforts. It is hard to live here on eight pounds a month, barely sufficient for food and rent. Our clothes are shabby and I have to buy blocks and pay the photographer. Esther does what she can to help and goes to the doctor's every day to massage one of his patients." He grumbled that the house at Epping was too small and inconvenient for his work. Also it would be better for his work to live nearer London, and he has decided to move. He asked Camille for three hundred francs (£12) to help with the removal expenses. Julie opened and read his letter, she scribbled at the bottom: "Tell Lucien you will send him the three hundred francs." But she must have changed her mind, for Camille wrote on 5th September: "Your mother insists that I should not give you three hundred francs. She must have spoken of this to you. For a long time she has argued with me about this. I try to reconcile everybody, but I don't succeed very well. All I can say at the moment is that you can be sure I will help you if conditions are not too bad. . . . So, for my part, I will do my utmost to send you the three hundred francs without speaking about it."

Lucien, impatient to move, found a house in Bedford Park and planned to go there in April. In debt, he again appealed to Camille for help who wrote on 10th March, 1897, "I will advance you money to move. I must tell you since we are on the subject of money, that I am changing my will and that Tessier (Camille's lawyer) is handling it. He tells me that, in order to prevent possible litigation, I must make, or rather keep, an account for each child to whom I send money, so that if necessary a reckoning can be made so that there will be no jealousy. As I want to spare you annoyance, I am doing it."

A few days later, Lucien sent Camille a copy of his third book, the second printed with the Vale type, the first volume of Jules Laforgue's *Moralités Légendaires*. "Your book arrived," Camille replied. "Very beautiful, very polished, the first page with the ornament of Salomé, the typography, etc., has the stamp of a master. The cover is charming. It is a beautiful book."

CHAPTER VI

Death of Félix. 1897

LUCIEN'S NEW HOME AT 62 BATH ROAD, BEDFORD PARK, HAD ON ONE SIDE a vista of open fields and a single railway track, on which infrequent trains used to clank to and fro between Acton and Chiswick, now long disused and overgrown with rank grass and weeds. Next to the house was a signal box, a level crossing and a wooden bridge. Perhaps Lucien's choice of locality had been influenced by Ricketts, who spoke of Bedford Park as a synonym for the elect of his art world.

He had not been well for some time. He had attacks of vertigo, sometimes his legs gave way under him. One afternoon in Bond Street he had to cling to Ricketts' arm for support until they reached a teashop where he was able to sit and recover. His doctor, McNish, feared these symptoms portended impending paralysis. Esther was alarmed, and she hid the diagnosis from Lucien, but told Camille, and so it became known to the family. Félix, not understanding that Lucien was unaware of this threat, wrote commiserating. Lucien was disturbed, but Esther assured him it was all nonsense; no doubt it was the mother who was to blame, she distorted everything. Lucien wrote to Camille that it was true he was not well: "But it is an exaggeration to speak of a beginning of paralysis! For over two years two fingers in my left hand have been numb and lifeless. I am told that it is nothing serious." But it was. He dined with Ricketts one evening in May, and came home by the last train. When he awoke the next morning, he was so tired that he stayed in bed; he told Esther he was enervated and unable to settle to work. In the early afternoon Esther found him crumpled in an armchair in the studio. His speech was indistinct, he complained of faintness. Esther fetched him a glass of milk and brandy. After drinking it he attempted to stand up, but his legs failed him, he fell over, retched distressfully, and vomited. Now he felt hungry and ate some cold meat, celery and apple rings, and drank two glasses of red wine. "He could not use his left arm at all," Esther wrote to Camille, "his right eye was almost closed, and he seemed drowsy. I had to feed him. I rubbed his arm and shoulder and after a great deal of persuasion got him to bed." She consulted the fat volume of homeo-pathic remedies—like his father, Lucien had a great belief in homeopathy—and gave Lucien opium and a salt water *lavement*. This had an effect, Lucien was able to grasp her hand with his paralysed one. For the rest of the afternoon he slept. The proscribed homeopathic doses of opium were repeated. The next morning, weak, but better, he only faintly remembered the events of the previous day. In response to a telegram, Esther's aunt, Orovida, arrived in the evening, and McNish began the first of many visits.

Anxious and alarmed at Esther's letter, Camille, who was at Eragny, abandoned his paintings of apple trees heavy with blossom, and hurried to London to be by his side. He could do little, but his presence was comforting. At the back of the house a flat roof overlooked the fields on the other side of the railway line, and here Camille set up an easel and painted *Fête de Jubilé à Bedford Park*, on the day of the celebration of Queen Victoria's Diamond Jubilee. His *motif* was a field thronged with people in holiday clothes, soldiers in scarlet coats, tents, and gay flags flying in the breeze. From this same vantage point he painted two further pictures of cricket being played on this field. In these canvases, against a background of trees, there was a ring of spectators watching the flannel-clad players in the middle. Camille had seen cricket before in England, and the game had a fascination for him. In one of his letters to Lucien, writing of a house he was considering renting, he commented that it had a field "where we shall be able to have some cricket". From a window in front of the house he painted a canvas of two children playing in the garden with a background of road and houses and another of the wooden bridge over the level crossing.*

Before Camille's arrival. Lucien had a relapse and fell unconscious. Esther sat by his bedside throughout the night, his sleep broken by hallucinations and deliriums. The coming of Camille was a tonic, but Lucien's progress towards health was slow. The weather being warm, Esther hired a bath-chair and wheeled him about the streets of the neighbourhood. When he was strong enough for the journey, Lucien, with Esther and the child, accompanied Camille back to Eragny, and here they stayed until October.

To Eragny, at the end of September, came bad news of Félix, living at Kew with Georges. He was ill, in an advanced stage of tuberculosis.

* Rodo's catalogue, numbers 1008, 1005, 1007, 1009, 1006.

Julie packed a bag and went to England to nurse him, it being arranged that she should stay in Esther's home. Three days after her departure, Camille received one of her frightful letters. She said she had arrived at Bath Road to find the linen and kitchen cupboards locked, the keys nowhere to be found. "That was a nice welcome!" Of course, Esther made these difficulties because she did not want her in her home. Camille being in Paris, Esther wrote indignantly to him—the mother's accusations were untrue and spiteful. If she hadn't wanted her in her house she would have said so, and she would not have been so disgustingly underhand as to leave everything locked. The mother knew that Mrs. McGregor had the keys—why did she not go to her and collect them? "Georges and the mother hate me. I should not mind very much on their account, but as I like you *very* much, I dislike the idea that you doubt me. Please do not listen to the things said about me and the things that are certain to be said about me when we are home again."

The McGregors lived at Stamford Brook House, a few hundred yards from 62 Bath Road. Archibald McGregor was the art master at the Crystal Palace Art School; Esther and Diana White had been his pupils, indeed Diana had posed for him, since he admired her beauty. The Lucien Pissarros and the McGregors were close friends. Lucien, after his return home, went to his studio to draw from the life. McGregor's ambition was to have a picture accepted for the Academy, an ambition never realised.

When, in October, Esther and Lucien were home again, Esther discovered she had left several things at Eragny. Camille wrote on the 30th to Lucien: "I sent Esther a little box with a pair of scissors she left here. Along with these I sent a pair of spectacles, which I found glinting in the sun under the seat of the large walnut tree; I saw them while I was making a study. Soon I hope we shall find, little by little, everything Esther lost in field and garden. . . . It is a pity that all the things she sows cannot take root and blossom!" Lucien wrote to Camille: "I am really better now, but unfortunately not well enough to be able to get such letters as the mother writes to me. It is Esther she is against, but she doesn't understand it upsets me as well." Julie was certainly rampaging at this time, harassing the patient Camille; no doubt it was she who nagged him to write and chide Esther. "In your letter you tell me that you have only seventy francs left in your pocket of the four hundred francs I sent you. I don't understand how you managed to go so quickly about it. It is not that I did not warn

VIIa. Reapers resting

VIIb. Ruth gleaning

Wood engravings from *The Book of Ruth and Esther*

VIIIa. Ruth and Naomi

VIIIb. Crowning of
Esther

Wood engravings from *The Book of Ruth and Esther*

you. The money I have got is only enough for my present needs. You must understand that I have Félix ill, and doctors in London and Paris to be paid. If I am not careful I shall not manage. As soon as you arrive you take a maid, but, Esther, how are you going to pay her?" Esther replied: "Dear Father, You are really quite unfair. Since we came back from France, I have kept my accounts *perfectly*, and can account for every penny spent and received. I have everything written down in a new book, and auntie went over it *all* to see if I had made any mistakes and there were *none*. The £4 disappeared within the last three weeks, and auntie thought Beatrice (the maid) must have taken it. Beatrice got tipsy and went away last Monday and then could not account for some of the money I had given her to pay bills with. Since she has left Ruth (Esther's sister) has slept here, and one evening when I went to buy provisions I found that Beatrice had been making me pay more for some things than she herself paid. So if people can take little sums they can take big, and I suppose she must have taken the £4. The money is never anywhere but in my desk, so it can be in no corners. Beatrice I would have trusted anywhere, and it was a real disappointment to find her turn out so badly. There were a few little things of mine when she turned her trunk out before me, my scissors for example. The things you found at Eragny I knew I had left about, but my silver buckle and buttonhook and the handkerchiefs, you never found and never will. However it is no good being angry, there is an English proverb, 'give a dog a bad name and you may hang him'. My bad name was given me years ago."

Poor Esther! She was certainly not the shiftless creature Julie depicted. True she was a bad manager but in so many things she was lovable and admirable. Her devotion to Lucien was steadfast, and her help in the printing-room, where she worked for long hours, invaluable. Obstinate, generous, enthusiastic over friends and the friends of friends she tried to do twenty things at a gulp, and was ever asking the aid of friends and relatives to help her lame ducks. Her integrity in money matters and artistic judgement was unquestionable.

Ruth, who was staying with her, was the sister who was surprised Esther had not stayed and slept with Lucien when it was discovered the wedding was not until the next day. She was a medical student. The two sisters had a great respect for each other; nevertheless within five minutes of any meeting, they quarrelled. Ruth believed progress was achieved by battle; her head was full of reforms, her method in argument not unlike the militancy of the later suffragettes. In the future, when she called to have tea with Esther, Esther would ask her to examine medically some new charwoman she had acquired. "If this happens again," Ruth once remarked, "I will never visit you again." Esther was not daunted. Soon after she sent one of her chars to the Royal Free Hospital with instructions to insist on seeing nobody but Miss Bensusan, to Ruth's embarrassment, since she was still only a student. Nevertheless Ruth admired Esther and considered her devotion to Lucien during his illness did much to prolong his life.

Félix died on the 25th November, 1897. Camille asked Esther to spare Lucien the shock of a letter and tell him as gently as she could the sad news. Aware of the affection between the two brothers she knew the blow could not be tempered. On December 15th Camille wrote: "I can't tell you how glad I am to see you have been able to brave the disastrous news of the death of our poor Titi, whom we loved so much, our hope, our pride. We were afraid to inform you and didn't know how to conceal our great grief from you, but in such fatal circumstances we have to be resigned and think of those around us. To give way to discouragement would be terribly dangerous, and we must surmount what we could not prevent. In our misfortune I was able to see how well Georges rose to the occasion, he evidenced great strength of character, for he kept your mother from making herself ill. Well, my dear Lucien, let us work. That will dress our wounds. I wish you strength, I want you to wrap yourself up, so to speak, in art; this will not keep us from remembering that fine, gentle, subtle and delicate artist, from loving him always. Mirbeau has written a remarkable piece about our poor child."

"An admirable family," Octave Mirbeau had written, "which takes us back to the heroic days of art. Camille Pissarro, in his old age, youthful and venerated, lives surrounded by his five sons, all artists and all different. Each one follows his own nature. Their father does not impose his theories, his doctrines, nor his way of seeing and feeling upon them. He allows them to develop by themselves, encouraging them to depend on their visual sense and on their individual intelligence.

"Lucien is a luminous and delicate landscape painter of exquisite sensitivity who does not confine himself to expression on canvas only. Having settled in England for the last few years, he tackles all sorts of mediums, woodcuts, book illustrations and engraving. Everything he creates he does with charming taste, discreet in his compositions.

"Georges, who resembles Félix very much both in temperament and ardent imagination, tends towards powerful and decorative lines. Enticed by the mystery of form and trying to translate it on canvas, wood or copper (all tools are good for him), he dreams of a new style for furniture. He works on materials, copper and enamels. Any little bit of metal or wood is a pretext for an ornament.

"Félix was a very young man, almost a child, with a serious and handsome face and expressive eyes, who gave everyone hope of being one day a very great artist. More than hope—certainty! Ardent imagination, originality, great vision, delicate taste; it was sufficient for Félix to want to do something for him to realise it: oils, water-colours, wood-carving or sculpture. With an old nail and a piece of zinc fallen from the roof, he made dry points of the most ingenious arrangement. My confidence in Félix Pissarro's future was extreme, but nothing remains of all the beautiful dreams that the poor child created around himself.

"Rodolphe, sarcastic by nature and always silent. At the age of ten he is always alone. What is he thinking about? Nobody knows. Where is he going? He is always away. He follows the banks of the Epte, gravely walks in the fields. Is he drawing horses like Félix? The river-banks, the sunny hills, the silvery mists, or the meadows like Lucien? No! One day in his room quantities of albums are found and they are an astonishment! Here is a disrespectful history of Punch and Judy and the Policeman. Authority is ridiculed in ferocious and cruel lines. The policeman and judges with faces of incredible deformation, resemble the neighbours of the district, they are recognisable, their characteristics exaggerated, a marvellous satire. Everyone laughs.

"And now to the youngest, Paul Emile, still in short trousers. One day a water-colour is confiscated by his father. It is of an old horse in the snow, it shows surprisingly original qualities.

"Such is this family, where art is at home and where everyone, whether young or old, cultivate the rarest flowers of beauty, without noise, without publicity and in proud and joyous independence."

A few days before Christmas, Lucien wrote: "I have little time for myself. The whole morning is taken with massage,* time for lunch; after dark, so early with the foggy weather we have, Esther is busy printing the cover of my new book. You are right, it is only work that will drown our griefs. What you told me about our poor Félix as an artist is really true." Only twenty-three when he died, Félix had hardly

* Esther massaged him, day after day, for many months. She was untiring.

started to live, yet he was already a gifted painter with a richer promise, Camille thought, than any of the family.

Lucien, Esther, and Orovida spent Christmas at Norwood with Esther's parents. Jacob's animosity towards Lucien had long since turned to liking. He now spent many days hawking Lucien's books from one London bookseller to another. He was not very good at this self-imposed task.

Before his illness, Lucien had walked with feline grace; after, he became awkward and clumsy. His restoration to health was long protracted—physically he was never the same, and the fingers of his left hand remained still and clinched. It was said of J. B. Manson's portrait of him, acquired by the Manchester Art Gallery, that the drawing of this hand was fumbled and unconvincing, unfortunately it was not, the hand was depicted as it actually was.

In December, Camille was painting from the windows of an enormous room in the *Grand Hôtel du Louvre,* where he had a superb view of the Avenue de l'Opéra and the corner of the Place du Palais Royal. On the 21st he wrote: "It is very beautiful to paint!... I am delighted to be able to paint these Paris streets that people have come to call ugly, but which are so silvery, so luminous, so vital."

1898

"I left Eragny very disturbed about your mother's condition," Camille wrote on the 6th January, "she has just recovered from the *grippe,* but what really worries me is her complete discouragement and state of nervous exasperation, such as I have never seen in her before. She weeps for our poor Titi (Félix) night and day. That is understandable, but what is less so is her belief that we are all indifferent, that none of us thinks of our poor little one. Because I do my best not to awaken our grief, your mother regards me as a bad father, lacking in sensibility and without affection for the poor boy. Everybody doesn't feel the same way. Georges and I live with Titi by arranging his drawings and pictures, and we feel his absence when we see what a subtle artist he was. Your mother's exasperation is of course the result of her grief and of overworking herself in London nursing our son. I have done my best to persuade her to rest, but she resists all advice. If I gave way to discouragement, what would become of us?"

Lucien, walking with difficulty, visited an exhibition at the New Gallery: "There was a room full of Rossetti paintings, mainly watercolours, very studied, bright colours. He appears to be a really great artist, greater than when he is painting in oil. Thank you very much for your offer to increase my allowance. It will help me a lot as I cannot earn my living at the moment, and it is impossible to economise on food as I have to be well fed."

Spring came, the trees blossomed, a *motif* which Lucien loved to paint, and he was sad he could not. It was difficult for him to hold a brush, drawing was impossible. Told that *The Queen of the Fishes* was regarded in Paris as a significant piece of beautiful bookmaking, his head full of plans for another book, the enforced waste of time vexed him. He wrote to Camille that he did not know he was so well thought of in France: he longed to get to work, but was badly in need of twenty pounds to buy a press. In May, the use of a house at Lowestoft was offered him by Mrs. McGregor's mother, Mrs. Miers, who had gone to Rome for Easter. "Not for my pleasure am I here I can assure you," wrote Lucien, "as I can hardly walk. However the air does me good. I feel better." On her way back to England, Mrs. Miers fell down the stairs in a Paris hotel and broke her leg, this enabled Lucien to stay in Lowestoft for a month instead of a fortnight. In August, Camille was at Rouen, and on the 19th he wrote: "For a long time now I have been casting about for some way to put five hundred francs aside for you to buy a press, but I haven't been able. Since I cannot always work at Eragny, I am forced to go to places where I can find attractive and interesting *motifs*, and this is expensive, very expensive. Fortunately I am still able to work." It was not until the 9th September that he was able to tell Lucien that he had written to Durand "to send you five hundred francs (£20) to buy the printing press". With this money, Lucien acquired a large press, but told Camille he was hindered, he had no money to buy the materials necessary for his next book. He ruefully added that his last book had yielded a profit of five francs. Grumbles about Esther's uneconomical housekeeping continued to flow from Eragny, and Lucien wrote to his father: "You may say that Esther does not organise as well as she should, but since we started the printing again, she is doing all the work I cannot do. She cannot be everywhere, and what she does do is a great compensation for what she doesn't. If I was alone all I could do would be to sit at the church door, cap in hand, for at the moment I could not even draw on the pavement. Poor Puvis has died. They said in the newspapers that he hadn't worked since his recent marriage. Is that true? I am really grieved. Alas! All the people we loved are going."

In December, Lucien sent Camille a drawing made by Orovida—
"all her own work, and not guided". "The deuce!" replied Camille.
"Here is still another potential artist. Orovida shows skill in drawing,
it was written that she would. Her drawing is already full of feeling,
elegance and unconstraint."

1899

"I long to be able to work," Lucien wrote early in the New Year,
"but it comes very slowly." He had been to the Royal Academy's
Winter Exhibition and seen some wonderful Rembrandt self-por-
traits, particularly one as an old man with grey hair. "Superb!" he
told Camille. "I could not help thinking of one you did of yourself
wearing your spectacles. It may seem ridiculous to tell you this, but it
seemed to me here, in the method of painting, is the same care as in
your approach. I started drawing again today. It was no good. I shall
have to begin all over again. I am sometimes frightened not to have
the strength to overcome this. I am able to do so little in a day." News
of another death saddened him. Sisley, the old comrade of his father
and Monet, died in complete destitution at Moret-sur-Loing on 29th
January from a cancer of the throat. Monet had hurried to his bedside, but Camille was unaware of his illness until a few days before his
death. Sisley left nothing but his pictures. His death shocked Camille
and Lucien; they had loved and respected him. "A great and beautiful
artist," Camille declared on 22nd January when he heard that he was
seriously ill. "A master equal to the greatest." An auction was
organised for the benefit of his children, and Camille gave a canvas.
Within a year Sisley's pictures reached for those days, fabulous prices,
Camondo paying forty-three thousand francs (£1,720) for his "Flood
in Marly".

"We are still without a maid," wrote Lucien to Camille. "We
had an ugly one for eight days: it was impossible to keep her." His
letter was unusually cheerful, he was working again and sixty copies of
his last book had been sold in a week, "more than the sales in Paris for
a year". But in July he complained that no one knew the trouble the
printing gave. "For example, I have just spoilt three hundred francs
(£12) worth of gold powder, without speaking of the waste of paper
and time." He had had to send away the printer he employed, because
he could not afford to pay him his wage of twenty-four shillings a
week. "Esther and I now handle the press. It works better this way.
But it is hot work this weather." It was July, Camille was at Eragny.

On the 28th, he wrote: "I have begun some *motifs* in the field." "How often will that field have been painted!" replied Lucien. "Our frontis-piece, which we are printing in three tones, gives a lot of trouble. It is difficult to adjust the blocks, they continually slip out of position. We have already taken two and a half weeks and it is still only half done. What is discouraging is that the effect on fine paper is not so good as on ordinary paper. Is the extra trouble worthwhile to get a result that is not clearly superior?" "Don't believe him," Esther wrote in the margin of the letter. "Lucien is quite blue at the moment. The impressions are beautiful." "No," Lucien took up the letter, "I am not blue, but red with exasperation."

A halt to the printing was called at the end of July when Esther's brother, Sam, offered the use of his cottage at Bradwell-on-Sea, and here Lucien began to paint again, but he could not stand, and had such difficulty that he destroyed what he did. Julie suggested sending some chickens to the cottage so that he could have fresh eggs, but wondered how the chickens would feed on the voyage.

In September, Lucien completed the printing of his two volumes of Jules Laforgue's *Moralités Légendaires* and sent copies to his father. "It is very well done and all to your honour," acknowledged Camille on the 27th. He had received the books "in perfect condition. . . . The ornamented page is without question the most beautiful you have ever made, it is full of style, very decorative and sufficiently like nature to go well with the fount; the gold blends admirably with the light greenish-grey tone, the drawing of the figures is charming, the lettering is firmly drawn, the geese very beautiful."

The end of the year approached, and Lucien's health returned, but slowly—his left side remained paralysed, and it was still troublesome for him to walk, but Esther had no longer to push him along the streets of Bedford Park in a wheeled chair. Day after day a thick London fog descended which choked his lungs and kept him indoors. Julie said it was the same at Eragny, the fog there was like a London one. She mourned the death of her son: "It is two years since Titi died. Why could not I have taken his place? he so young to go the first! It is horrible having to bear all this."

1900

Throughout the winter Esther worked at the printing, Lucien being unable to do this hard work. He said her help saved him two pounds a week. In the spring of 1900 he was well enough to go to the exhibition of the New English Art Club where he saw George Moore, "but he did not recognise me". It was a bad show, "worse than the Academy", he commented. "Our leading young artists have discovered that black paint is the last word in art." He and Esther again stayed a few weeks at Sam's cottage in Essex. McNish, his doctor, had advised hot sea-water baths. The sea was a mile away, and every day buckets of sea-water were carried to the cottage. As it was important for him to take exercise, he walked in the afternoon, but painted in the mornings. He wondered if he would ever be able to paint standing again. Nevertheless he wrote to Camille: "the air is doing us good."

"The books are bringing some money, but it is always the same, one needs money to start a new book." But he had enough to begin the printing of *La Legende de Saint Julien* and of *Les Ballades de Maistre François Villon*. His work was disturbed by a letter from Julie: "Come quickly. Quarrelling at home. Georges has a new wife." Lucien went, and was told Georges had remarried the previous month in Jersey, and this had greatly upset and angered Camille. Georges wrote Lucien a letter apologising for not letting him know about his wedding and the birth of a girl who had been named Camille Athée (!). With Lucien at Eragny, Camille recovered his composure. Several of his pictures had been sold at recent auctions, and Camille, fairly well satisfied with the prices they fetched, hoped this would induce collectors to come to him and buy. Soon he was at Berneval, "a pretty little watering place an hour's drive from Dieppe," he wrote on the 11th July, and here Lucien joined him. It was four years since he had been able to complete a painting, now with his father's sympathy and encouragement, he regained confidence and painted three pictures which satisfied him. His fears that he would never paint again were dispelled.

Christmas was again spent with Esther's parents. During their stay Lucien and Esther heard that their house had been entered by burglars. But when Esther returned home she found nothing had been disturbed. The burglars had been frightened by a lay figure. "Before leaving," Lucien told Camille, "I did a sketch and left the lay figure in the position I had used: the arms had a threatening gesture."

1901

In March, his old friend, Verhaeren, came to England to lecture at Oxford on the French Symbolist poets. Lucien went to hear him. "He read some of his own poems. It was marvellous. He is one of the great ones of the new school." *La Legende de Saint Julien* was completed, and

Lucien commented: "When I have finished my wood engravings, I cannot bear them any more." Once more he was often at Ricketts', and there met W. B. Yeats who talked of Lady Gregory and said he had heard one of her peasant tenants say: "She is plain and simple like the Mother of God, and is the greatest lady who ever lived." Lucien showed Ricketts his first attempt at a type. Ricketts showed him a sketch for his King's Font, and gave him a drawing of a portion of the Avon Font. Ricketts made a note of this visit: "One is sometimes puzzled at one's avoidance of other persons, yet the benefit one gets from them may perhaps be summarised by this trivial episode: Pissarro walks to a chair on which is placed a drawing by Van Dyck. His eye does not focus it, but slips to the floor where there is a small sketch in oils of my 'Bride and Bridegroom' moonlight picture. This he slowly picks up. 'Whose is it? Yours?' 'Yes.' He then puts it back again without a word." Perhaps Lucien could find nothing to say. The old sympathy between them was fading. Lucien had been shocked when Ricketts had said: "Impressionism? Open your paint box, shut your eyes, and see what Zeus will send you."

CHAPTER VII

Esther's Dream House. 1901–1905

SO THINGS RUBBED ALONG, LUCIEN FRETTING OVER HIS BOOKS, TAKING infinite care with their preparation, fretting over money, never knowing how to manage and always the stream of letters coming and going between London and Eragny. Periodically came a grumble from Julie. The boys were home and did not work. She had no time for lazy people. "It's always the same thing and poverty in the house. I get in such tempers that it kills me." The boys "wasted their days" painting; but Lucien wrote to Camille: "Georges is really a lucky fellow to be able to be with you alone, so tempting to be able to paint with you. You will have to come to England to do a series of paintings, not in London, but in the country. Somewhere where you can get a cup of tea at seven in the morning." Lucien was working under difficulties, his landlord choosing this time to repaint the interior and outside of the house, but his irritability was soothed when the carrier brought him a gift from his father, three paintings, a Renoir, a Monet and a Puvis de Chavannes. That afternoon Esther returned from a walk greatly excited. She had seen the house of all houses where she would like to live. It was at Stamford Brook, near the "Queen of England", over the level crossing and just along the road. Two seventeenth-century cottages had been turned into one, set back from the road with a garden which could be made beautiful. It was remote and quiet, surrounded with orchards, and in the garden she had heard wonderful bird-song. Lucien must come and see it at once.

Lucien caught her excitement. With the growth of his printing activities the present house, like the last, had become small and inconvenient for his work. But at first he was dismayed at Esther's dream-house. The garden surrounded by a red-brick wall was buried in rank grass, thistles and docks, and amid this desolation straggled a hazel nut tree and four old apple trees. In a corner was an old vine house with three climbing vines. The house was equally abandoned, corrupt with cobwebs, decay and dilapidation. There were gaps in the pantiled roof, and in an upstair room water dripped from the ceiling into a rusty tin bath. There were no drains, and water had to be pumped from a well in the garden. All the same, this old Georgian-style house attracted him, and he visualised the conversion of the stables and the brew house into a printing-room and a studio. Even its sad state could be an advantage and induce the landlord to let at a low rent. Who the landlord was, was obscure; no one knew. When, at last, he was found, he offered to sell the house for £1,000. Lucien refused. He had not the money and he dreaded the entanglement of a mortgage. The landlord then suggested a long lease with a repairing clause. Camille offered to lend the money to put the house in order, and this was accepted. But months elapsed before all the repairs and conversions were completed.

The two cottages had been made into one by Admiral Blackmore, who had lived there attended by an old sailor. They had covered the walls with fishing-net on a painted canvas, the effect resembled a lattice-patterned wallpaper. When this, falling to pieces, was removed by the workmen, newspapers of 1760 were found behind the rotting canvas.

Whenever she could get away, Esther was at The Brook, as the house was named, supervising and planning. The house became her obsession, and continued to be for the greater part of her life. If she had money, whether to spare or not, she spent it on The Brook. If it was not the house it was the garden: she became an ardent gardener. She exchanged views about gardens with Monet, and collected cuttings wherever she went. She made lawns, planted trees, shrubs and flowers, and at great cost made both the house and garden beautiful and charming. This obsession for improvement even extended over the years to the cottages which she and Lucien rented, Melton Lodge at Norwood, left to her by her parents, and the house bought near Toulon. This caused many financial crises, when there should have been money and there was not, and gave rise to justified grumblings by Lucien at Esther's lack of forethought and thrift.

Sam, Esther's brother, inspired by Lucien, had written the only obituary of Sisley to appear in the English press, and this now fired him to launch on art criticism. Lucien was amused and said: "He does not know anything about it, but no doubt he will come to me when he is in trouble." In April, after many months, The Brook was ready for occupation. Drains had been installed, water-pipes led into the house, the roof had been made weather-proof, walls and ceilings had been stripped and shone with new paint, and the stables had been converted into a printing-room and the brew house into a studio. "We are delighted with the house," Lucien wrote to Julie. "There is only one blemish. No money." He was at work designing the Brook type, and a maid had been found who was a treasure. "She gets up in the morning at six-thirty." But Julie was not so fortunate. Camille was painting at Dieppe but at Eragny she had no maid, and "there is so much work to be done". She was old, unable to manage, "and there is the garden where the grass grows so quickly".

In the summer, Lucien, Esther and Orovida went to France, and stayed with his mother at Eragny, or Lucien painted with Camille at Dieppe. When he returned to London he chided Julie for her conduct to Esther, particularly before the nine-year-old Orovida who had artlessly said: "Why doesn't grandmother like you?" "I admit that you are extremely kind," wrote Lucien, "but, *bon dieu*, if you were not kind one could not stay five minutes in your company. You are like a volcano. So touchy, so severe. Don't get cross with what I tell you. You know these are but words, we love you from the bottom of our hearts."

Jacob Bensusan's feather business collapsed, ruined by a change of fashion and the disappearance of ostrich feathers on feminine headgear, and he retired to Bexhill. Esther's aunt, Orovida, who, from her lodgings in Herne Hill, had gone daily to assist in his office, now came to live at The Brook and stayed there until her death from typhoid in 1912. Soon she was the pillar of the house, reliable in stress—her calmness and sense of humour had a steadying influence. If anything was lost or wanted, "ask auntie" was the invariable solution. During the day she tied a black satin apron round her waist; under this her skirt bulged with a large bag in which she kept her oddments. On state occasions she changed to a heavy lilac silk with leg-of-mutton sleeves trimmed with yellow lace, a large fichu over her bodice. She was loved by Orovida. Although her aunt had little money she was always able to find some in her purse to give her niece a treat.

In December, Lucien presented to the British Museum an almost complete collection of his engravings in their choicest impressions, showing his handiwork in every stage of the process from the first sketch to the printing of the proof. Early in 1902 he likewise presented to the *Musée du Luxembourg* 45 prints of his wood engravings and a folio of *Les Travaux des Champs*, a replica of the collection given to the British Museum.

Most of the year was spent in printing, he and Esther working together on the books, Esther making some of the engravings and managing the machinery, throwing out the defective printings, and Lucien mixing the inks to get the precise colours. A printer, Thomas Taylor, was employed to pull the press and set-up under the guidance of Lucien. He grew devoted to Lucien, and stayed over the years until the printing of books was abandoned.

Lucien designed three types—one for himself, "The Brook," and two, one roman, the other gothic, for Dr Van Royen, an amateur printer of books at La Hague. He also made two press marks for Van Royen, whose press was known as *De Zilverdistel*. Some examples of his beautiful work are at the Ashmolean, part of the Orovida C. Pissarro Bequest. Van Royen died during the Hitler war, a martyr of the Resistance. Lucien was dead when Mrs Van Royen wrote to Esther in January, 1946, from Delft: "It is only yesterday your letter reached me. Since three years our house is empty, damaged by the Germans who destroyed the whole district. I wept as I recognised on opening the letter your well-known handwriting my husband so often received in former days. So, *hélas*, the great artist that Lucien Pissarro was, is no more alive. To us Death came in another way. In the second year of the war my husband joined all Dutch societies, painters, sculptors, musicians, actors, etc. (in resistance) into one large organisation. But when the *Kultur Kammer* was established, he, the very soul of the artists' resistance, was taken a prisoner on the 5th March, 1942. They took him to the Scheveningen prison and afterwards to the wretched concentration camp at Amersfoort. There he died within six weeks, starved, and exhausted by illness and misery. I never saw him again. I was told how he behaved like a hero, never complaining, always with the vigour of his high spirits, helping and comforting the others. In the summer of 1940 he began to print again after a twelve years *intermezzo*. In the few hours he could spend with his beloved press he could feel happy, then he could forget the deep depression under which we lived. His last marvellous book of seven poems by Boutens (written during the war, he was our best poet) was ready four days before he was made a prisoner."

With Lucien, money was never plentiful; too often there were bleak periods when there was none at all, but living in those pre-war days was incredibly cheap and Esther could always get credit. As long as the printing continued, money trickled in, but considering the time and immense labour which went to the making of Lucien's beautiful books, the return was incredibly poor.

1902

"I am very happy," Camille wrote on 11th August from Dieppe, "to learn that you are going to begin to print with your own types of font"; and, on the 15th he wrote: "You can get your alphabet made. I have swung a little deal which will bring me exactly the necessary money, two thousand five hundred francs (£100)." In October, he wrote two letters to Lucien, the first, dated the 3rd, recorded the death of Zola. "It is a terrible loss to France! And coming after the Dreyfus case, it is, as you see, a serious event. I sent my condolences to his widow, but I do not believe, considering my age, that I can attend the funeral. I would not dare", and on the 20th: "This morning I have received your volume of Ronsard.* This time you have surpassed yourself. The whole thing is simply superb. . . . The letters engraved by Esther are of great delicacy and admirable workmanship."

During this month there was a death in the family. Esther's sister died of tuberculosis. Poor Jacob Bensusan was greatly distressed and, like Job, thought the hand of Jehovah heavy upon him. At The Brook the maid who delighted in getting up early in the morning had long since departed. The girl filling her place left without notice, taking with her the only clock Lucien and Esther possessed, and McNish, Lucien's doctor, presented a bill for sixty pounds, covering attendance for three years. "I can pay it," said Lucien, "but not at once."

1903

In January, Julie went to the South of France "to find out how life was there, perhaps the place for your father to spend the winter. It was nice, the climate good, the weather beautiful, but the sons said it was ugly, so your father doesn't want to hear about it any longer. He would have been well there". Two of the boys were at Eragny, "so it is hell here. I came home to do the washing since it is always me who does the slaving."

The first book printed with Lucien's Brook type was *An Account of the Eragny Press* by T. Sturge Moore. In March, the next two books, Milton's *Areopagitica* and *The Descent of Ishtar* by Diana White, were sent to Leighton's for binding. Here, 150 of the 200 copies of each book were destroyed by fire, and Lucien was faced with the labour of reprinting the lost sheets. The books had been insured for £100, but the insurers only offered £60 as compensation, and after protracted correspondence, Lucien had to accept this.

* *Choix de Sonnets* de P. de Ronsard.

Orovida was now ten, so thought was given to her future. Despite her inclination to draw and paint, Esther decided that a more remunerative career would be music, and most unwillingly Orovida continued her piano lessons with Madame Henry. She didn't want to be a musician, she wanted to be an artist. At the beginning of July Camille went to Le Hâvre. Lucien wrote that it would do him good to work near him. He would like to come and paint in the suburbs of the town. "I was hoping to tell you that we could live without your allowance, but the time has not yet come. It is terrible to have to tell you this, but we must wait, wait, wait, until I can recover what I was able to do before my illness," and he stressed, "you have no idea of the work needed to print a book." Later in the month, accompanied by Esther, Orovida and Diana White, he arrived at Eragny where he showed Diana Camille's paintings, water-colours and drawings. She was impressed. She said she had learnt a lot, and she was fired to get to work again. Julie's personality disconcerted her, but she realised her "rough kindness". Lucien amused himself riding a tandem bicycle with Paul and they planned a tour in Burgundy. Instead, he joined his father at Le Hâvre. He grumbled that the weather was dreadful, he had to pay five francs a day at the hotel and the water-closets were indescribable. Despite the weather he painted three pictures—a view of the estuary, a canal with a church, and a road winding downhill. "The series that father is painting in spite of the bad weather, is marvellous, but as he works from his window the weather does not matter. There is one picture of people with umbrellas watching the boats returning to harbour, it is wonderful." In the autumn Camille returned to Eragny. Julie wrote that he had been ill, but nothing serious, an apartment had been rented in Paris, in the Boulevard Morland, and there he would spend the winter, painting from a window. But this was not to be.

"Be careful he does not catch cold when you take him to the Boulevard Morland," Lucien warned Julie. But this is what happened. Standing for a few minutes at the door of the hotel watching his bags being taken upstairs, a chill wind blew, and he collapsed. Rodo wrote on the 22nd October that he was very illl: "The greatest surgeon in the world has been consulted, but he did not say what the trouble is. He only wrote a complicated prescription." For three weeks Camille was in great pain, often unconscious. Julie never left his bedside. "It is better for you to come at once if he is to recognise you again," Rodo warned Lucien. Lucien, in Paris the next day, found the family assembled, with the exception of Georges. "When I came," wrote

Lucien to Esther, "it was terrible to hear him moaning and groaning. It is now one-thirty, and the three doctors and the surgeon are in consultation. I am afraid it is the end. Dr. Cartier thinks the abscess should be opened as soon as possible, otherwise the infection will spread. They will operate tonight." The inflammation in the bladder extended to the rectum, and an abscess had formed. But there was no operation. Camille's homeopathic doctor objected. The result was blood-poisoning.

Lucien was bothered because there was no ready money, as Camille was unable to sign a cheque. He did not know what to do. On the 11th November, Camille had a fearful night. "The trouble was a constant hiccup," Lucien wrote to Esther. "We have a nurse and that brings complications for our mother who is in a dreadful state, as you can imagine. Dr. Cartier refused to come unless in consultation with Dr. Léon Simon. Simon, in spite of father's condition, has never even raised the blanket to see the condition of the patient. What a fool! Do not come. The flat is so small there is no room for anybody. I sleep on a bed in the dining-room, and there is no room for the nurse."

Camille died the next day, the 12th November. He was buried in Père Lachaise. A contemporary account described the funeral as "a modest one without any of the pomp which attends the obsequies of officially recognised mediocrities".

After the funeral Lucien returned with Julie to Eragny. Here he went through some two thousand of Camille's sketches. "No one knows the value," he told Esther. He and Julie visited Monet at Giverny, Monet meeting them at the station in his car. "He showed us his series of London. Marvellous! Effects of mist and fog." Monet advised a good exhibition of Camille's paintings, with pieces gathered from the amateurs and those in the possession of the family. Above all they must not be sold at bad prices, certainly higher than those of the dealers. Monet not only offered to lend money but went to Eragny to help value the pictures.

1904

Camille's death was a catastrophe to Lucien. Not only had he lost his wise mentor but, until the estate was shared, his main source of income had abruptly ended. His position was indeed deplorable. He had no money and no prospect of any for some time. In March of 1904, leaving Esther at The Brook to continue with the printing of

C'est d'Aucassin et de Nicolette, he went to Paris, hoping to interest booksellers in his books. He walked the streets, calling on one after another. He saw many people "but nothing comes of it. I do not have a moment of tranquillity". Monet was sympathetic and tried to help, but his efforts were also in vain. Nothing came right; one small irritation succeeded another. He found he had lost a pair of trousers, serious indeed with his limited wardrobe, and could only imagine that they had been left on the boat. In the evenings he worked at a wood engraving of his father from a photograph. After days of frustration he went to Eragny and was amused that Julie now "receives" every Thursday. Esther sensed he was bored, and suggested he should paint and have a model. Nothing he would like better, he replied, but he feared that the models in Paris were not respectable, and he hesitated to introduce them into his mother's house. "Even father was not allowed to have models," he added. Esther's letters were of difficulties and requests for advice, but as ever he left her to solve the problems and said: "Do what you think best."

Nothing having been solved by the journey to Paris, it was now decided to let the living quarters at The Brook. Lucien went to the country to paint for three months while Esther and Orovida stayed with the McGregors, Esther making daily visits to The Brook to work in the printing-room.

Lucien stayed on a farm at Finchingfield—eighteen shillings a week ("extraordinarily cheap for England", he commented), but the weather was dreadful. The village was ten miles away from the nearest railway station, but he had the luck to see the carrier as he got off the train who gave him and his baggage a lift. On unpacking he found that his two hats, a straw and a felt, had been squashed and damaged. "I told you it would be so when you packed," he wrote to Esther. Also a cake had been flattened into crumbs, nevertheless he would be able to eat it. He thought the country beautiful, and the house was clean and comfortable, but it poured with rain and he was only able to make sketches for water colours. "It is all to the good," he wrote. He would start pictures when he knew the country better. He fed on bread and cheese and drank cocoa made with water.

In June the family assembled at Eragny for the *partage* of Camille's pictures. At first there was dissension, since all the family needed money quickly, and it was argued that the best course would be to have an immediate auction and divide the proceeds. Julie was against this. It wrung her heart to think that Camille's pictures would be dispersed. Lucien, for a different reason, agreed with her; he and Julie consulted Monet who strongly advised against selling. He said it was too early, and if the family would but wait the pictures were certain to appreciate in value. His counsel prevailed. Values having been agreed, the sharing was done amicably, the pictures being divided into equal piles and choice determined by the drawing of lots. But it was a slow business, there were delays, and M. Champly, the lawyer, did not arrive. Lucien fretted; he was worried that the books were not selling. He depended so much on the money, and he was depressed at the waste of his time at Eragny. "I don't like all this," he wrote to Esther, "I want to work." He painted a water-colour and, enraptured with a moonlit night, jotted down notes, and from them made woodblocks for *Christabel*, the book he was then engaged on. These were sent to Esther with a request "for prints in the cold tone of moonlight".

Lucien rolled the canvases, his share of the *partage*, and returned home. He and Esther lived on credit and he wondered what would happen. Hugh Lane called, anxious to buy one of Lucien's Camille pictures for Dublin, but Lane said the price asked was too high, also he had seen a picture at Durand's which he liked better. But Lucien thought he did not buy because the picture was badly framed.

Three Cézannes, from the undivided pictures, were sold to Bernheim in October for fifteen thousand francs (£600). Lucien's share of this was one thousand two hundred and fifty francs (£50). Julie's share was a half plus a sixth, now, she wrote, she was no longer obliged to sell her Camille self-portrait, indeed not any more pictures of his. It was a great consolation to be able to see them, it would hurt her to have to part from them. "The poor father is dead now a year. Nobody thinks of him, not even his children. I have asked Rodo to take some flowers to the grave." The house was cold, so she was going to Paris for the winter, but sad to leave, for it was here she had had the company of Camille for twenty years. "But what else can I do?" She enclosed the money due to Lucien after deducting what she had spent for him, but there were two centimes which, she said, she did not know how to send.

Esther paid the bills, and when she had done this the Cézanne money had gone. Julie wrote that all the money she had was ten thousand francs (£400), she intended to invest this at 7½ per cent which would allow her to live frugally without the necessity of selling her pictures. "So, you see, my dear Lucien, you must not depend too much on me to help you." But now hope came from Mary Cassatt, who wrote that she had found an amateur wishing to buy some pictures—she thinks he will give one thousand five hundred francs for Lucien's Degas and one thousand five hundred francs for the two Manets. But the amateur offered only one thousand five hundred francs (£60) for the three. Mary Cassatt would not budge on the price, and the amateur retired. Lucien appealed to Julie: "You may find it strange that I am so short of money in spite of what I got for the Cézanne, but it is because my last book did not sell well and I lost money on it. Also we let the house for Christmas, but at the last moment the people did not come." Julie replied: "I am not rich, but tell me what you need, especially if it is not a lot."

1905

The old lady came to London and stayed with Lucien and Esther during January of 1905. On her return to Eragny she complained of the conduct of Georges. Lucien replied: "Do you want me to tell you what you did to Georges? Well, you spoilt him too much." Soon she had a grievance against Paul and Cocotte: "They sulk since I have been back and do not take the trouble to talk to me. I am very unhappy. I wish she would get married. But to whom?" She continued to grumble about her children: she said they were rude and indifferent to her. But she was not easy to live with. She dominated, scolded and tried to make Cocotte a kitchen drudge. Her family tolerated her ways, but occasionally there was resentment and bitter recriminations shook the house. Julie found solace in her garden. "It is lovely, beautiful," she wrote to Lucien, "poppies and irises of all colours; they look like coloured fireworks." Now Lucien fell out of favour. She said he only wrote when he needed money. "No, that is not fair," replied Lucien. "I am quite sure that, in spite of all, I am not the one who is most indifferent of all your children." In a few weeks she was writing: "You don't seem lucky, my poor boy, and the poor father is no longer here to provide." Lucien had promised to go to Eragny, she begged him not to delay: "Here are plenty of strawberries, peas, artichokes, but when you come they will all be gone." After his stay, the correspondence resumed. "Monet came with his family to see us and brought some plums. He told me you had sent him your book, and he thinks it very beautiful. He has a son-in-law, a bookseller, who lives at Cannes, he will sell some." A month later she censured Lucien. She said he was unable to live on his earnings and would not manage according to his means: "But then I am only a peasant and have had to work hard all my life." Nevertheless, worried that Lucien was in distress, she made journeys to Paris, called on the amateurs, and tried to persuade them to buy one of her pictures. She succeeded in secretly selling a Manet to an American, and sent Lucien the proceeds, five thousand francs (£200). "When you get my letter, let me know that you have received *the seeds*. I will know what you mean. I don't want the children to know. It is not their business." She said she must somehow save enough money to leave to Lucien to pay for her funeral: "Otherwise I don't know how you will manage." She returned home from Paris to find the house empty: "No lights, no fires. I was tired. It was not cheerful, and all alone in this big house I had to make a fire. I was very sad." The house was full of memories. She was startled, thinking she heard a footfall and it was Camille's. The past was more vivid than the present, her thoughts always on Camille.

CHAPTER VIII

The Eragny Press. 1906–1908

THE YEAR BROUGHT NO CESSATION OF FINANCIAL FRET TO LUCIEN.
Expenditure exceeded income: time after time he was in desperate need
of ready money and could only meet the crisis by borrowing. The
Société des Cent Bibliophiles commissioned a book, a high honour, and
a price was agreed, but the unbusiness-like Lucien greatly under-
estimated the costs. He only discovered this when he was actually at
work on the book, too late for him to bargain further or withdraw.
As usual, in his determination to make the book as beautiful as possible,
he spent so much time and money on it that the profit was reduced to
a minimum. The *Histoire de la Reine du Matin et de Soliman Ben Daoud*,
by Gérard de Nerval, restricted to 130 copies, with a frontispiece,
twelve initial letters printed in gold and colours, and thirty line illustrations, is one of the loveliest examples of his craftsmanship and crea-
tion, all the more remarkable considering the mental anxieties besetting
Lucien during its making. He told Julie: "I have to make so many
more wood engravings than were planned, and all this costs money
and I have a heavy sum to pay the printer. He is in urgent need of this
and I am afraid he will leave. This will stop my work completely. I
need one thousand five hundred francs (£60). Can you help me?"
Julie did not know how to help. She considered selling her house.
What did Lucien think of this? He replied, rather ambiguously, that
the house only existed for him because she was there. Then should she
sell her pictures? That would be a dreadful disaster Lucien said. Julie
now suggested that he should write to Monet, "that good friend", for
a loan. Lucien replied: "I take up my courage and will write to him."
He asked Monet for two thousand five hundred francs (£100), offering
as security a picture by his father and the still-life dedicated and given
to him by van Gogh. Almost by return of post Monet sent the money,
"together with a charming letter written just as if he were father. He
does not speak of any guarantee or security, but asks that the loan be
repaid when I am able to do so. So try and sell my van Gogh so that I
can send him the money quickly". But he wanted only one thousand
francs (£40) for this picture, quite inadequate to repay the loan.

Again the money was swallowed in paying bills. In May, Lucien worked without Taylor, his printer, to save his wages. Funds were so low that a young girl was taken as a boarder for a pound a week. Julie wrote of the death of Cézanne, "It makes me think of the days past. Another one gone," she sadly commented. She had seen Fénéon, and said he was like a monk who had left his order. Paul had been called up to be a soldier, but was not accepted: "He is very happy about it and so am I. He is a thorn in my side, but it is a weight off my mind." She was still trying to sell Camille's pictures in Paris to the amateurs but with no success. To add to her small income she thought of letting the ground floor at Eragny to summer visitors, but hesitated: "I don't want anyone to go into the studio where are all dear father's things and which is a sanctuary for me," but she asked Lucien if he could find her suitable and nice Englishmen as guests. Lucien recommended Albert Rutherston, an admirer and buyer of his pictures. Rutherston was delighted with the idea, but there was a hitch as Julie remained adamant about the use of the studio. In the end he did not go as his father fell ill and died.

Lucien complained that he worked hard and got no money in return. At the end of June there was another crisis. "This time I really don't know how we are going to manage. We have to let the house and I will go and paint in a little village. The printing business brings us no money." He had come too late on the scene, he said. "Beautifully printed books are now out of fashion. My work gets gold medals in the exhibitions, but I am starving! The man has just called to ask the money for the daily newspapers. I have twenty-five francs ($£1$) left." The next day he heard that the family estate at St. Thomas had been settled. This had been long awaited, Lucien had thought it would bring him a considerable sum. Far from being so, his share amounted to $£6$ $11s.$ $7\frac{1}{2}d.$

Late in the year Lucien published *Verses by Christina Rossetti*, reprinted from G. Polidori's edition of 1847. In view of the date of the original publication, he thought the copyright had expired, but was disillusioned by W. M. Rossetti, the executor of his sister's estate. Pointing out that the verses Lucien had published were still covered by copyright, the edition of 1847 having been privately printed, and the actual date of publication not being until 1896, he demanded a fee of $£25$. Lucien was advised to pay and did so. But it left him sore and he related the transaction in a letter to Andriemin, a friend and a subscriber to his books. Andriemin replied: "What you say about the cost of your copyright of your Rossetti should not surprise me as I have heard very strange stories about that family's grasping tendencies. You would not expect it from Italians so artistically inclined. It is true that the Neapolitans are only half Italians. Dante Gabriel's dealings with William Morris are not looked upon favourably by surviving friends whom I have heard speak of them. Biographers are silent on the motives of their cooling friendship, but I know that it was based upon certain financial transactions.* This was a case when a businessman like William Morris was over-reached by an artist. So, at least, I was told."

1907

The pattern of 1907 was much the same as the previous year. If Lucien did not live in the abject poverty of the artist exploited by novelists and exemplified in *La vie de Bohème*, he yet had continuously to contrive makeshifts to satisfy the needs of his household. His was a genteel poverty. The dread of disaster was ever in his mind. He worried, crises came one after the other and were overcome: bailiffs were expected, but they did not arrive. Left timid and shy by his paralysis, unfitted for the hurly-burly of money-making, he relied on Esther. Everything was left to her, but unfortunately she was as unpractical as he was. They lived moderately. She was not extravagant, and did not spend money on clothes. Indeed many of her garments she made herself, but she was house-proud; her linen and china had to be of the best. To her, tomorrow was remote. When money came in excess of immediate requirements, it was too often spent on some long-visualised improvement to the house. She dismissed from her mind that their income was uncertain, and it might well be a long time before the elusive money again came their way, and that it would have been wiser to have put the money aside for rent and rates and fuel and food.

* Biographers are also silent on Morris's reactions to the relationship which existed between his wife, "the ox-eyed Janey", and Rossetti. They could not know them. Morris never permitted even his closest friends to glimpse his inner life. Significant, however, is the pregnant line in *Love is Enough*: "Because for love's sake, love he cast away." Nevertheless, this relationship may well have been the real cause of the "cooling friendship" which was to lead over the years to the two men avoiding each other. Later Lucien wrote a book on Rossetti, but here he was more concerned with Rossetti as an artist than as a man, and Mrs. Morris is only mentioned as sitting for several important pictures. With equal reticence Lucien made no reference to Fanny Cornforth whom he had met and knew to have been Rossetti's mistress.

Lucien's work at this time was rarely adequately rewarded. Scrupulous, conscientious, the soul of integrity, everything he did must be as perfect as he could make it. He worked for months on a book on Rossetti, commissioned by T. C. and E. C. Jack and included in their Artists' Series, and when at last his manuscript was completed, received a cheque for twenty guineas.

Julie could only help with trifling sums, and said it broke her heart the way the dealers treated Camille's pictures. Even his friends, she wrote, said he was now old-fashioned. She had again tried to sell some of her pictures, but "nobody wants any of them". Lucien replied: "I got your two hundred francs (£8) this morning. I am showing a few of father's pictures. There was an article about them : that was all. Perhaps they looked poor in their frames. To impress, they should have been well framed, and made to look like something very precious. Don't be surprised if the prices do not go up. The framing is another matter ; they can always be well framed, if one only had the money ! The dealers say that the time has not yet come for them to make business. Don't worry about father, *he will never be forgotten*. Like Corot and Millet, when he does come up it will be for good. Father is, among all the impressionists, the man who represents the nineteenth century most significantly. His philosophy, which you know so well, can be perceived in his art. As for me, who knows his ideas better than any of the impressionists, every day I realise more and more how much his art reflects his ideas. So don't worry, dear mother, his day will come. It will be a day of glory, I assure you. Those who are to be pitied are ourselves, for meanwhile we have to be devilishly hard-up."

Lucien missed the services of Taylor, his printer. The manual work took all his time. "I must have time to paint," he said. But there was no time. Also he and Esther were not quick enough. "Must have a book soon, otherwise no money," he wrote to Julie. "We can't pay the bills and are trying to let the house. It is Esther's mother who has been helping. We are living on credit, and the taxes are not paid. This could be serious. I do not know what we will do next week." Three weeks later he wrote: "How wrong I am to worry you with all our troubles. A friend has written an article which was published. He said what a pity that my books should come to an end through lack of money. This made an editor write to me that he would take our books and publish them. Esther and I went to see him, he said he would make us a proposition in a few days' time. For one week we lived full of hope, we thought that the purse would be filled again, but nothing came of it: nothing happened. The editor said the public would have no interest in our books. Our last hope is gone. But do not do anything desperate yet to help us (Julie had offered to sell some of her shares). Esther considers taking up massage professionally and will consult McNish." McNish was not encouraging. A few days later Julie sent five hundred francs (£20). "This will pay the butcher and the baker," said Lucien. "All my worries come from my obstinancy in believing that my books will come into favour again. They bring in two thousand five hundred francs (£100), and this does not cover the cost of production." At the end of the month, some relief came from John Quinn, a New York attorney, a great collector of pictures and manuscripts, who bought one of Lucien's paintings for thirty pounds.

1908

Early in the New Year Julie wrote that Rodo had been through the accounts: "It is cruel to see how we have sacrificed such beautiful things for so little." In March she was in Paris: "I am getting so dull and bored with Eragny. I feel lonely in that big house, and don't know what to do with myself. Here it is worse. Life is a burden to me. How sad it is to get old. One is annoyed by everything and annoys everybody. You should send me some of your prints, I should be pleased to see them. Don't be afraid of my criticism." Three weeks later she went to the *Salon des Indépendants* with Paul. "A real mess!" she wrote. "Painting is decadent. It is ridiculous what is now being done: worse than Luce or Signac." She commented on a wood engraving Lucien had sent her: "I like your washerwoman best, but her arm is so thin that it makes me shiver to look at it."

Frank Rutter, the art critic of *The Sunday Times*, was introduced to Lucien, whom he subsequently described as "that exquisite landscape painter from whom I have learnt all that I know of the science of colour",* and, in July, Lucien showed at the first exhibition of "The Allied Artists' Association" at the Royal Albert Hall at which over four thousand pictures were displayed. The A.A.A. had come into existence through the enthusiasm of Rutter, and was in many respects similar to the *Société des Artistes Indépendants*, every member having an equal right to show their pictures without submission to a jury. Lucien had been a member of the Paris group since its inception and had shown

* *Since I was Twenty-Five,* by Frank Rutter. Constable. London, 1927.

at all their exhibitions. His knowledge and advice was invaluable to Rutter. Sickert also took a leading part in the formation of the Association, and typically proposed the one rule which did not follow the French pattern. In Paris, the works were hung in alphabetical order. This had caused dissatisfaction, and Sickert argued that lots should be drawn for the order of hanging and place. One artist was on his feet at once. That would never do. "The best work of the best artists should be given the best place," he declared. "Not at all," replied Sickert. "In this society there are no good works or bad works. There are only works by shareholders." Sickert had his way.

Forty members hung the pictures, which varied greatly in size and merit, as well they might. Theodore Roussel was not happy with those in his sector; one of his lady admirers asked: "However could you hang those dreadful pictures?" "My dear lady," replied Roussel, "we have the same obligation as the Royal Academy to hang bad pictures; only here we have not the right to refuse the good." The A.A.A. survived until 1919, but long before had led the way to the Camden Town and London Groups.

Sickert had already established at 19 Fitzroy Street a centre which he optimistically hoped would enable artists to sell their works direct to the public, thus side-tracking the dealers. Here a group was formed, each member having the right to a picture rack in the studio, jointly rented, to store their pictures, and on Saturday afternoons exhibit them to friends and guests. Although prices were low there were few sales, nevertheless these afternoons were enjoyed, and Spencer Gore amused himself painting a portrait of the girl who dispensed the tea and cakes. Lucien had first met Sickert in 1891, and subsequently they became friends, Lucien a little suspicious of Sickert's charm, but Sickert greatly interested to listen to Lucien's theories on impressionism and his first-hand knowledge of the movement. Although Lucien was a member of the Fitzroy Street group, his attendances were spasmodic, often not having the money to pay his fare to London. But here he made friends with the other members—Spencer Gore, Augustus John, Henry Lamb, Robert Bevan, Charles Ginner and Harold Gilman. Sometimes, in the evening, a few of them would dine together at some cheap restaurant like *L'Etoile* in Charlotte Street. At a time when Esther was staying with her mother, Lucien wrote to her: "In the afternoon I took three shillings and went to town. Plenty of people at Sickert's. After tea I was asking myself whether I should stay to dinner as I had the other day with Rutter and the others. Well, I had two shillings in my pocket, sufficient for the dinner we then had, so I will stay. We all went out together and walked in the direction of the fashionable district, which made me uneasy. We reached Regent Street and I thought there is no pub around here. Gore was walking with me and I asked him where we were going. He said the Café Royal and I asked if he knew the price of the dinner. Three shillings, he said. When we reached the door I said to all of them: 'Now I must leave you. Good-bye.' It seemed rather queer to Sickert and still more to Gore. Well, I was hot all over. There is really only one crime in this world and that is to be with an empty pocket."

That empty pocket made him miserable. Julie was miserable because she was alone and Camille dead. The house at Eragny was pervaded with memories. Julie, unable to escape from them, would not leave it. In letter after letter to Lucien she wrote of her unhappiness and discontents. Lucien was not always able to console and was chidden for writing so seldom. He tried to rouse her from her apathy, but she replied: "I shall not write to you again. Your last letter was so cruel to me." But write she did. The children, she grumbled, "break my back", they would not do a thing for her. These children for whom she had slaved all her life so they should not lack anything, now only made fun of her and even accused her of neglecting their education. "I gave them all I had, but they are ashamed of me because I am ignorant and not the blue stocking they would like for a mother." She brooded over these sons who only fretted her and earned no money. "It is always the same thing," she moaned, "poverty in the house. But what will happen to them?" These outpourings were extraordinary. Rodo and Paul were devoted to her, if resentful of her nagging and bullying. And, indeed, she was devoted to them.

Cocotte was no comfort; Julie's rough domination estranged mother and daughter. And Julie continued her lamentations to Lucien: "It is not very cheerful for me. I sit alone and cry." She lived in a world of memories, pining for a lost happiness and a distant tranquillity. She hid herself in Camille's studio, and there, surrounded by his paintings and the testimony of his working days, relived their lives together. Here Camille had painted so many portraits of her and their children, here she had stormed and blustered over their hardships and anxieties and found strength in his courage and determination. Now there was no one to whom she could turn. The studio was her holy place. There nothing must be touched: everything must remain as it was.

CHAPTER IX

Cocotte's Wedding. 1908

COCOTTE, NOW TWENTY-SEVEN, LONGED TO HAVE A LIFE OF HER OWN, TO be married and escape from Eragny. She was not happy. Long before Camille died, Julie had written to Lucien: "Cocotte has gone to be present at the communion of a little cousin. It will cheer her up, for life for her at home is not amusing. No friends: an old father, a bad mother, and grumbling brothers. She is to be pitied. I would like her to get married. If you have a good friend who could be a husband for her, you should introduce him to us." But Lucien had no such good friend, and Cocotte's life at Eragny continued to be discordant. Often she was alone with Julie, and Julie was not easy to live with. Warm at heart she might be, but she could not help being cantankerous. Young men were attracted by Cocotte, but these affairs came to nothing, for although Julie was anxious to get Cocotte married, she could not bring herself to be amiable to these would-be suitors. Cocotte declared that only a millionaire would find favour with her mother. In 1904, Tessier, the family notary, a widower, proposed marriage, but Cocotte had no inclination to play the mother to his children. Tessier withdrew, but in the following year introduced a young man to Cocotte, whose intentions, he said, were serious. Julie sniffed at the young man: "He is a Tartuffe, an idiot, but Cocotte loves him deeply." Tessier prepared the marriage contract, and Cocotte, Julie and the young man met at his house at Macon. Minor alterations in the contract were agreed, the marriage was fixed for eight days ahead, and the young man departed to Paris where he claimed to have urgent business, saying he would return in good time for the wedding. But he did not return: instead he sent a letter to say he had changed his mind.

Now, in 1908, the young man who changed his mind had been forgotten, and Cocotte was in love again. She told Lucien she had met a very sweet and nice young man, the sweetest of all, and an enthusiastic amateur painter. "We fell in love three weeks ago, but the mothers are not pleased. We are to be married in June, but mother says you cannot come until August, but, oh, I beg you, please help us. Come in June even though I should have to pay for your journey. I would rather do that than wait. I am the happiest of women. At last I have found someone who loves me." The young man was Alexandre Bonin, a clerk employed on the Bourse. Julie did not like him. "He is funny," she commented, "and looks like a peasant dressed in his Sunday best, a small-time speculator! Poor Cocotte is not difficult to please." Rodo met him. "He looks all right," he said. But Julie was anxious for Lucien to come to Eragny; his head being screwed on the right way, he would find out all she wished to know about the young man. She wanted to be assured that the young man was healthy and free from disease, and so a plan was made. Cocotte was to bring him to Eragny and Julie would have a doctor waiting to examine him. Horrified at this plan, Cocotte wrote to Lucien: "Come quickly. Mother wants it to be a white wedding. Only twelve days more to happiness! Then, at last, I shall start living." Lucien arrived, and he went with Cocotte to help her hang the curtains in the house at Houilles, her future home. Here he met Bonin, his mother, and a sister. Lucien considered the mother a good sort, rather like Julie—plump, a frank expression, very proper, and from Normandy. "I managed quickly to conquer her," he wrote to Esther. "Bonin told Cocotte that she is quite in love with me. The sister is the head of a boarding school in Paris, a spinster, plain but good-hearted, quite in love with Cocotte. Bonin is open and frank, black eyes, black moustache, and he looks strong; in a word he is a nice fellow. I believe Cocotte will be happy and have a nice little home." Bonin had an income of some twelve thousand francs (£480) a year: "they should be comfortable with that. Mother is much better since I am here; she has given Cocotte a bad time, behaving stiffly, and just stopping short of being downright rude to the young man. At the dinner of the *fiançaille*, Julie rebuked Madame Bonin in a way which must have made her think: 'Ah, she considers my son is not good enough for her daughter.' These sly pinpricks of the two mothers are very amusing. Cocotte wants me to wear a top hat, so I will have to buy one. If I do not she will take someone else as the *garçon d'honneur*. It is a dreadful bore and a waste of money. When I have spent the francs on this hat I will have remaining almost nothing."

This time there was no hitch, the wedding was accomplished at Marguerry on the 11th June; one of the courses at the breakfast was the famous *sole à la Marguerry* which Lucien enjoyed. In the evening there was a "little dance". Lucien returned to London and soon after Cocotte wrote: "The house and the garden at Houilles are lovely. We went on Sunday to Eragny, but mother did not speak to Alexandre at all, not a word. Notwithstanding, we have not yet reached our first quarrel." But Julie said they did not speak to her. "I wanted to ask Cocotte how she was getting on with her mother-in-law and if she was happy, but Bonin gave me no chance to be alone with her. He was like her shadow. Then, when at last I was alone with her, she answered my questions by turning her back on me and saying 'I have to go to the lavatory'."

Julie continued to worry over her sons. Georges showed Paul a system he had invented which could not fail to win at the roulette-tables. "Paul does not work," wrote Julie. "He went with Georges to Nice and Monaco in order to gamble and lost the few thousand francs he had from our poor father. Now he has nothing and no employment." She added: " In case I should die suddenly I have left my papers and shares in a tin box hidden under a heap of coal in the cellar."

A young German museum official called on Lucien. Shown the studio, he was attracted by a small picture by Camille. He thought a friend of his would buy it for one thousand francs (£40) and present it to his museum. He took away a photograph and wrote that the purchase would be completed when his friend returned from a holiday in Italy. But his friend did not return. Suddenly taken ill, he died in Florence. But Lucien was glad he did not let the picture go when he received a letter from the *Société des Cent Bibliophiles*: the President wrote that Lucien's book had given such satisfaction that it had been decided to increase his remuneration from ten (£400) to twelve thousand francs (£480). Also enclosed was one hundred francs for "M. Taylor". But Lucien had already received the greater part of this money in advance.

1910

Money anxieties persisted in 1910. Sickert heard of Lucien's difficulties and offered to try and sell one of Lucien's Degas etchings. Lucien also offered one of his Camille pictures to a German dealer, this with misgiving, since he was loth to part with his father's pictures. Not only was sentiment involved, but he regarded them as his capital, certain to appreciate in value, an insurance for the future. Another crisis was threatening when Danze wrote asking if he would make a book for his

Société du Livre Contemporain. Lucien accepted and went to Paris to discuss the offer and to endeavour to get an advance. He also had in mind to persuade his mother to lend him an insurance policy, lodged with her as surety against a debt he owed to Camille's estate, which he required as a guarantee to back a loan from his bank. He arrived in Paris on 25th January and stayed with Rodo in his studio in Montmartre. He wrote to Esther★ that he travelled second class on the boat, sleeping in a "dirty, stuffy hole, my *couchette* retaining some dry remnant of a previous crossing. Well, I put myself on my back, my head on my portmanteau, *entortillé dans ma couverture*, and in spite of the swell I was not ill. When I arrived at St. Lazare it cost me a franc to have my luggage taken to the cloakroom". Then he took a cab to Rodo's and was horrified at the fare, 2.25 francs (a penny over two shillings), but the driver assured him it was correct, it was the legal night-service charge. The letter concluded: "*J'ai vu, j'ai combattu, j'ai conquis!*" This jubilation seemed to have little justification as he had climbed the many stairs to Rodo's studio with but a franc left in his pocket.

Early in the morning of the next day he was at an exhibition of Camille's pictures: "It is quite beyond my powers of writing to explain the extraordinary feeling I had in front of these paintings. You could see the descent of Corot, Turner, Millet, but finer and more masterly in synthesis, more poetical. I became increasingly certain that our dear old man was really one of the rare genius's of painting. I always knew he was a great man, but this time I mean something like Titian or Velasquez." Rodo was upset at the setting of the exhibition. He complained that it was appalling, the effect of the pictures lost in "Durand's enormous luxurious hole", so cluttered up with senseless furniture and sculpture, and the pictures badly displayed, hung on oriental carpets and propped on chairs.

★ It was at this time he began to write his letters in English, but with occasional lapses into French.

CHAPTER X

Cries of Love and Despair from Riec, 1910

AS NOTHING COULD IMMEDIATELY BE DONE ABOUT HIS BUSINESS AFFAIRS, Lucien and Rodo decided to go to Finisterre to paint, taking Julie with them, but departure was delayed. The streets were flooded, and the place du Hâvre in front of the *Gare St. Lazare* deep in water. The station could only be reached by way of a narrow passage in the rue d'Amsterdam. The station at the *Quai d'Orsay* was also flooded. "This morning there is no milk. The situation gets grave," Lucien wrote to Esther. Two days later, without Rodo, but with Julie, he was at the *Hôtel Cadoret*, Riec-sur-Bélon. "We are here at last," he wrote on the 31st January. "The village is quite paintable, tho' I have only seen one side of it. Quimperlé, where we slept last night, was lovely. One could work there an eternity." There the hotel was clean, the food good, and the lavatory an English invention with water and lavatory paper: *que veux-tu de plus?*

"I went out this morning early. Imagine : white frost, mist and sun as an effect. It is a hilly country with rough, grey, stone buildings, each stone irregular and surrounded with white plaster. Pollarded trees, foothills beyond disappearing in the mist, on top a church, and a town *en amphithéâtre* against the sky. So lovely, it has spoilt everything I have seen since." They paid little, the food was wonderful, the hotel clean and the landlady adored artists. He had not yet investigated the lavatory. The weather was not good, it threatened rain, but if he was unable to go out there was a view from his window which made a good *motif*. Duret owed him £20, he had written to him asking that the money be sent to Esther. He warned her not to spend the money before it came, otherwise it would have no advantage. The next day Lucien confirmed that "the place is spotlessly clean, the food gorgeous, the lavatory clean, with English lifting-up seats". There was no bath-room, there was a place for it, but it was not yet fitted. "It seems too

Portrait of Jeanne by Lucien Pissarro, 1889 (*Oil on Canvas* 28⅜ × 23)

Jeanne in the garden at Eragny, 1889 (*Oil on Canvas* $18\frac{3}{4} \times 13\frac{5}{8}$)

good you should succeed to let the house and come here. The idea alone makes me shake with excitement, fancy having your dear comfortable person to cuddle and kiss and . . . No more. I get too silly and must be satisfied with kissing you on paper." Two days later he sent a postcard. He anxiously awaited a letter, but urged Esther to be "explicit and orderly in her sentences". When a letter arrived, Lucien replied (5th February) : "I would be very wretched to know that you are without money, but Duret writes that he sent to you a few days ago." It rained continuously.

At the hotel were two young men, artists, one a Russian, the other a Pole. That afternoon Lucien walked with them through a Scotch mist to the sea, five kilometres away. It was beautiful, Lucien said, the coast reminded him of Diana White's Cornish sketches. "I was thinking of you all the way there, and I did wish more than once to have you near me, I felt so affectionate *dans le vide!*"

Again he hoped Esther and Diana White would come to Riec for a holiday. "It would be so nice," he wrote on the 8th February, "to have your dear little person near one. I tell you I feel ridiculously affectionate." Three days later it still showered, but the weather was on the mend. He was at work on two pictures of sun and cloud effects. "There are nice spots about, quite wild, one perfectly quiet where it is lovely to work, *ce qui ne gâte rien!*" He wrote to Esther daily, his letters a mixture of events, affection and reproof. "I am sorry you miss the Purcell, and I feel hurt that you think fit to tell me that in order to be economical you deprived yourself of that pleasure. My dear, I hope you realise that I do not grumble at the cash you spend for your pleasure, but at what is spent and could be well saved on soap and globe polish and such things. A little less of that spending and a little more of concerts, paints, or books, would please me very much. I do think as intellectual people we do not have our share of intellectual pleasures that are within our means." He wanted envelopes in which to enclose prospectuses of the Eragny Press. Esther sent them, but they were the wrong size. She defended her choice. Lucien replied on the 10th February: "The reason you gave for the envelopes is absurd, ridiculous, idiotic. When I am in London you won't listen to my advice and do as you wish. You are as obstinate as a mule." He was sorry to have to write such a letter, but this "envelope business is really too silly. I was feeling most affectionate to your memory and when I received your letter I was quite upset. All the same many kisses and love. Do not send any money. Mother has given me some."

Rodo arrived and at once said it was ridiculous for him to have come. A waste of time, and "*il l'avait bien dit*". He disliked the countryside and wanted *motifs* which were not there. He grumbled that the old water-mills, the cascades, the great lumps of stone, merely resembled the setting of an *opera comique*, but Lucien was well satisfied, and said he could work in the village for a long time, Despite the rain, he had finished two canvases, one a *temps gris*, the other a *matin soleil*. He worked every day unless there was a downpour.

Lucien and Julie had been happy together, "getting on splendidly all the time we have been here", he wrote on the 17th February. "The poor old thing is easily contented, provided you show her a little sympathy." She had asked for a small room where she could be warm, Lucien had a much larger room, but soon the mother moved into his room, which now became their sitting-room, and Lucien slept in a room which opened into it. When Rodo arrived he was given a room on the same floor, but he complained that his neighbours were noisy. He could not sleep, and so he and Lucien changed rooms. Lucien was not disturbed by his neighbours but regretted the room he had, and "*l'intimité* with the mother".

When Esther received the money from Duret, Lucien again warned her: "Be careful to make it last as long as you can, for after that there is nothing more to expect." Julie was to return to Eragny at the end of the month. She must go to look after her garden, but she promised Lucien money to remain at Riec if his pictures were not finished. "Your last two letters," he wrote to Esther, "were, for you, so very affectionate that I felt quite touched . . . you say you let the place at four guineas a week, and that one week will be paid in advance. But with only four guineas, how can you pay some of the bills, buy clothes you need, have your travelling expenses and have something in your pocket for the unexpected?" Esther told him a friend had met with an accident. He commented: "Poor M. has no luck, but I must say I do not understand the kind of woman who faints at such awkward moments. If I felt faint I should not take a tin out of the oven just at that moment." Now he gave way to one of his periodical moods of profound dejection. He had no confidence in his work, and it did not satisfy him. On the 22nd February, he wrote: "I realise very much what a hopeless struggle I am engaged in, for I am not a painter. I have no side quite my own. My personality is only a weak extension of the poor, dear, old father. I have no facility, the slightest thing gives me an enormous amount of effort and, above all, I am not over-industrious.

You see, I know myself." This distorted self-portrait was the outcome of a brief feeling of frustration, common perhaps to all artists, when it seems impossible to satisfy oneself and paint a good picture. "Early in life," Lucien continued, "I thought that perhaps I could do something, and I dragged you into the pool in which I struggled. I am much too weak to be able to save you and myself." He dared not think what the end of it all would be. He said the success of his book, *Soliman Ben Daoud*, meant nothing, and he feared the book for the *Société du Livre Contemporain* would be a failure. He sent his love: "I am sure that our union is one very much alike to Charpentier's ideal. If we were not so often irritated by the difficulties of life, I mean money, we should be really happy together." In his next letter, dated two days later, he wrote: "I am awfully sorry you regret your affectionate letter. Please don't. It is not so very often that you let yourself go in a letter, and you must imagine how pleased I am when some of your *real self* comes to me in that way. Your foolishness in that letter made me quite foolish also, and it is a very sweet feeling."

By the beginning of March his mother and Rodo had gone. Julie had paid his *pension* until March 12th and had given him his fare to Paris. He paid three francs (half a crown) a day *tout compris* at the hotel, but this he told Esther, was a favour. He was writing his daily letter to her in his room just before going to bed: "I am alone and lonely. It is at this time I miss you. You will say that's just like me, that is all I care for. No. A thousand times no! But you will not think so." The weather had changed, the days were bright and sunny, but he continued to have a "ghastly time" with his canvases. He did not "feel" his brushes, the way to paint seemed strange, and every picture had to be worked at differently. Although he found fresh *motifs* every day, "I dither about and lose a lot of time."

He had heard from Danze. His committee had agreed to commission the book, he could start work. It was to be Emile Moselly's *La Charrue d'Erable* and it was to have ten head-pieces, and the same number, also in colour, of initial letters and tail-pieces. In the evenings, Lucien worked at the designs and sent them to Esther to make into blocks.

There was still a possibility that Esther would join him at Riec. He wrote to her on the 6th March: "I think it would be a good plan when you come to bring me a new Norfolk suit as mine is getting shabby, and will be still more so if we remain here any length of time." As he was stock size Esther should have no trouble in getting one.

Then he had an afterthought: "But there is the Custom's business. I tell you what to do. For a few days you could wear the knickers instead of your own, that would be sufficient to prevent them to look too new. But I wonder if your seat would go in?" He was still at Riec on the 15th, and Esther had not come. On that day he wrote: "I am sorry I gave you such a douche about the Degas, it is only because I knew my Sickert. I am afraid all his fuss means very little. Of course, I do not mind selling the Degas. I did care for the other etchings: but they are all gone." It appeared, he said, from Esther's letter, that wonders were expected of him. "It makes me frightfully nervous. I am afraid everybody will be greatly disappointed. So far I have only one canvas which satisfies me. It is all very well to paint, but no one ever buys anything. All the time I showed at Sickert's studio in Fitzroy Street I did not sell one single picture."

The new problems set by his painting was partly explained in his letter to Esther. She had written to say that an editor of one of the weekly reviews had asked him to contribute an article. "My dear, an article from me on *l'esthétique en général*? Well, I must say that I am passing through a phase where I do not know if we are not all wrong with our *travail d'après nature*. It may have been a *réaction nécessaire* at the time of the impressionists, but are we right in doing the same thing again? For what is my purpose in painting landscape from nature? To learn, so that I can do my blocks for the books away from nature, and so bring to them a sort of résumé and synthesis? The whole of art would seem to be in that mood just now. In wanting to do impressionistic landscape I believe I made a big mistake: it has already been done so well that it cannot be done again. The father's exhibition was a glorious affair, beyond anything I can tell you, and we, the queue, are nowhere." Nevertheless he affirmed that he had a technique which was his own. He had made a decision with his painting, and no longer followed strictly the theories of impressionism. At last he was weaned. His pictures in future will reveal his own individual personality, and a devotion, poetical in its intensity, to the beauties of nature. His life would have the austerity of a sacrifice offered to a noble ideal.

"If you send me any money," he wrote two days later, "let it be £2 10s. instead of £2, because although I have not much opportunity to spend, I have all the same a certain amount of incidental expenses. For example, I had to buy five more tubes of white, I have already gone through ten. I use a considerable number of stamps, there are, of course, my cigarettes, today I had my hair cut, and there was the washing. So, you see. But if at the end of the month you have neither let the house nor sold the Degas, I go away because I do not want to be so far without cash, the position would be too horrible. My darling, you seem to count too much on my work: it makes me quite nervous. What I am doing is perhaps useless. So far I am pleased with only one of my things. The weather changes so that I cannot work two days running on the same *motif*. It is very trying." He did not mind Esther trying to sell his Jongkind painting if this would pay her travelling expenses. "My dear, I think of it, three months' holiday with you and Diana [White] would be ideal. I should be satisfied to have you both, but it is so wonderful that I fear it will not happen. Things one wants too much do not happen. But in spite of all that I say I wish ardently for it and especially for you. So many days away from you diminish the little time of happiness I have left, for I am fast getting very old."

In his next letter he again complained of letters which reached him unstuck, the gum on the flap of her last was unlicked. And he did not understand why she was upset at the mother's letter which he had sent her. True, it was abusive, but she wrote only from sympathy and a desire to help. He is about to look for his folding stool which he has left somewhere in a field. He hoped to be successful, as he had already found the cork of his turpentine bottle and a pair of gloves. Brittany, he said, was amazing, you could safely leave anything in the fields and know that the peasants would not touch it.

Madame Cadoret had the police magistrate from Quimperlé and his wife to lunch, and she invited Lucien and Shaluta, the Russian painter, to join them. They would fare better, she said, than if they took the table d'hôte. But, wrote Lucien on the 19th March, as it was Friday, the menu was not plentiful, only oysters *à la Cadoret*, soles, crème caramel, salmon and Dutch sauce, green peas, a cheese, and wine and champagne. But, afterwards, it was impossible for him to go to his *motif*. This letter created a bad impression. Esther was convinced that Lucien did not work that afternoon because he had drunk too much at lunch. She had a horror of drunkenness as a result of an unpleasant experience. Shortly after their marriage she and Lucien were going to see a performance of Planquette's *Les Cloches de Corneville*. At dinner they entertained a cousin and were very merry, the cousin continually filling Esther's glass with wine on the sly. She felt no effects until they reached the theatre, then the reaction was so violent that Lucien had to take her home after the first act. She had never forgotten that evening, and it was hateful to her that Lucien should give way to drink. Her next letter was angry and abusive.

"Your letter made me very sad," Lucien replied (23rd March). "Fancy you treating me so hard! That day I did not work after *déjeuner* is the only day I have lost. I hope you can say the same. Having nothing to do, you can occupy your time as you wish and without reproach. Since I am here I have nearly completed five paintings, two colours of a block, and I do not count the sketches. If this is not enough, *I do not mind*. I have done it because it pleases me, and if I choose to stop work one afternoon, *quelle qu'en soit la raison*, I will do so, if you do not like it, so much the worse. I will not be turned into a picture-producing machine. Yes, my dear, there was wine at that lunch, and I also had a glass of champagne. Shocking! But I have made no abstainer vows, and I do not like your remonstrances at all. I finish my canvases this week and I am surely going away on the 31st unless you wire me to stop, but do not put me in the position to have to beg for cash of the mother. After all she has done I cannot ask for any more. I hope your next letter won't be so nasty, you can be so very much so when you choose. I write at night, I go to bed sad and in bad temper. You spoiled my evening thoughts. Love and kisses you nasty little woman."

The day before he received the "nasty" letter, he had written: "You tell me to cheer up, that things can't be worse. It seems to me that when things are at their worst it is no time to cheer up, before we do that the tide must turn. Tell Orovida that I know now from who she takes her love of letter-writing. The other day as I was walking I made for her, in my mind, a beautiful letter, but unfortunately it remains there, and it was such a fine one, talking of cows and pet dogs, and flowers and *gâteaux, le tout arrosé de* wonderful jokes, but alas! *mais où sont les neiges d'antan?*"

Esther's next letter brought further vexation. "It arrived open and had not been stuck", Lucien wrote on the 26th March, "The gum on the envelope was quite shiny." Everything was hopeless. "I am frightfully sorry that you sent me that extra pound and you remain with nothing. You must abandon the idea of coming to Brittany, it is hard, but, my darling, when one has no money, one does not build castles in the air. If we start the new book with debts, we are finished!" On his last day at Riec, 3rd April, 1910 he wrote: "I realise that debts and difficulties are in front of us until we die, for I will never, but never, be able

to earn enough money to give you all the sort of comfort you require—
the comfort of a well-to-do English, middle-class person!"

With these bitter, despondent words, Lucien departed from Riec and
for the next weeks was either staying with Rodo in Montmartre or
with his mother at Eragny, all the time trying hopelessly to solve his
money problems. At Eragny he unpacked his pictures. When put
into frames they were better than he thought. "When dry, I will take
them to Paris and show them to Durand. I can only hope he will be
interested. So I am not going to send you any of them for the New
English unless I fail to sell in Paris. As for putting the father's pictures
to the *mont-de-piété* you must not dream of it. They would not
lend us much, two or three hundred francs. Fancy asking prohibitive
prices in Germany and ending on that!"

He approached the subject of the insurance policy to his mother, but
she neither understood nor listened. She wept. He was like the others;
he thought only of money. Finally Julie said that nothing could be
done until Champly kept his promise and gave her the insurance
policy when he returned to Paris. But Lucien did not think he would
get it. "She will put it in her tin box under the coals with her other
papers, and it will be *à la merci du premier qui le trouvera*!" In 1902
Lucien had signed an acknowledgement that he owed his father ten
thousand francs (£400). To cover the claims of the rest of the inheritors he had taken out a life insurance for this sum. After Camille's
death the policy was endorsed to the effect that it was the property of
the heirs. Champly, the notary, retained the policy and with him it
remained.

Esther thought it was his mother's obstinacy that prevented Lucien
regaining possession of the policy. She wrote that Julie was hard
with him, but Lucien would not have this. It was Esther his mother
was hard with, because she was convinced they were in such a dreadful
hole through Esther's mismanagement. "Being messers, we can't
help it," said Lucien. He was longing to go and try his luck in Paris.
"My sweet old *compagne*," he wrote. "I am only grieved that I can't
give you much comfort, except a reminding of the love of your silly
old lover. For you know I am quite as silly as ever, although I am
forty-seven. I have been reviving in my mind all the good moments of
high exalted emotions I had near you, when my heart seemed so big
that it nearly hurt! The intellectual times when we got excited by
artistic ideas, and last, but not least, the sensual times when we seemed
to be a single being, with that lovely penetration which makes all one's

organism as being a single one, with a sort of unity of pleasure. You see, my sweet one, I am quite raving today, and I try to make my 2½d. stamp useful in giving you my inside thoughts, for of late our letters have been the contrary, with all sorts of business matters, leaving little room for one's feelings. There is a lot of pear and apple blossom this year."

So love and worldly affairs alternated in his letters with chiding and rebuke. "I received this morning two letters of yours. You should not spend so much in stamps. I write as often as I think I have something to tell you, as I cannot afford to spend the stamps for nothing. Again you send me one of your letters open, as you will see by the enclosed.* Just now, with all our money bothers, it is not very nice." But the next day: "My dear old girl, how dreadful to think you are alone in such a pass. You don't know how it worries me. I don't seem to be able to think of anything else ... Much love from your own distressed friend and lover, Lucien." Esther suggested that he should persuade Julie to buy her pearls. He was appalled. "Every day your letters are more and more distressing! I began to have a sort of fear at posttime." Of course, Julie would not, or rather could not, buy her pearls. "Why don't you try and sell them in London or, failing that, pawn them? It is easier to pawn pearls than pictures." He complained that he was old, worn out, and had the ill-luck to have been born under an evil star: "When I think how I was hopeful when I asked you to join my misery! I thought that hard work would be enough, but hard work is nothing without luck, and that has always run away from me."

"I wish I could write to you, my own darling, some good news, but nothing. Nothing!" He wrote on the 27th April from Paris where he was trying to sell one of his Camille pictures. He hoped Signac might buy it, but when he visited him on the 26th April, there was company at dinner, and he had no opportunity to speak about the picture. But Signac showed him a Camille bought for eight hundred francs (£32), "a lovely thing". He feared the one he wanted to sell was beyond Signac's means, or indeed the means of any of his friends, "for they are not rich. So I went to Durand this morning, took my courage *à deux mains*, and ask him if he will buy one of the last pictures the father painted, and show him a photograph. He ask the price, not to frighten him, I said three thousand francs (£120). He tell me all sorts of things and finally he was not able to pay more than one thousand five hundred

---

* Esther's sister Ruth had the same failing. Licking the gum was thought unhygienic!

francs, if, when he sees the picture, it is a fine one. I told him I could not entertain the idea. I was not surprised". Esther lost hope. Nothing, she said, will come of these efforts to raise money. Now she had the fear that Lucien was minded not to return to England. "Do you imagine I won't come back?" he replied on the 10th May. "If I don't, it is simply because I fear the dreadful life we have together when we are worried." But he would not return until he could bring some money. "I confess that I dread to be with you and be miserable. I want to be back with relief to our anxiety in order to be able to love you as I feel I would like to do, without a shadow between us."

"You have not achieved a better success in England," Esther had written, "because you do not take an active interest in the various art societies." "What rubbish!" exclaimed Lucien. "Attending silly society meetings is a waste of time. The truth is I have had the stupidity of settling in the least artistic country in the world. If I was in Paris, after a certain number of years, I would be in a different position, even without going to the cafés or the dealers. Look at Lepère and his books. He started printing much after me, and see where he is! As for Sickert, he is preparing his way for the Academy, as they all do. He has never said he is against it,* and it would give him a much better standing as a teacher. If he writes it is in order to get a certain influence, as Ricketts has done. Do you want me to do the same? Poor you and Orovida, you deserve to have a good husband and father on the stock exchange, robbing good guineas to make you happy. My poor dear, I see my letter will turn as nearly nasty as yours, but I will stop it now, for if we spend postage it must be for something other than abuse." Esther was not to be fobbed off. She wrote that he achieved nothing. What does he do in Paris? "My dear," Lucien replied, "I simply go about, and as Paris is small and confined, I meet a lot of people, and that is how business is done. In London, I may walk for days, and meet no one. Perhaps this is because I know so few people, and even then I cannot talk to them easily, as I am a foreigner and feel out of place. I see now quite clearly the enormous mistake we have done to settle in London. There the game is over." "You are right," he said in a further letter, "not to discuss the mistake of living in England. We can do that when we meet. But really, England is so dull to me. I mean from the artistic point of view. In Paris, there is a wonderful life, and the snobbism

---

* Sickert was not against the Academy. He once remarked to Clifford Hall: "I am proud to be a member of an institution of which Turner was also a member."

for art among the silly bourgeois is far more developed, which gives a much better chance to artists. But, maybe, a reaction will take place in England."

He went to Bernheim's, "with a stout heart, knowing I was playing my last card," but without result. He must go again. "My *pauvre vieille*, you don't know, or rather you must know, how I miss you, for it is in the moment *de crise* when I am most *découragé* that I need your comfort." The next letter was an exclamation of despair. Lucien said all his efforts had been in vain, catastrophe was upon them. "*Hélas!* my dear, my last hope has gone! The Bernheims won't take my things. They are good, they say, but there is such a crisis in modern painting that they can't see their way to add to their stock. The only thing they can promise is to keep a few, show them, and endeavour to sell. My sweet Esther, I don't know what to do. My cash is finished, I go back to Eragny on Monday. The one result of my trip to Paris is the offer of Durand of 1,500 francs (£60) for father's *Hâvre*. This time it is the end. Our home will be destroyed, our little belongings will be sold, and I have a feeling of nightmare that we shall never meet again. I want your dear person so much: I can't tell you what I feel. Not only about the money matters, but I am so disheartened and everything is so rotten here. The art movement is in a frightful crisis. I doubt if I will try again to do any landscapes. It is useless, *je suis désemparé, découragé—vide—fini ! ! !* I must stop as all I would say would be in the same key. What would I not give to have you in my arms and have your comfort. Your sad Lucien." The letter had a postscript. "I wonder, my sweet darling, if you had that fit of fears while I was writing this distressed letter? Ugly, fat old woman of nearly forty, that is all very well, but dear, one's feelings don't get as old as one's outside envelope! Whatever happens, you are always for me the sweetheart, and I always have the vision of what you were. I see myself walking by your side, your enigmatic face ornamented with an Egyptian smile. No fat can take away that vision from me. The hours we have lived together are more important than the present and I bring them back. I am hardly now in the present, luckily, for it is a beastly thing. I had a word from mother, she comes to Paris today, I am meeting her at the *Gare St. Lazare*. I shall do my best to persuade her to do something, but we must not count on it, she has already done so much."

Bonin, Cocotte's husband, brought optimism. He thought he could sell the Camille picture to a *député*, a M. Sembat, and on the 10th May advanced Lucien two thousand francs (£80) on the security of the picture. Lucien at once sent Esther the greater part of this money. "I hope the enclosed will relieve your immediate anxiety, but we must be awfully careful, I cannot tell when the next money will come, therefore we must not pay out much and be again with nothing for the current expenses. The cheque of one thousand eight hundred francs is from Bonin's two thousand. I keep two hundred to pay for my expenses while here and for my fare back to London. Also I must get some oil-colours, they are cheaper here than in London. I will give Bonin an I O U on which, if he succeed to sell the picture for three thousand he will give me the remaining one thousand. Dear Esther, I hope you will be careful in order not to put us again in such a pass." Previously Esther had deplored that she was not trained in some profession which would enable her to be of service to the community. "You have a most powerful way to help," Lucien commented, "but you won't do it, and that is on account of your English education." He recalled how Enid Verity, when she and her husband met with difficulties, cut down her expenses, "wonderfully. In other words, one must not go for STYLE, for that is an expensive luxury in the land of the Angle. In a word, if one has a certain amount to live on, to spend a little less instead of much more, is a very useful profession. The whole rotten system is contained in a nutshell: you like a wonderful display of dinner china to eat nothing: the entire business is conducted on these lines, and that is why we can't manage. I tell you all this because the cheque will be a relief, and you will feel strong to hear some kind of truth. I know you will answer you are right, and things will go on as ever. I must put up with it. Well, my dear, I kiss you very dearly all the same". Esther was not mollified with the cheque, nor was it a relief making her "strong enough" to read Lucien's home-truths. She did not defend, she attacked. "All you have done," she replied, "is to obtain a loan." "You are quite unkind to me," answered Lucien. "I pass my time, running all the day long in the hot weather, doing my best, and you grumble." He felt as if he was in a nightmare, wanting to move, but unable to do so. Nothing more could be done about the picture until Bonin, who was *en vacances*, returned. Only then could he get the picture and take it to M. Sembat. "What else can I do? No, I don't like your letter, because I think it is very unkind. I am killing myself with worries and efforts to try and succeed, and you imagine that I do not come back because my bad will stops me."

Bonin returned from his holiday, Lucien collected the picture and took it to M. Sembat. But no one answered his knocks, the house was shuttered and empty, and a neighbour told him that M. Sembat had gone to the country. "What do you think one can do, when everything goes that way? Meanwhile, all day, I run in the hot sun, trying to make things *aboutir*."

On that note the flow of letters to and fro ceased. The picture was not sold. Bonin retained it, and Lucien returned to Esther, having achieved, with the loan, a temporary truce to their difficulties, and with the commission for the new book.

CHAPTER XI

Lucien Meets James Bolivar Manson, 1910

AT THE BROOK, ESTHER, HER PURSE AGAIN FULL, ENGAGED A NEW SERVANT, Emma Ruddick. She was to stay with the Pissarros for sixteen years. Born in a Suffolk village, her mother and father were in the service of an employer who owned a large racing stable near Newmarket. Emma remembered how starved the "little" jockeys were, she was sorry for them and gave them food. Emma was just twenty when she came to London. The family at The Brook then consisted of Lucien, Esther, Orovida, aunt Orovida Bensusan, and Orovida's governess, Miss Hurley, who also acted as housekeeper. Emma at once became one of the family, immersed in its affairs. Over the years she frequently gave notice to leave, but never went. If a book was unfinished she would not take her holiday until it was completed. Writing from Canada, in 1959, at the age of sixty-nine, she remembered Lucien as a good man: kind, quiet and gentle. "He was fond of animals, and they liked him. Orovida's Siamese cat used to perch on his shoulder. Esther was the kindest, cleanest and most truthful person I've ever known. She was never selfish, her own wants always came last. She aimed at perfection in everything she did, and she expected the same from everyone in her household. I don't think I ever saw her idle. In those days there seemed so many poor people who came to the door hungry and asked for something to eat, they were always given cocoa and food. Esther was the only woman I've met who, when her purse was empty, would borrow a shilling from me to give to the needy. This happened many times. She was devoted to Lucien and took great care of him when he was ill. She loved her home and garden and knew the name of every plant and shrub. I always think of The Brook as a happy place, many friends came on the "at home" days and other times. It was an interesting family. At The Brook I learnt to make a French omelette and I remember the salads that Lucien mixed for himself at the table."

Esther was at home on every other Sunday, and on these occasions there assembled relations and such friends as Francis Dodd, Ethel Walker, Spencer Gore, Harold Gilman, Robert Bevan, Walter Sickert, Aitken of the Tate Gallery, and Campbell Dodgson, the Keeper of the British Museum Print Room. Miss Hurley made the cakes, Esther handed round the cups of tea and whispered to a favoured guest: "You'll stay to supper?" After tea, the unfavoured departed in ones and twos. A withdrawal was then made to an inner room for supper, usually a cold collation. At this a ritual was observed. A large bowl of salad was placed on the table, and Lucien, surrounded with condiments, mixed the dressing, a hard-boiled egg being one of the necessary ingredients, Emma, with solemn face, stood by his side, as if ready for an emergency. After supper, music was made in the drawing-room, the company sitting as comfortably as they could in cane wicker armchairs, their chatter broken by a cry of: "Silence!" from Esther. "Mrs. Voynich is going to play!" Everyone was then expected to keep perfectly still, disregarding cramps and muscular reactions. If the slightest movement was made, the chairs would creak. Mrs. Voynich having played a Bach Prelude and Fugue from one of the Forty-Eight, Esther would ask a relative to sing—a soprano with a repertory of the sentimental ballads then popular in drawing-rooms. But Esther did not care for this kind of music and as the first notes trilled through the room she would begin a conversation, only made inaudible by the hum of talk that immediately followed. On many evenings Lucien would get out his portfolios of the family drawings, and pass them round.

Esther was absent-minded. On one occasion at a dinner party, when the bowl of soup was placed in front of her to serve, she helped herself and began to eat, oblivious of the rest of the guests. Lucien motioned for no one to say anything. Presently Esther asked: "Would anyone like a second helping?"

The musician of these occasions, Ethel Voynich,* was Esther's closest friend, married to a Russian whose political opinions had twice incurred banishment to Siberia and two escapes. She was an accomplished pianist, but an injury to her wrist had prevented a professional career. She also composed, but most of her energies went into her novels. These had a wide vogue, particularly The Gadfly, which had a phenomenal success when Mrs. Voynich was over ninety and it was translated into Russian. She was frequently at The Brook, either as a

* Ethel Voynich died in 1960, in New York, at the age of ninety-six.

guest, or paying rent when Esther was away. Ethel Voynich was friendly with Lilian Manson, principal of music at the North London Collegiate School, who was at this time producing Purcell's *Dido and Aeneas*, the performers and instrumentalists being her pupils. It was an ambitious project, coming as it did some sixteen years before the revival of interest in Purcell's music. Mrs. Voynich persuaded Esther and Lucien to go with her on the 5th February, 1910, to the first performance. Afterwards she introduced them to Lilian and her husband, an artist. There was at once a mutual attraction, and when Esther invited the Mansons to one of her "at homes", they accepted. Lucien and Manson had much in common; there was a sympathy between them, and when Lucien returned from Paris at the end of May they became close friends. This friendship was to last throughout Lucien's life. It was the one intimate contact with another man that Lucien made in later life. Lucien gave impetus to Manson's impressionist enthusiasm: Manson heard from him of Camille's indomitable integrity and struggles and he read the letters which Camille had written to Lucien. They talked of the early days of the movement and the theories which flowed from it. This was to lead to the formation at the Tate Gallery, when Manson was employed there, of the Impressionist collection. As time went on, Lucien relied more and more on Manson for advice, help and friendship.

James Bolivar Manson, sixteen years younger than Lucien, was the son of a poet who earned his living as one of Cassell's editors. Manson had left school at the age of sixteen to become an office boy and a packer in the employ of George Newnes, the publisher. Having, like Lucien, little taste for the tying of parcels, he found a fresh situation as a bank clerk, but this also had no appeal, and he spent most of his time playing practical jokes on his colleagues. His real interest was painting, for which he had a natural instinct and facility. When, in the evenings, he was free of the Bank, he went to Heatherly's and drew from the life. In 1900, Lilian Laugher, his future wife, after studying music in Berlin, came to live with his parents at Dulwich. With her help and the little money he had contrived to save, Manson resigned from the Bank, went to Paris, and studied with Jean Paul Laurens at the *Académie Julian*. A year later he married Lilian. He was then twenty-two, she eight years older. Manson, when he met Lucien, was living at Hampstead with Lilian and their two children, Mary and Jean, sometimes selling a picture, more often not. His uncertain income and Lilian's salary were inadequate for their needs, Lilian grumbled, and not long after his meeting with Lucien, she bullied him into accepting a clerk-ship at the Tate Gallery as assistant to Charles Aitken, the Keeper and Director. Although, in 1930, when Aitken retired, Manson was appointed to his place, he never became reconciled to an official career, his heart being elsewhere. Sir Alec Martin said of him that he was not a Civil Servant but an artist. He became an unconventional curator, gay when solemnity was expected, his eyes always twinkling, and on occasions, near to being submerged in official hot water. Nevertheless the Tate blossomed during his stay, and it was he who persuaded Aitken, whose taste in art had hitherto been for crucifixions and annunciations, early Italian painters and pre-Raphaelites, to open its doors to the Impressionists and the New English Art Club.

When this friendship began, Lucien had reached the age of forty-seven. He was rosy-faced, someone said he had a well-soaped look—his thick and prominent eyebrows, which remained black long after his hair turned white, jutting raggedly over scrutinising dark-brown eyes, his long beard black but streaked with white. In town, and out of doors, he invariably wore a large black hat and a cape: he said he liked to feel his arms free. Only late in life did he take to an overcoat for the sake of its warmth. Normally, he dressed in greenish tweeds, a green cloth cap on his head, and a yellow tie round his neck. He selected his ties with care; they were beautiful, but unseen. Young John, the son of Ruth, Esther's sister, once asked him if he wore a tie. The answer was a sweet smile, and a lift of the beard. On state occasions, such as private-view days, Lucien appeared in his black hat and inverness cloak over a dark-blue suit. He spoke English fluently, and if it was sometimes incorrect, his meaning was clear. Orovida remembered Manson at this time as a fine figure of a man, handsome, with abundant hair. But he looked ill and strained. Although devoted to his two children, his home life was not happy. His character differed widely in many ways from Lucien's. He liked good company. He was a man of the world, at ease in any company, while Lucien was unworldly, dreamy, vague, shy, often embarrassed. Manson had a penchant for mischief, his contempt for self-importance, pomposity and pretentious-ness often betrayed him into pricking these bladders with a devastating wit which made him enemies. Lucien was kindly, and reticent in speaking of other people, and rarely indeed had his remarks a sharp edge. Once, however, when a popular artist explained to him: "If you want to succeed like me, Mr. Pissarro, you must keep one eye on the public and one eye on your work," Lucien flashed: "You must have a dreadful squint!" He was always gentle. Orovida remembered only one occasion when he was physically aggressive, and that was when in the street he saw a French peasant beating a worn-out horse. Lucien knocked the man down. Although he liked joking, his jokes were simple ones, a little childish. If for example there was a sudden crash of breakage, he would exclaim: "Something has fallen down!" or he would take the spoon from his saucer at tea and say: "These be stirring times!" Manson had a flair for imitating bird calls and the noises of animals. Both he and Lucien loved animals. Often Manson would suddenly start singing,—ribald music-hall ditties—and this would recall to Lucien his father's delight in singing the Creole songs he had heard as a boy at St. Thomas. Lucien would hum the tunes, and then recite the words in a flow of extraordinary French gibberish.

The economic position at The Brook showed no improvement. Bonin's loan was exhausted, and Lucien wrote to Julie: "Had I not been so short of money I would have been able to produce another book, but I cannot make a book without spending money, and since I have only debts, I dare not increase them." Julie replied: "I am very sorry to hear of the mess you have put yourself in since the last book. You must cut your expenses down. You should do without a maid. Housework is not shameful, better than debts." In October, 1910, Lucien thanked Julie for sending him one hundred francs (£4). The rent and the taxes had been paid by Esther's father; her mother paid for Orovida's schooling. "We beg on all sides. I hate it." He was working on his book for the *Société du Livre Contemporain*, making wood engravings for it after drawings by Camille. The project would take two years. Julie had planned to go to Riec in December, but did not do so—it was too far. What would happen if she were to die there all alone? Trouble and expense for Lucien. "When I die," she wrote, "I want everything simple. No priests about, please. It is nothing to me if I do not even have a grave."

CHAPTER XII

The Camden Town Group. 1911–13

EARLY IN 1911, LUCIEN SOLD ONE OF HIS CAMILLE PICTURES, *La Jetée du Hâvre, Haute Mer, Soleil, Matin* (No. 1298 in Rodo's catalogue), to John Quinn for £220. In March, he was in Paris to sign the contract for the book for the *Société du Livre Contemporain*. The payment was fifteen thousand francs (£600) to be made in three instalments. Lucien also arranged for an exhibition of his books and prints at the Maison Goupil the following spring. "The future looks a little brighter," he wrote to his mother. Before going to Paris he had been painting at Colchester, most of his old assurance had returned, and the result was four of his finest landscapes.

Lucien and Manson met frequently, Manson persuading Lucien to emerge more frequently from his isolated life at The Brook and regularly attend the weekly gathering at number 19 Fitzroy Street. This was to his liking, and recalled to him his life in Paris in the 'eighties, when he had so many friends and the opportunity to discuss and live more actively in the art movements of his time. But his enjoyment of this new pleasure, the arguments at number 19, and the occasional dinner at *L'Etoile* in Charlotte Street, were tempered, as ever, with the need for money, the prick that he could not afford these jaunts. Often he stayed at home because he had not his fare to the West End. His opinions were greatly respected at number 19. Here he "found an English audience capable of appreciating the novel principles of colour and design which he had absorbed twenty years earlier during his brief association with the neo-Impressionists".*

"Pissarro," wrote Sickert, some years later, "holding the exceptional position at once of an original talent, and of the pupil of his father, the authoritative depository of a mass of inherited knowledge and experience, has certainly served us as a guide, or let us say, a dictionary of theory and practice on the road we have elected to travel."†

---

* Douglas Cooper. *The Courtauld Collection. A Catalogue and Introduction* University of London. The Athlone Press, 1954. Page 47.
† *The New Age.* 28th May, 1914.

No subject, at number 19, aroused more argument and dissension than a mention of the New English Art Club. Most of the group showed at its exhibitions, but the more adventurous, those who refused to submit to the Royal Academy, had become dissatisfied with the N.E.A.C. as well. They considered it had become safe and conservative, its standards akin to the Academy. The formation of a new group was suggested, Gilman taking the initiative, but John, loyal to the N.E.A.C. favoured a peaceful penetration of the selection committee. Lucien, although sceptical of such an attempt, supported him, and took the opportunity to remind the others of *un peu plus de variétié,* and of his father's dictum of orchestration of colour.* Gilman was tooth and nail against any compromise, and all for forming a new group. Gore supported Gilman with characteristic gentleness and mildness. Gilman's persistence won—it was decided, at a meeting at Gatti's, that a new Society be formed. A good dinner had been enjoyed with a flow of wine, when Sickert strode out of the restaurant waving his arms and vociferated: "We have made history." Two more meetings were held before the group was finally launched. Sickert suggested the title, saying: "Camden Town has been so watered by my tears that something important, sooner or later, must spring from its soil." When members were asked why it was called the Camden Town group, they answered: "Because some of the members live at Hampstead, and others at Chelsea and Hammersmith."

The tactful Spencer Gore was elected president, and Manson secretary, and the following were elected as members: Walter Bayes, Robert Bevan, Malcolm Drummond, Harold Gilman, Charles Ginner, Spencer Gore, J. D. Innes, Augustus John, Henry Lamb, Wyndham Lewis, M. A. Lightfoot, James B. Manson, Lucien Pissarro, W. Ratcliffe, Walter Sickert and Doman Turner. The majority of these artists represented the cream of that brilliant pre-Kaiser war period of English painting.

In 1898, The Carfax Gallery in Bury Street, St. James's, had been opened by young John Fothergill, later to become an innkeeper, eccentric in dress and in the food and wine he provided. When Robert Ross took over the Gallery he retained Arthur Clifton, the

---

* "The thing which impressed me was the immense respect with which John and Sickert, as well as the rest, always listened to anything Pissarro had to say about painting: I felt, and I believe they felt, that Pissarro was the master of us all, the man from whom we could all of us learn." *Since I was Twenty-Five,* Frank Rutter, Constable, London, 1927.

business manager. Sickert had exhibited there from the first and was on the most friendly terms with Clifton. It was not difficult for him, with his engaging talk and charming manners, to persuade Clifton to open the doors of the Carfax to the group, and it was here that the three exhibitions were held, the first in June, 1911. Lucien showed three of his Colchester landscapes and his impressive *Well Farm Bridge, Acton*, depicting a train thundering under a bridge, although he had already expressed doubts about the new group. "If they exhibit at the Grafton *en bloc*," he had previously written to Manson, "I should, of course, be glad to join as one of them, tho' I think we are all better out of it."

1912

Money was a little more plentiful in 1912. It was an uneventful year, mainly devoted to the preparation and printing of *La Charrue d'Erable* for the *Société du Livre Contemporain*. In January, Julie, winter-bound in Eragny, complained of loneliness and that only Lucien of all her children wrote to her for the New Year, but in May she wrote: "If you could see how beautiful the garden is, the trees in blossom: it is a lovely sight. To think that the poor father does not see it. And to think that Papa Durand is still alive, eighty-two years old. Poor father should have lived longer, he was more useful than this Papa Durand. This proves once more that there is no justice, neither above nor below." She still hoped to let the house to visitors and stay with Madame Cadoret at Riec, but as the house had no electric light, no gas, and no bath, it was useless to hope it would do for the English. Kikite, Georges' child whom she looked after, had been given a prize at her boarding school in Paris, a book, and Julie commented that it could not have been more appropriate for a Pissarro. It was called *Mademoiselle Sans le Sou*.

On the 20th April, Lucien wrote to Manson: "I can't help being astonished that my work should seem to you capable of giving any help. I feel so hesitating myself, and I really never know how to manage each time I start a new canvas. . . . We ought really to manage to go somewhere to work together for a while. I should like it so much. I feel isolated since I have been working in England." He was able to help Epstein who had a show in Paris with letters of introduction to his friends there, among them Georges Lecomte, art critic of *Le Matin* and Félix Fénéon, "a man of great intelligence and taste who has made of criticism an art".

"You are right, my dear old mother. I should have written, but my excuse is that I work very hard, and am so exhausted at the end of the day that I have not the courage to do anything. The wood engravings tire my eyes so much that when night comes I take a rest, especially as the artificial light is not good for my eyes."

Madame Monet had died the previous year. This loss, and his fear of approaching blindness, turned Monet, already a recluse, into a misanthrope—convinced he had been a failure. Lucien had this in mind when he wrote to Julie: "Think of this poor Monet, whom we all believe to have had luck on his side: talent, success, fortune. Well, in spite of all this, I am quite sure he is absolutely miserable." He added: "I am just as worried as you are that you are all by yourself." In August, Lucien was painting at Rye, but he wrote: "I must get back home soon to finish the book." There he found friction between Esther and Orovida. Orovida, now nineteen, had no liking for the career in music planned for her by Esther, and demanded to be allowed to paint. But Esther remained obstinate. Julie surprisingly wrote: "What do you want to do with poor Orovida? Since she likes drawing, why worry her with other things she doesn't like? Poor father used to say that one could not make pictures and at the same time make shoes. Why force her to learn what doesn't go into her head?" Julie was alone again; this and her "ungrateful children" were the themes of her next few letters. Lucien replied: "I would like you to become reasonable, my dear mother. Now that you are no longer a small girl it is time to act seriously. You see that now I have become a grown man, and you have turned into a little one, here is my turn to scold you. You know nobody is happy that you are all alone in Eragny, so when you have finished with your cider, go and stay with Cocotte." On Camille's birthday Julie wished to go to his grave. She asked Georges to take her, but he wrote to tell her she was an old fool, a mad woman. As for himself, he would go and pay homage to Zola's grave. Words that can only be judged in the light of Georges' reputation as an eccentric wit.

The anniversary of Camille's death approached. Always at this time Julie wrote to Lucien and recalled this unhappy day. Lucien knew she would grieve on the 13th November, and he wrote to her the day before: "It is tomorrow that another year will be added to those which have followed the cruel parting. You are going to be sad and alone in Eragny. Think of my last letter, finish with your cider-making, and go and wait for me at Cocotte's place. I do my best to get on with my book, but there are difficulties, it is the bad time of the year when the printers are over-busy, and we can only get our workman on odd days." However, the book was finished at the end of December and Lucien received the final payment of five thousand francs (£200). "That is all very well," he told Julie, "but, in effect, this represents my profit on two years of hard work."

1913

Lucien was unable to join his mother at Cocotte's house as he was prevented by a new anxiety: Esther was ill, her change of life difficult and complicated. A specialist advised curetting, and she went, as a paying patient, to the Royal Free Hospital where her sister Ruth had been trained. An operation was considered to be successful, and after a fortnight she returned home. A few days later Lucien was in bed with congestion of the lungs. Orovida made a pastel drawing of him which Esther thought "strikingly like". But Lucien, bored with inactivity, thought only of getting to work again. Meanwhile he wrote time and again to his mother urging her to come and live at The Brook, but Julie refused. She was rooted at Eragny.

In March, Lucien, convalescing, was painting in Devon at The Mill, Blackpool, near Dartmouth. With him was an amateur painter, James Brown, a musician, an arranger of early chamber music for small orchestras. As usual, Lucien was dissatisfied with his work. "No, the real fact is," he wrote to Esther, "I am out of training. I no longer know how to begin, to go on, to finish." And he could not decide how to frame for his next exhibition. He thought white and gold mixed. "People won't buy a picture if framed in white as they imagine it will clash with their furniture."

In a letter to Manson, dated the 7th March, Lucien wrote: "You express my superiority to you all, it is only old age, having more experience: but be patient, it will come soon enough. I was fifty the other day! You are all ever so much younger. However, you are right, it is no good to try and skip over the period of drudgery. There is no short cut."

Esther's health continued to cause anxiety. Despite the operation, it did not improve. McNish advised a stay in the clear air of Switzerland. Lucien would have liked to have gone with her, but this was not possible, as there was not the money for both, and also he must work. He had begun to sell, and he must paint new pictures for his exhibition. So it was arranged that Esther would first go to Eragny, whence Julie would accompany her to Switzerland, and Lucien would paint at Rye. Manson, hearing of this, suggested that he, his wife and children, should share a rented house with Lucien and Orovida. Brown also wished to be of the party and to bring his wife and small boy. Esther, hearing of a likely house, went to Rye to view it. She wrote to Lucien: "I do hope you will like the place. There is a bathroom, arrange to take a cold bath every day. They will respect you more if you do." On her return home, Lucien went to Rye and was alone for a time. He wondered if he would be able to work without hindrance when Brown and Manson came. "My sweet girl," he wrote to Esther, "you are perfectly ridiculous to be ashamed of spending thirty-five shillings on a hat. It is awfully cheap. So many women spend so much more." Esther departed to France, and Lucien, expecting Manson and Epstein for a week-end visit, hoped they would not be late as a good dinner had been prepared for them. When they arrived, the ladies of the house were impressed with Epstein. They thought that despite his untidy, unkempt appearance, he was a handsome man.

Finally all the party was assembled. Lilian Manson and Mrs. Brown, with the assistance of Emma Ruddick, did the chores and the cooking, while the men painted and the children played. Orovida painted with the men. On the anniversary of their marriage, Lucien wrote to Esther: "Yes, my dear, twenty-one years. That seems a long time, and only one serious quarrel, so serious, that I am at a loss to remember what it was. We all work together. Manson has made good progress and is, I believe, very pleased with my help. The only one who does not progress is myself."

Esther wrote from Eragny that Julie was amiable, but that it was sad to see her limp with her bad knee every day to the post office hoping to find letters from her children, "so miserable if there is not one. She is old, easily tired, and often relapses into dignified silences". Esther still opposed Orovida's wish to be an artist. She wanted her to be self-supporting, and urged that she should be sent to Germany for six months to learn the language, a valuable asset for her future. "Look at Manson who is able to draw a regular salary at the Tate and paint at the same time. She must make up her mind how she intends to earn her living, for she will ruin her painting if she thinks to make money out of it. I know that Diana (White) does not agree, but then she does not know what it is to have nothing a year." Lucien replied that Manson dreaded going back to the Tate. He was not free to paint, except at the week-end. The job worried him, led nowhere, and compromised what future he had as a painter. Orovida did not want to go to Germany and worked hard, believing that if she showed sufficient progress at painting she would be allowed to continue. "If she is going to paint, she must do it seriously, and not as a pastime." Lucien reverted to Manson. Manson sacrificed himself for the sake of a small salary, and Mrs. Manson was now distressed that he had given up everything for so little. He had no hope of advancement, and it had not been worth it. "She is most unhappy about it. If you want to be an artist you must work more than on Sundays and holidays."

Esther arrived at the Haute Savoie, Vallorcine; in her next letter to Lucien she ungraciously capitulated. "Yes, Manson is a good example. The poor fellow is about thirty-five years old and up to now, or rather to a year ago, has not been able to earn a living for himself, let alone for his wife and children. Nothing hindered him from working before he took the Tate post. He is not a pusher and I trust Orovida is not a pusher. The better the artist, the less able is he or she to sell their work. Well, I suppose I must give in. I only hope the child may not feel the misery of having to beg for every sou as I have." But was it she or Lucien who had had to beg?

Lucien could not understand why Esther had no money. She explained that her purse with seventy francs in it had been stolen. The purse was in her coat, left on a chair in the hotel dining-room, and she thought the waiter had stolen it. But Lucien was not to bother. Julie had made good the money, and advised her not to tell Lucien of the loss. But that was not the sort of secret Esther kept from him. At Rye, Lucien packed to return to The Brook. He had finished nine canvasses, but would not know his achievement until Diana White had seen them. "Now that the sure judgement of my poor dear father is not here, she is the only one I can consult." Julie returned to Eragny, leaving Esther alone at Vallorcine. Her health was improved, but McNish advised a four weeks' extension of her stay. Esther worried about the expense, "how can we manage?" It turned cold, she was bored. "I do nothing but walk about, sit about, mend old clothes. Could you not send me a block to do? I have my tools with me." If Sam knew of a publisher she could translate a Brieux play.

In the previous December, the Camden Town Group had held its third and last exhibition at the Carfax. The exhibitions had not been a success financially; only a few works had been sold, and the director of the Carfax had no heart to continue with them. Now, in November of 1913, Marchant of the Goupil Gallery, who knew many of the "Camden Town" painters, became interested. But he wanted a larger exhibition than those hitherto held, and he disliked the group's title. He thought it had "vulgar associations". Epstein suggested the group be renamed the London Group, and this was accepted. Lucien remained a member for a while, but being out of sympathy with the Vorticist element which came into the exhibitions, did not show. Carfax had an interest in Lucien's painting, and whilst Esther was still in Switzerland, Lucien had occasion to call on him to discuss business. But Esther did not trust his acumen and warned him not to go alone. "Ask Manson to go with you." She complained that at the hotel she was too much alone, beyond a word or two with the *bonne*, or an occasional chat with the peasants working in the fields, she talked to no one. She thought most of the time of Lucien and wrote long letters. In October, Lucien went to Vallorcine to be with Esther for the last week of her stay, delighted to find she looked so well.

"Sad anniversary!" wrote Julie on the 13th November. "Ten years ago today that the dear father died. Poor man, he was so afraid that I would sell his pictures for nothing! My poor paintings! Be assured that I shall not let the sharks have them for nothing." At an exhibition in Paris of Camille's pictures, sales amounted to one hundred and twenty thousand francs (£4,800). "Bernheim came to collect the pictures yesterday and paid thirty thousand francs (£1,200) immediately." But it was doubtful if Lucien would get any share of this money because of his indebtedness to the estate. It was the undivided pictures that had been sold. "It is cold and I have a cold," Julie wrote in a further letter, "so don't expect me for Christmas. I don't feel I have the courage to go to your place: it is too far." She said Joyant was not pleased that the pictures had been sold to Bernheim, and now did not think it worth while to have an exhibition. "It would be as well if you came to deal with the matter. What I do, according to Rodo, is wrong. He says I am an old fool, and he makes difficulties about sharing the money. I want to wash my hands of it all." She was distressed because Rodo made her believe he thought she was cheating, and putting some of the money aside for herself. Of course, Rodo had no such intention. She was thin-skinned where her children were concerned. Nevertheless: "I am absolutely indignant about this," she wrote. "I have got beyond caring how many one-thousand-franc notes there are in my chest. I prefer the sight of my dear pictures. You had better come. I will give all the pictures to you to deal with—my dear friends, because it is they who are my friends and my only company."

At the end of the year, the weather being fine, Lucien was painting, effects of mist and sun. "I work as hard as possible," he told Julie. "Now that I start to sell, I must produce." Julie's reply was an offer to pay his debt to Monet.

CHAPTER XIII

"The Sensation." *1914—1915*

IN JANUARY, SICKERT LEFT FITZROY STREET AND THE LITTLE GROUP AT number 19 was disbanded. Lucien observed that this was because Sickert, as a respectable drawing master, could not associate himself with the cubist recruits. In January and February, Lucien, with Orovida, stayed at Eragny preparing for the Camille exhibition at the Manzi-Joyant galleries which Joyant, despite the Bernheim purchases, had decided to proceed with. Whilst Orivida and Paul experimented in etching, Lucien found frames for his father's pictures and arranged for the cartage to Paris. Usually this was done in an old-fashioned four-wheeled carter's wagon, but as it was market day at Gisors, it was not available, and Manzi sent an auto-car. In Paris, Lucien finished cleaning the pictures and hung them. His mother had sent her good ones, and Bernheim had promised some of his collection, but now made difficulties and was dilatory in delivery. The exhibition was not a success. "The rooms continue to be empty," Lucien wrote. "It gives me the blues to see that big room so full of magnificent pictures quite empty. Not one critic has said a word."

He sent Esther "a ridiculous article" describing Monet's poverty in early life. He said it was quite wrong. "I remember Louveciennes very well. When we went to see the Monets they seemed to me quite bourgeois compared to us. Little Jean Monet had a cupboard full of the most magnificent toys. That does not sound like living on potatoes! And when the mother went to buy meat at Marly the butcher teased me because he said I had such large eyes. He would not have been so amiable to me if the Monets had not been good customers. And the large 1870 picture in the exhibition, the portrait of Madame Monet in a black silk dress, does not resemble poverty. *Mais cela fait bien d'avoir l'air d'être mort de faim!*" When Lucien wrote this letter, Orovida, at Eragny, saw in the studio a picture by Monet unsigned. "What a pity!" she exclaimed to Julie. Julie wrote to Monet at Giverny, and he replied: "Bring me the picture and I will sign it." Julie and Orovida went together, Julie in her black bonnet with the glittering sequins; and the black silk dress she wore when she went to market, and put in her false teeth. Orovida was startled at the change, Julie looked twenty years younger. Monet gave them an excellent lunch. He and Julie recalled bygone days. Monet asked if she remembered the pancakes? His thoughts were back in the 'sixties when, one morning, he had no money and no food, and he called on the Pissarros hoping to eat with them, but the Pissarros were also without money. But Julie had a couple of eggs and some flour, she borrowed milk and made pancakes. Monet said he often thought of that day when he was so hungry and Julie cooked such an appetising meal.

Lucien was a small boy in those now faraway days, and did not know Monet had suffered as much as his father, indeed he was but five when, in 1868, Monet, unable to sell a single painting, had all his pictures seized by creditors, and he, Camille Doncieux, and his small child, were thrown out by the landlord, and Monet had tried to commit suicide.* He was only kept from starving by the bread which Renoir stole for him from his mother's table.

When Lucien was home again at the beginning of April, Julie wrote to thank Esther for her offer of artichokes, but she was no longer, at the age of 77, able to look after her garden. So she would not be able to plant them. She said that Esther did not devote enough time to her house, "do you think you are a daughter of Jupiter and a goddess!" Surely, if she mended her own linen she would save money on the servant and her food. It was impossible to accept the invitation to stay with them; she was too old, and can hardly walk or see. A few days later, in a letter to Lucien, she wrote: "Your Esther would be more courageous if she would do her own work and get rid of the servant, but she is a good-for-nothing, much too superior. No, I do not need any artichokes."

In April and May, Lucien was at The Chip, Chipperfield, King's Langley, Herts. Combinations of yellow gorse, pine trees and fruit blossom enchanted him, and he painted furiously against the changing weather, for cold winds scattered the blossoms and night frosts nipped the early flowers. In June he shared an exhibition at the Carfax Gallery

* Letter from Monet to Bazille dated 29th June, 1868: "I am writing . . . to ask your speedy help. I was certainly born under an unlucky star. I have just been thrown out of the inn, stark naked at that. I've found shelter for Camille and my poor little Jean for a few days in the country. . . . My family have no intention of doing anything more for me. I don't even know where I will have a place to sleep tomorrow . . . PS. I was so upset yesterday that I was stupid enough to throw myself into the water. Fortunately, no harm came of it."

with Manson, Malcolm Milne, Harold Squire and Diana White. In the short-lived but brilliant *New Weekly* Frank Rutter wrote of his exhibits: "The impressionism of Lucien Pissarro is profoundly learned in the secrets of nature, but it is never harshly scientific like some neo-impressionist landscapes. It is before all else emotional, the work of a man who moves us because he has been deeply moved himself." Lucien's sales at the Carfax amounted to £133. 7s. The gallery's commission having been deducted, he received a cheque for £100.

One Sunday in July, van Royen came to lunch at The Brook. "It was like this at the Pissarros," he wrote. "The nice little house is well back from the street . . . you go through a white gate and find all sorts of strange and attractive leaves and flowers just like those that appear in his books; on your left is an extension, formerly a stable . . . low, small, with four deep windows in which there are all kinds of flowers. On the walls paintings by Camille Pissarro, Lucien Pissarro and others. The dining-room is even smaller. When you sit down there is no room left. On the walls old Japanese woodcuts, engravings by Durer, Ricketts and Pissarro. Above the fireplace are shelves of well-read books—apparently quite extraordinary books to judge by the titles. . . . Madam is very sweet, yet, very cultured. the daughter is a strange little creature, twenty years old I believe, but looking more like fourteen, plump, very black eyebrows, large, childish eyes and wearing steel spectacles. But she draws extremely well and makes lovely woodcuts. . . . We spent the whole day with them and in the evening the room was hardly large enough for all the guests. Pissarro, hidden behind his beard and thick eyebrows, sat there enjoying everything so heartily and yet so quietly. He is an extremely sympathetic man. Refined and very clever everything he says is well considered and exact and yet at the same time so simple and modest."*

On the 14th July, Julie was sad with self-pity. There were celebrations in the village, everyone was laughing and gay, fathers and mothers had their families around them, "but as for me, poor old woman, I am alone". She had asked Esther to spend the holiday with her, but Esther, she said, had not troubled to answer. "If you need a few centimes, send me an envelope marked registered, and I will let you have what you ask." At the end of the month Cocotte and the children were with her, waiting for Paul to arrive before going home, for there

* Hammacher, A. M. *Jean François van Royen*, 1878–1942. The Hague. Nederlandsche Vereeniging voor Druk-en Boekkunst, 1947.

was anxiety and rumours of war. Two days after the rumours were confirmed and the German army was marching through Belgium.

That August Lucien was painting at Swindale Grange, Brough, Westmorland, when the news reached him. Esther wrote: "Brown has been. He is certain that the Russian troops are not a myth. It is well known that they have come but it must be kept a secret. People have taken food to them. They are black-bearded men who have travelled in troop trains from the north of Scotland." But Lucien was not interested in mythical Russians in England; his thoughts concerned his mother's safety, Eragny was on the German's line of advance. But Julie would not come to England. She replied that she had left her home in 1870 and had lost everything: rather than run away a second time, she would remain, even if it meant being buried in its ruins.

Now, there was no question of Orovida going to Germany. In the late summer she worked in a toy factory organised by the Women's Emergency Corps, and later went to another toy factory in Wales. Then she was employed as a clerk at twenty-five shillings a week in the Claims and Records Department of the Ministry of Pensions. Rodo came to England and worked with the Morland Press as a wood engraver. He lived in London and painted the suburban streets. Cut off from his friends in Paris he was miserable.

On 24th August, Julie wrote: "The Germans are in Belgium. If they go on like this they will soon be here. I am much afraid that the poor pictures of your dear father will be once more in the hands of the Prussians as in 1870," and on the 29th: "The Prussians are at Douai, that is very near! They march quickly. It is likely I will never see you again. Paul and his wife leave tomorrow and want Cocotte to go with them. Cocotte is terribly afraid for her children, but the husband (Bonin) does not want them to go." Two days later the Prussians were at Amiens. "All the men have left Eragny, there are now only the old women. I can hear the guns. I am alone. Here I must stay to keep the pictures for you. I wait for the end." Paul and Berthe, his pretty young wife, abandoned their home at Evron and set out to cycle to the Spanish border ("we have not the money to join you (Lucien) as you suggested"), but the roads were congested. They got nowhere, and returned home. "We hear there are no Germans in Eragny although they are very near." On 13th September Julie wrote: "I do not leave the place because I am old enough to die. I stay to prevent the Prussians destroying the pictures of your poor dear father, so that you will be able to enjoy them one day." "Well, my poor dear mother," Lucien replied, "if the Prussians want to rob the pictures, by being there you will not prevent them, so I advise you to leave before they come. Go to Dieppe get on a boat, and come to us. Your life is more precious than the pictures. It makes me so unhappy that you are so obstinate as to stay at Eragny." On 19th September Julie wrote to Esther: "Don't worry about me. I am all right. The Prussians didn't come this way. Feeling I would get killed by them I wrote to Lucien that I wanted him to keep his father's portrait." At the beginning of October she told Lucien: "Today is the day I was born. I am seventy-six. My poor mother brought me into the world with a lot of trouble, and since it has been trouble all along."

Paul wrote: "I think you are too much of a pessimist. Life will always exist and art as well. Father's pictures will keep their value. Mother advises me to start selling chocolate, that is to be a grocer. Thank you! I cannot paint outside, I should be taken for a spy." A few days after he and his family returned home, an anonymous busy-body denounced him to the police. "As a result a gendarme called to ask me if I was a spy, and wanted to see my papers. The upshot is that I am now on good terms with *le brigadier*, I am drawing his portrait and we go fishing together."

The war killed the Eragny Press. It was impossible to get the right kind of paper, production costs became prohibitive, and even if these difficulties could have been overcome, Lucien could not replace the loss of his continental subscribers. Earlier in the year, Lucien had printed *Whym Chow*, a commission from Katherine Bradley and her niece Edith Cooper, who collaborated in verse under the name of Michael Field. They were friends of Ricketts and others of the Vale group, and this book was a memorial by the two poets to their pet dog which had recently died. The last of the thirty-five books had been printed, but it was not until after the war that the presses were sold. In 1947, three years after Lucien's death, following the example of Ricketts, the Brook-type punches were thrown into the sea by Esther and her nephew, John, during a crossing to France. Nothing in private presses has ever surpassed the exquisite and delicate colourings of the wood blocks of Lucien's Eragny Press. The prices that the books now fetch would have astonished him.

Lucien was hard hit. He had begun to sell, but, in the prevailing war fever, sales abruptly stopped. No one bought pictures. He had hardly any money left, and his life again became one of day-to-day make-shifts. James Brown, at Esther's suggestion, wrote to his friend Arnold

Bennett, described Lucien's difficulties, and asked him to buy a picture at half-price. Bennett replied that the effect of the war on him, financially, had been "terrific", but he would do what he could. He examined Lucien's contract with the Carfax Gallery and said it was "iniquitous". As so it was, for it imposed a commission on every picture Lucien sold, whether by the Gallery or not. Lucien sent Bennett four paintings to select from. Bennett replied that although he had only seen them by electric light he perceived "that all would give me very great pleasure". He would keep two. "The understanding is that I lend you £30 without interest, and that if I am not repaid within a year of the end of the war, one of the pictures becomes my absolute property in discharge of the loan. The other is to be returned to you. I enclose cheque." Bennett did not record this act of generosity and kindliness in his Journals. His letter was dated 4th December. At the end of the month Blackwell agreed to pay forty-five guineas for *The Yellow Tree*, painted at Epping in 1893. Blackwell had seen this picture at the Carfax and bought on the understanding that it could be changed if, within two years, he saw a picture he liked better.* He was not sure of his choice and would rather have one of Camille's pictures. Lucien replied: "I would not like you to buy anything you do not really want. As to my father's things, I have already parted with one, and unless I am absolutely obliged I will try not to sell any more." Lucien then plunged into an important confession of faith. "Now with regard to my painting, it is very difficult to defend it. I always paint my pictures entirely out of doors, and being a pupil of the impressionists try always to render the feeling that the subject gives me. When at work I never, or very rarely, consider the execution, and my best things have always been entirely subconscious. It is the colour and tone which specially attract me, and to me an atmospheric effect cannot be truly rendered by a bold sweep of paint, but by touches of subtle difference which suggest the delicate variety of nature."

Blackwell replied: "I am much interested in your remarks *re* your own methods of painting, and note what you say, although I don't agree with all of it. Surely you would grant that Turner rendered atmospheric effects by a bold sweep of paint with success? How do you mean you paint subconsciously? Subconscious is a very popular word nowadays and used, or rather misused, I think, in more than one

---

* It must have been changed, as the picture is still in the possession of Orovida C. Pissarro.

The Yellow Tree painted at Epping, 1893 (*Oil on Canvas* $28\frac{5}{8} \times 23\frac{1}{2}$)

(*Collection Orovida Pissarro*)

The Mill, Blackpool Sands, 1921 (*Oil on Canvas* 25$\frac{1}{2}$ $\times$ 21)

sense. I personally admit that I don't know what it means unless it is a superior word for imagination or soul. A man must within be completely conscious of what he is doing, or perfectly unconscious: unless he is tipsy, and then I suppose his subconscious mind has full play." Lucien replied: "I find it very difficult to answer your criticism. To explain my meaning would require a lengthy analysis of the development of landscape painting from the classical Claude Lorraine to modern times, passing through the influence of Turner, Constable, Corot, etc. Such an analysis would require a clear mind in words. Certainly I recognise that Turner rendered atmospheric effect, but you must remember that his landscapes are mostly conventional, they were painted in the studio, and you will find that the atmosphere is rendered by a careful glaze applied over the bold sweep of paint. A careful and elaborate way of working impossible to do in front of changing nature. Turner's way is perfect in attaining his own aim; but we are looking for something different, although he is to be considered as one of our ancestors. Our tradition is on the other hand indebted to Constable on account of his ardent love of nature. I mean by nature, aspects of things for their own sake without too much arrangement disturbing the logic of their true relation. Did you notice how convincing Constable's little oil paintings in the National Gallery are compared with his more elaborate large pieces? Do you agree that those little masterpieces are far superior to the large studio canvases? The large pictures in comparison look like frozen enlargements. The same remark can be applied to Corot. Why? We explain the difference in this way: the large pictures are self-conscious, and the little nature studies subconscious. Our traditions come down from these two great English masters, that is we do not try to go farther back. It is those two influences which were at work at the time the old impressionists were beginning. Having noticed that Constable's, as well as Corot's, nature work was far superior to their studio work, they chose to study from nature, and found ways of painting suitable to their aims.

"I fear I will fall into a trap in using the word subconscious about painting, but it describes a state which I cannot express otherwise. My father would have said that he painted instinctively, and Claude Monet has actually said he painted *comme l'oiseau chante*. Your suggestion of tipsiness is not altogether wrong; intoxication would be better. Unconsciousness is used for instinctiveness, which is explained as a process of reasoning so quick that we are not conscious it is working, and when, on the rare occasions, one can work so, it is a sort of submerging of the

F

149

painter in the thing he is painting, and he is for the time not conscious that he is painting at all. I hope all this does not sound pretentious to you. I really only try to explain what I mean."

1915

Early in 1915 Lucien was at Sam Bensusan's, the Brick House, Duton Hill, Essex, "I really don't know what to tell you," he wrote to Esther. "My life is monotonous and regular. Only the price of food goes up and up, and if it continues, what shall we do? I am frightfully anxious about our future if this awful war lasts much longer." A day or so later he wrote: "No sooner am I here than I begin to think that I did not make enough of the pleasure of being near you. I found the letter from the mother with the recipe for cooking rabbit. Please take note of it." He said of a letter from Julie: "Yes, the mother's letter is funny. Don't you know that nothing is good enough for her lovely sons? Fancy not one of them marrying a wealthy bourgeoise! That was her ambition. She does not realise that if that had happened, she would have been the first to suffer." He sympathised with Orovida: she has had to accept a commission to paint the portrait of a dog. He would like to return and paint in London, but cannot without being taken for a spy. He told Julie: "I don't know what would have happened to us if one of our amateurs had not had pity and bought a picture." In April, The Brook having been let for three guineas a week, a place had to be found where he could paint and Esther be with him. Esther received particulars from the landlady of Sea View Cottage, Fishpond, near Charmouth, in Dorset, a detached cottage, "with a nice garden, vegetables and flowers. The water is very good and pure from a spring just inside the gate". There were two bedrooms, and the landlady, a Miss Apthorn, the daughter of a clergyman, enclosed with her letter postcards of the cottage, "which you can return or pay one penny for each". The terms were half a guinea a week until mid-July, then fifteen shillings a week until October. It seemed cheap and reasonable. To have fresh vegetables from the garden was an attraction, and at the end of April, Esther and Lucien went to live in the cottage with a sea view.

Manson wrote from the Tate: "I shall be very glad to take care of your father's pictures here. They will be as safe as possible. I have been frightfully upset. My dear brother has been killed in France. He was shot in the head by a German sniper. Fortunately he died instantaneously. It was his first day in the trenches."

Lucien's money troubles continued. Manson staunch in friendship and goodwill, spent his spare time in going to one collector after another, urging them to buy a Lucien Pissarro: he wrote optimistic letters of promises made, but despite these, there were no sales, only excuses. One collector hesitated and moidered, but when Manson thought he had at last screwed him up to buy, finally backed out. He said that although the picture was beautiful it had a pine tree in it, and he did not like pines. Another would not buy because the colour of the picture was out of harmony with his collection.

In July, Manson, granted three weeks' leave of absence from the Tate, came to the cottage to paint with Lucien. He and Lucien were, as usual, good company for each other. They shared childish jokes, the weather allowed them to paint, and they sat up late at nights, smoking and endlessly discussing art and the absurdity of war. When Manson returned to Hampstead, he wrote: "I got back safely and find it quite hateful to be in London again with its grime, its dirt, its noise, its officialism, and its countless nerve-wearing distractions. Already it has seized me again with its octopus claws, and I am feeling so far from art, nature, and your kind companionship as though I had never known any of those blessed things. I had a lovely time with you and you were both unspeakably kind to me. It did me much good, but, alas, the time was too short."

The thatched cottage was not all that had been claimed for it. There were no drains, the rooms were damp, and the stove was so old it would not burn. Miss Apthorn agreed that a new one should be installed. Esther was suspicious of the so-called pure water. As it trickled over the fields, it could not be pure. Miss Apthorn said it could always be boiled. Not content with this, Esther wrote and complained of the water to the Home Office. Esther's letters to Miss Apthorn pointed out other deficiencies, nevertheless she picked a bunch of flowers from the garden and sent them to her in Essex. There was a regular flow of letters from Manson. On the 13th August he wrote: "Your pictures arrived safely. They are beautiful, particularly the one of the hills, which is very fine indeed. Aitken likes it very much and thinks that perhaps the Contemporary Art Society will buy it. Now do cheer up. I am sure that something will come of all these efforts." On the 16th: "I like the charmingly reckless way in which you offer me your valuable pictures. I should love to have *The Ghost of the Broom*, or indeed any of your pictures, but I *cannot* accept it. You want all your work, it represents your fortune, and if you cannot sell it easily just now, you will later—or your family will." At last Manson managed to sell a picture to Dr. Sadler. On the 28th September he wrote: "I enclose a cheque for £45 from Sadler. I also send his most charming letter, in which he offers to *give* you the £45 in acknowledgement of all that you and your family have done for art. I told him I was sure you would insist on his having the picture." Two days after: "Go it, my dear old man. You are surpassing yourself. I think the *High View** is a *masterpiece*."

Julie remained at Eragny. She was not well; she trembled all the time, and the slightest thing was an upset—"*c'est la guerre*." Georges wrote to her that he had no money, and she sent him one thousand francs (£40), but later he was again without a penny and his children were ill, so she sent another thousand. She was alone. Georges promised to send his children for company, but did not. She grumbled about Rodo but did not say why; perhaps it was because he did not write. "You are the only one, my poor Lucien, who thinks of me. I don't know if I will see you any more. I am very old and cannot travel any longer alone. Remember me as an honest woman and a good mother." Although she complained of her health, she said she could do nothing about it. All the homeopathic doctors had gone from Gisors, and the others were no good. She went to Vézelay to be with Paul and Berthe, and was sad that in the streets she saw only soldiers without arms, without legs.

In December, Lucien and Esther left Fishpond and moved to Cold-harbour, Holmwood, Surrey where their landlady provided them with rooms, attendance and light for a guinea a week.

* Now in the cellars of the Tate Gallery.

CHAPTER XIV

Soldiers at Eragny. 1916–1918

LIKE CAMILLE, JULIE CONTINUED TO FINANCE HER CHILDREN. IN JANUARY she sent Lucien one thousand francs (£40): "I know that in wartime you cannot earn much. When I am able to send some more I will." Paul was at Eragny. He had been to the cellar where he had secreted some of Camille's pictures. Many were damp, and those which were varnished were covered with a green mould. The damage was not serious, but another place must be found for them. In 1914, Paul had packed all the pictures in boxes, an enormous job, and had tried to get them away, but he had been unable to find transport, and so had hidden the boxes behind a false wall in the cellar. In 1915, Julie had called him to Eragny to unpack them. He then advised her to send them for safety far away from Eragny, he suggested Uzerches. This was before the battle of Verdun, and it was then possible. But Julie said: "Go away. I will do what I like with my own pictures." "She won't listen to my advice," Paul said. "She thinks I am still a child."

Julie received money from Bernheim, part of the price of the pictures bought in 1914. She wanted to give each of her children two thousand francs (£80) out of her share, but Cocotte did not understand Julie's offer, and remonstrated. Her mother must stick to the terms of the inheritance. Julie was annoyed. "My poor boy," she wrote to Lucien. "It is difficult to please everybody." She sent his share "and a little extra".

In London, Rodo was troubled and in fear of arrest. He had been to the Danish Consul who said he was French, and then to the French Consul, who said he was Danish. Rodo did not like the way of life in England, and longed to be back in France, but if he returned he feared he would be imprisoned as a deserter. In April, Julie complained that she suffered much from rheumatism. Her house was full of soldiers. "They do their cooking here, six officers are in the drawing-room, together with those who bake for them. In the stables are fifteen youngsters. It is like a barracks here. They will go to the trenches. How sad to see all these boys as cheerful as chaffinches, who will be killed as they sing." Six weeks later the soldiers departed. "I did my best to be pleasant to them, some have written to me." The house was empty, the old lady again alone. Meanwhile Lucien grumbled that living was twice as expensive as it was, and that he has had to pay five shillings for his washing—"that will make a big hole in my cash". In June he was naturalised. On 25th October Julie wrote and reminded Lucien that she was seventy-nine. Aunt Estruc and Kikite were with her, and there were more soldiers, and the house was full. She had sold further pictures to Bernheim for ninety thousand francs and had received ten thousand (£400) on account. How could she send Lucien his share? At the beginning of December she enclosed a hundred-franc (£4) note in a letter. The soldiers had gone. She was alone again, she did all the work herself, and received no letters.

In October and November, Lucien was painting at East Knoyle, near Shaftesbury. His old vigour had returned, he worked unceasingly and completed twenty-three magnificent canvases. No longer distracted with the strain of his printing press and of producing books to a schedule, his mind was now entirely free to grapple with the problems of paint. The result was a series of superb pictures. But the time had not yet come when he would be able to sell nearly every picture he painted.

1917

Lucien remained at East Knoyle painting for the greater part of the year. During January he worked at winter *motifs* for his forthcoming exhibition with Marchant at the Goupil Gallery. Esther, with him over Christmas and for a few days in the New Year, was told that her father, Jacob Bensusan, was seriously ill, his life ebbing away. She packed a bag, putting into it the cheque-book and the accounts (she was preparing Lucien's Income Tax return), also a letter she had written to Orovida explaining her departure from East Knoyle. She decided to travel to Bexhill by way of Portsmouth where she would have a five-minute wait. When she got out of the train at Portsmouth, she was met by a railway official. "Are you Mrs. Pissarro?" "Yes." The man took her bag. "You are wanted in the stationmaster's office." "What for?" "You will see!" Esther followed him along the platform, and he went into the office, while she was told to wait outside. Time passed; she saw the Bexhill train pull in and steam out. Finally she was called into the office to be confronted by a group of men. Her bag had been opened and its contents strewn on a table. Esther was furious. She had lost her train, and was now put to this indignity with all her intimate feminine possessions exposed. "What is all this about?" she demanded. Her question was not answered. She was asked about her movements. Why had she come to Portsmouth? "You should know," she said. "You have obviously been through my bag and my personal papers, and no doubt you have read my letter to my daughter. I'm in Portsmouth because it is my shortest way to Bexhill. And all this nonsense has made me lose my train." "You seem to have plenty of money," commented one of the men. "I wish I had," said Esther. "You have looked at my accounts. You must know I haven't." "What's your husband? Isn't he a foreigner?" "He was born in France, but he's lived here for nearly twenty years and is a naturalised Englishman." "Really? Have you any proof?" "Certainly not with me, but if you phone the Home Office that can be confirmed." The Home Office was rung up, and after some delay, a man said it was all right, she could go. He became more pleasant. "Have to charge you with the call." "Oh, no," exclaimed Esther. "Why should I pay?" and she would not. Her bag was repacked and handed to her. "Now," said Esther, "perhaps you will be good enough to explain what all this foolery is about?" "You'll know after the war," the man said.

Rumour was the trouble. The villagers at East Knoyle had become suspicious of the Frenchman, Lucien, who made sketches of the neighbourhood. He lived in the cottage up on the hill, a submarine was in the bay, and a light had been seen at dusk waving across the hill. Of course it was the foreigner signalling the position of the boat to the enemy. When the village policeman saw Esther getting into the Portsmouth train he had telephoned the police station there. It wasn't Lucien who had waved the light. It was his landlady who went along her garden at night, a lighted lantern in her hand, to see that her chickens were safely housed.

Jacob Bensusan died two days after Esther's arrival at his bedside.

Esther had only been gone a day when Lucien wrote: "It is now I realise what it means to me not to have you by me when I come back from work." But a week later: "I curse myself for being so weak and for being always directed by you as if I were a child." This outburst was occasioned by Esther's well-meant efforts to conduct his business, which had resulted in upsetting Marchant. This became apparent in a letter which Manson wrote to Esther in March.

At East Knoyle, the weather was bad. It was cold with an east wind, there was ice on the ground on which Lucien slipped when he went out. This stopped him from painting outside. The water was frozen in the cistern and it was difficult to get any. Notwithstanding, he painted a snow effect from the open window in his little room. Concerned at the success of the German submarines, he feared that soon there would be a famine. In February there came a fresh anxiety. Marchant had promised to provide frames for his pictures, but now found he could not do so. He had only English stock sizes, and Lucien painted on French canvas sizes. Lucien would have to have special frames made, and as he was sending forty pictures to the exhibition, the cost would be one hundred and sixty guineas. To help meet this expense he reluctantly sold a fan painted by Camille to Blackwell. He told Esther: "I have had a most sweet letter from Blackwell, he has sent £84. So I may have a new suit with this money which is not a luxury as my knickers have a hole between the legs where the stuff rubs when I walk." Manson wrote: "Your show must bring you relief. It is a shameful thing that an artist of your rare gifts and attainment should be worried about money."

A new group was to be formed and Manson suggested a Miss S. as one of the members. Lucien thought this unwise. Manson now wrote a shocker to Esther: "It is a difficult matter to write about. It is subtle and intangible. To explain at all, I must be frank. To start with, there is a *general* feeling that you are inclined to interfere in matters which are strictly speaking not your business, and that you seem to wish sometimes to manage other people's affairs. Those who know you know that it is the result of your desire to do the best for Lucien, but on others you make the impression of being interfering. I don't know really whether it is what you do or the way you do it. The Camden Town Group, on several occasions, resented what they called interference as to their affairs on your part. They felt also that you tried to ram a certain lady candidate down their throats, it aroused bitter resentment and opposition. I mention this to show that the general impression is not a new thing. Then, Mr. Carfax, at the beginning of Lucien's agreement with him, asked me several times if you deliberately meant to insult him, and said he could do nothing if you would interfere. I don't wish to defend Mr. Carfax. In regard to Mr. Marchant, I did not *mean* to say that he was upset or that you had done Lucien any harm. Not at all. Some of the things you had proposed to say to him on which you had consulted me about, I thought were injudicious, and I said so at the time, and you certainly agreed and did not say them. He appeared to me, rightly or wrongly, when I saw him, to be perturbed, and I thought it best to tell him that if you appeared pressing and over-anxious it was because you were so keen on doing the best for the exhibition. He was *not* upset, but I feared that if things had been left to themselves he *might* have been. I thought it best to mention this to Lucien (this may have something to do with Lucien's letter of the 26th) as people have said so often it would be better if you left Lucien to do his own business. I fancy that men don't like doing business through a third person, unless that person is a lawyer. People like Lucien so much and are favourably disposed towards him. Also it is possible that businessmen dislike to discuss their business with women, particularly if they are, unconsciously, a little overbearing. My desire in this matter, as you know, is simply to do the very best for Lucien. With regard to the other matter, I immediately thought you had inspired Lucien's objection to the proposed candidate, as I thought, to speak the truth, it was what you would do. It is quite immaterial to me whether the person in question is a member or not. I write all this reluctantly and because you have asked me to do so. This, you will understand, is the stranger's point of view, those of us who know you, know that you do not spare yourself, and what you do for Lucien you would do, in case of need, for any of your friends. It is a case, purely and simply, of the impression made on strangers and that may, it is quite conceivable, have unfortunate results. Your kindness and unselfishness has never been in question."

It was not an unfair letter, and did reflect certain aspects of Esther's character. Esther did interfere, often unwisely. Lucien was much to blame; he wanted only to be undisturbed to get on with his painting, and was only too pleased to leave his business affairs to Esther. It said much for Esther that she neither resented Manson's letter nor allowed it to affect her regard for, or friendship with, him. But whether the letter did any good is doubtful.

After the bad winter, spring came with softness and sun. Lucien wrote: "The country looks lovely, but the apples are not yet in bloom." In June, Manson wrote a more cheerful letter to Lucien. The Trustees of the Tate Gallery had accepted Lucien's *High View, Fishpond*, but had rejected Sadler's offer of Lucien's *Eden Valley*; but Sadler had presented this to the Contemporary Art Society. The Trustees, Manson said, were hopelessly hostile to modern art: "they make me furious. They have the point of view of fifty years ago. Gilman, Ginner and Gore were rejected." Lucien sent Manson some of Monet's letters to read, but Manson said he found them difficult to decipher. "He practises division of tones in his handwriting"—an apt description—but Monet was almost blind when he wrote the letters. Manson was now Assistant Director at the Tate. "Lately my interviews with people have emphasised the *rarity* of really nice people. All that makes you appear even more valuable, if possible, and I hold myself lucky to have the privilege of your friendship."

At the end of the year Lucien went to paint at Hastings, and found rooms on East Hill. Orovida was also at Hastings, staying with Esther's mother at the Medlow Hotel.

1918

On the first day of the New Year, Julie wrote that she was being punished by not hearing from Lucien, not even on her birthday, and that she did not like Esther interfering with her affairs. But she was pleased that Orovida had got work and could earn her own living in some way or other. "Is it that you have no money to write?" In March she saw from her window a pathetic procession of refugees fleeing from the Germans. They passed her house and went on through the village, a trudging unhappy flow of old men, women and children, with household goods and treasures and the necessities for their journey pushed in over-laden handcarts and prams. On the 21st of the month Hindenburg had begun his last offensive. The collapse of fighting on the Russian front and the release of his armies engaged there, gave him a numerical superiority in the West, which he retained until the Americans reached the trenches. All was staked on a stupendous thrust which penetrated and bit deeply into the allied lines. Julie heard that the Germans had reached the outskirts of Beauvais, and she was again in an agony of alarm that the events of 1870 would be repeated. No longer trusting to her own resources and courage to defend the pictures, she summoned Paul for help. "I took all the canvases off the stretchers," he wrote long after, "and rolled them. It was a longish job and took twelve days or so. They made two fat rolls, and there were also my own pictures. Then I set off for Brantôme in the Dordogne, the home of old Durand-Ruel. You cannot imagine all the wanderings of the journey, mostly at night, by bicycle, by rail, and by goods train, the lack of food, and the fatigue, the long nights in the open air. It was a terrible nightmare."

Esther, to help lighten the anxieties of lack of money, now courageously found employment at Woolwich Arsenal, and went to live in a hostel, spending her week-ends at The Brook. Emma Ruddick and her sister were also there—they were working on night-work at a munition factory at Acton.

The dark nights and the black-out troubled Lucien, but although he had no torch "I managed to find my way all right twice" through the streets to have his dinner with Orovida at the Medlow. "I had only one collision with a group of people. I nearly swallowed my pipe! Now I know the way very well and there is no danger." Julie sold Camille's picture of *La Mère Larchevèque*,★ "that extraordinary picture of the washerwoman with blinking eyes" for ten thousand francs (£400), and a Swedish Gallery offered twenty-two thousand francs (£880) for the portrait of Cézanne. But Lucien warned Esther: "My dear, do not dream about the amount that may come to me, and remember I am not entitled to a single penny until my debt [to the estate] is paid. We must go on being careful, for it may be that in the near future food will become so rare that it will cost a fortune to have a piece of bread to eat." He was afraid that he "will go through a lot of money here". The weather was bad, and being unable to go out, he started two pictures from his window. Visiting friends who lived some way from the town, he missed the last bus back and had to walk many miles through pouring rain. In places the water in the road was ankle deep, and he thought that in the dark he had left the road and was walking along the bed of a stream. The next day the rain continued and he bought a macintosh, but, a day or so after, wrote to Esther: "My new, nice-looking macintosh, tidy, and matching my stockings and green suit, is spoilt. I was in the bus when all sorts of fisherwives come in from market with their parcels. Nothing extraordinary in that, but wait. When we arrived at the top of the High Street the one sitting next to me, said, 'Oh! I have upset my bottle of oil.' I look. The seat by my side is covered and I have two patches on my new mac! I could say nothing. I rushed home, took some boiling water, soap, and a nail-brush, and rub as hard I could, but the place is still visible. Now I am sorry that I got it."

Lucien heard that there had been an air raid on Paris over Montmartre. He feared for Paul and Berthe, and for the pictures if Julie had been so foolish to send them there. One evening he thought he would begin to put the account books in order and prepare a balance sheet, but it was impossible as Esther's private bank-book was "such a perfect muddle, you have the bad, the very bad, habit of not putting the dates

★ Painted in 1880. No. 513 in Rodo's catalogue.

of the cheques received. I cannot find enough money from Marchant to balance the exhibition account". But a greater grievance against Esther now followed. She had interfered again. Money was coming to him from Julie's sale of *La Mère Larchevèque*, but he was in debt to Paul, Rodo and Cocotte. He had written to them, and they had agreed to let the debt stand. It was at a time when they did not need the money. But Esther wrote and told them that of course Lucien would pay what he owed from his share of the picture. "What a muddler you are!" wrote Lucien. "I wish you would let me arrange my own business, I mean the money which is from my side of the family. How can I, in elementary decency, ask Paul to pay up Rodo when he and Cocotte give up their own shares in order that I should get something out of it. My dear, with the turn events take, I don't feel that I should reject the prospect to have a little cash in front of me : things may turn very bad, we may have a famine and a rush for food. Of course, as usual, when I receive some cash, you carefully dispose of it for me. I don't think I would like very much to have Rodo here, he is too depressing. I must not have disturbance in my work, only one disturbance is good for me and that is you. You, your dear face would cheer me up. Mind, my sweetheart, be careful, and do not ruin our dear life by making me feel I am a mere tool in your hand. Be reasonable, my sweet little wife. I do love you so much, and I don't want to pain you, but on the other hand I cannot give up altogether my own will."

Esther now wanted him to persuade Julie to divide the pictures, but Lucien replied : "You must not bother my poor old mother with the *partage* of the pictures. She cannot possibly do it : it is too complicated and she will lose her head over it." Esther suggested Monet would help. "And you cannot bother and disturb poor old Monet to do such work. You don't seem to realise what it means. Remove the idea from your head."

"What a misfortune to live to be so old and see so many unhappy things happen," wrote Julie mournfully. She was now eighty. "The poor people in Paris have been shelled again in a dreadful manner. What a terrible war it is with so many people in mourning." A Cézanne water-colour had been sold for two thousand six hundred francs (£104): "You take my half-share," Julie wrote to Lucien, "but don't tell the others. Tell Bonin (Cocotte's husband) you have sent me my share, but let me know how much you say in case he asks." She still suffered much from rheumatism, the weather was cold (her letter was dated 3rd March), the snow fell, and she had no coal, "which is very sad when you are old. No sugar, no butter, no bread, here one cannot get anything. Three hundred crumbs of bread per person per day is the ration! What bad luck for an old woman like me. It is no good praying to God, he is also old and does not listen".

In April and May her house was once more filled with soldiers. "You ask me what I have done with the pictures? Well, they are still in the same place, hooked to the walls, where I have the pleasure of seeing them, which is a comfort to me. Bernheim wants me to sell them, but I am too old to bother. What I shall do if the Bosches come is I will burn them rather than those pigs should have them. You can imagine how I shake all over thinking of this, and I think of it all the time."

While at Hastings, Lucien kept a diary, a working record of his days. Some extracts, taken at random, reveal his struggles and the time it took him to paint a picture, dependent as he was on the moods of the weather:

18th March: Morning. Worked at sunny effect, T.15,* old church. Afternoon made an attempt to do a sketch, but I am quite out of it.
19th March: Missed the day—*indécis* in the morning, rain in the afternoon.
20th March: Morning. Worked at sunny effect, T.15, old church. Afternoon went to see the old castle. Lovely view with both old and new town.
21st March: Worked at sunny effect, T.15, old church. Afternoon, thick mist. Went for a walk.
22nd March: Morning. Had a splendid effect with sun and slight mist in the background. Thought I was going to put the old church on its legs. Started to work, half demolished the thing, then the sun disappears and the mist changes into impenetrable fog. Damn it all!
23rd March: Same effect as yesterday, but steadier. Worked at the old church although it was Saturday.

Lucien disliked working at the week-ends. There were too many onlookers and small boys who gathered around, made inane remarks, and disturbed his concentration.

* This refers to the French size of the canvas he works on, $25\frac{5}{8} \times 19\frac{3}{4}$, a *toile de quinze.*

24th March: Same effect for third day running, so work at old church. The picture is out of the wood, only foreground to complete.

25th March: Alas! Wrong weather, east wind and no sun, could not complete the old church.

26th March: *Morning*. Had a go at the old church. Worked foreground but could not finish. Shall have to leave it behind.

27th March: Go to London.

16th April: Return from London.

25th April: Finished old church at last!

26th April: Got up at five to go and investigate where I can find a nice *motif* for a sunrise, but the sun did not rise the whole day, it was a lot of energy spent for nothing. After breakfast, finished the sketch started on West Hill on the 24th.

27th April: Got up early, again to be faced with the same trick as yesterday, though I found a likely spot when it is fine.

But the weather did not permit a start on the sunrise until the 14th May. Meanwhile he made sketches in the prevailing grey light around the neighbourhoood.

13th May: Raining all day. No work. Afternoon had my hair cut.

14th May: At last had early *séance* at the East Hill, the effect is so rapid that I could only cover part of the canvas.

15th May: No *séance* in early morning, too dull. Went and looked at the fish market. After breakfast finish the sketch of gorse in Ecclesbourne Glen. Afternoon went again to try and do a sketch of the subject I saw yesterday, but was too hot, too tired, and made a mess of it.

While painting on East Hill, a young lady, after watching him, asked if he would give her lessons. He replied he did not give lessons but would be glad to give her advice. "Is it not curious that, if you have a palette in your hand, the shyest young lady who, normally, would not talk to you to save her life, thinks it now quite correct to come and do so," he commented to Esther.

Soldiers came and went at Eragny. In October, Julie wrote: "Even the studio is now occupied. Soldiers are in the stables. Better than the Bosche!" In November, the long-drawn-out war came to an end, the armistice was announced, and Julie commented: "What a weight off our shoulders, but what a number of victims, how many useless misfortunes, why all this misery? And this is what is called a victory! What an irony. What fools people can be." The soldiers remained at Eragny until December. Julie said she had given Paul a thousand francs (£40) to send to Lucien. "If the poor father had not left pictures behind, how could you have managed, my poor son? For the last fifteen years you have lived on his work. What a piece of luck that I am not a woman who smokes, or eats sweets, or spends money on dress." Now the war was over, Lucien and Esther were anxious to see her. "I would prefer if you would come at Easter. Then the house will be more comfortable, now it is filthy after the soldiers, everything to be scrubbed, every wall. I wait for better weather. It is cold and we have no coal; the wood burns too quickly and gives no heat. Bernheim is willing to buy your picture. How much do you want for it? Meanwhile, if you need money, let me know."

CHAPTER XV

The Monarro Group. 1919–1920

EARLY IN THE YEAR LUCIEN AND ESTHER WERE TOGETHER AT THE BROOK, Lucien recovering from an operation on the prostate gland. Rodo was with him. He told Lucien that recently in Paris he had examined the plates of Camille's etchings. They were in a bad condition, the only chance of getting any further good prints was to do so at once. He and Lucien went to the Leicester Galleries and arranged for an exhibition of these etchings and some of Camille's paintings for the spring of 1920. The plates were obtained from Paris and a successful printing made from them in London. Julie raged when Paul told her of the proposed exhibition. "What!" she exclaimed. "You are going to move my pictures again!" Just previously Rosenberg, the art dealer, had been at Eragny looking at the Camilles, and had offered seven thousand francs (£280) for a large canvas. Julie had indignantly refused, she was not so poor as to be forced to accept such a ridiculous price. "He must have thought I was low and without even a cent to buy bread with," she commented. She still thought of selling her house. "What a funny idea. What a disaster!" Paul said.

That June, Lucien went to Paris with Manson—"the heat terrific". They stayed in Rodo's sixth-floor apartment in Montmartre, the highest point in the city, the view wonderful. But the six flights of stairs were exhausting to climb, especially at the end of a tiring day. They cooked for themselves, the restaurants were too expensive, until an eating place, dark and dirty, was discovered, frequented by cab-drivers and porters. Here the atmosphere was friendly, the talk amusing, and they were treated as of the company. On one occasion a prodigiously fat woman came in. She had just bought some scent. She went to their table and insisted in sprinkling their handkerchiefs. Meanwhile Orovida and Esther awaited Lucien and Manson at Eragny. "Come quickly," Orovida wrote to her father. "Grandma is in a filthy temper and treats me as she treats mother."

Emma Ruddick had been left to look after The Brook. She was perturbed when strangers knocked at the door and demanded to be shown over the house. She did not know what to do. Esther, troubled and agitated at Emma's news, wrote to the landlord. She was informed that he had died and that his executors had decided to sell the property. This dismayed Esther. She could not bear the thought of losing her house—it would be too great a wrench—but what could be done? How could she possibly raise the money to purchase? Over anxious weeks, she wrote here and there, asking for loans.

On 19th June, Lucien had lunch with Monet. Two days after he wrote: "Dear M. Monet, Just a line to thank you for your warm welcome. I can't tell you the good it did me and how much I admire your courage and energy. At the time I was returning from Paris full of doubts about myself and quite sick of the art I had seen everywhere, shown me as expressions of the contemporary trend. After seeing you I am more certain than ever that 'the sensation' is the foundation of everything, a noble thing as long as it comes from a real feeling. Those among us who have only a little talent are to be respected as long as we are sincere. Your example, so noble and powerful, is a medicine to an art which, in our times, is sick. It is a beacon to the artists of my generation who are trying hard to re-act against the substitution of intellectualism for the sensation. As Signac so rightly described your work, painting should be as a bird sings, and this is why I allow myself to trouble you again and to try to express more clearly on paper what I was unable to put in words to you. 'As a bird sings!'—that is now the motto of us all. It doesn't really matter if sensation arises from work painted in front of nature, or not, as long as the sensation is there. Is not Cézanne's slow and strong work full of sensation? Van Gogh, also Gauguin, are highly instructive. Seurat and Signac were enthusiastic to apply scientific laws to their painting, all the same there was something in their art that was alive, not sick—the sensation. I am grateful for both the good and the illumination you gave me. Your really sincere admirer, Lucien Pissarro."

Lucien remained at Eragny during July and August, Manson staying with him for a while, but Esther, restless while the fate of The Brook was undecided, returned there, Julie going with her. Here Mrs. Voynich played the piano every evening to the old lady. She liked classical music. But she was not an easy visitor. As ever, she disapproved of Esther's ways and nagged at what she called the muddle and mismanagement. Esther had no defence against her rough tongue. "She is always making trouble," Esther wrote to Lucien. He replied, "If she did not grumble she would not be herself."

"We have been able to secure our house," Esther told Manson. "You know how I longed for it in the old days. The terrible nightmare of being turned out is over." After prolonged negotiation the house was offered to her for £1,400, and the money was raised with help from Esther's mother, a loan from Julie, and a mortgage of £400. Lucien damped her joy. He said he was happy to know she had realised the dream of her life, but his "sad disposition" saw the danger ahead, and made him fear for the future. "How much remains in the bank?" The unpredictable Esther evaded the question, but replied that she is sure he would not mind, but she had just given £5 for some rather bad cases of misery. This did not hearten Lucien. "The situation of things is getting very desperate. I feel convinced that we shall pass through a time of revolution. This morning a grocer of the rue Lepic had his shop wrecked by an angry mob because he overcharged a woman for a rabbit. And it is precisely at this time we become landlords!" Orovida had gone with him to France to paint. It worried him she passed her days in her room, drawing tigers— "tigers," said Lucien, "no longer connected with life or psychology". But Orovida obstinately continued to go her own way. She did not paint from nature, but transmuted her vision of reality through an inner world of her own. Her influences, if any, were derived from the paintings of Persia and China. Lucien, once convinced of her sincerity, approved and encouraged. Impervious of theories and 'isms, coteries and cliques, she came to be recognised as an original artist. Her exhibitions were a success; she sold her paintings.

It was not a good year for Lucien; slow in recovering from his operation, his health precarious, he painted with difficulty. He paid another visit to Monet, walking the ten kilometres to Giverny with Manson, "Monet was very nice, he showed us his pictures, also the other studio where he keeps his earlier paintings. Manson was impressed. Orovida has a good holiday, she stays in a gorgeous country to draw a tiger which could have been done at The Brook. I have lost my summer in a place where I could not do a scrap of work! I shan't have anything ready for the most important exhibition of my life. How will I come back without the necessary cash to buy my ticket?" His letter was a cascade of misery. He told Esther he detested holidays, "uncomfortable, distressing, disturbing, and the enemy of work. To work I must have my quiet routine, no pre-occupations of any kind to disturb my mind". But he was no longer troubled that he would not have his fare home, as Julie had given him five hundred francs (£20).

Lucien "worked sedately" going through his father's letters. He thought he had broken the back of the collection. "I have a pile of Monets, Mirbeaus and Gauguins. The Gauguin ones seem extremely interesting, he shows fight for the impressionists, and considers himself one of them. But these letters are of the time prior to going to Tahiti to do his best work, in fact, a time when he was only a student. Time! I do not remember when it has been so long, it seems to me an age since you went away. Everything can go to the devil as long as I have your dear person." The "dear person" was, of course, Esther.

Orovida was at Méricourt with Paul and Berthe, etching and fishing for her Siamese kitten, Sekmet, "Metou", which Madame Fénéon had given her. Blanche Monet wrote to Esther and said Monet was working and in perfect health, and asked for seeds for his gardens. Esther sent them, together with three different kinds of climbing roses for one of Monet's five gardeners to plant. "Not a day passes," Lucien wrote to Esther, "without my remembering a smile, a kiss, a perfume, and many other things I cannot describe, and brings me a vivid recollection of what I miss by being away." Julie in the bleak days of November when Lucien was once more at home, wrote: "We have snow. It is very cold. I went all the same to poor father's grave, on my way back I fell. My old legs don't carry me any longer. My knee was hurt and I cannot walk."

In December, Lucien, Rodo, Manson and Miss Hassell met. There had been many discussions before; now they finally decided to go ahead with a new group to be called Monarro, a portmanteau title derived from the names of Claude Monet and Camille Pissarro, the *Président d'Honneur* to be Monet. Marchant, of the Goupil Gallery, gave the use of his gallery for the first exhibition, but did not like the name Monarro, and suggested instead "The Cosmopolitan". "No," said Rodo. "That sounds like a low pub or a Swiss hotel on the Riviera. Marchant would go into a circus ring for publicity." The original title was kept. The aim of the group was defined in the foreword of the catalogue: "It is to concentrate the work of those artists who have derived inspiration, more or less directly, from the leaders of the French impressionistic movement, Claude Monet and Camille Pissarro." At the first exhibition, 131 pictures and some sculpture were shown, the exhibitors being Lucien, Manson, Paul Emile, Rodo, Orovida, Paul Signac, Pierre Bonnard, Théo van Rysselberghe, Ivan Mestrovic, Claude Monet, Maximilien Luce, H. Clement Hassell, Léon de Smet, E.M. Henderson, Diana White, Marcel Jefferys and Walter Taylor. It was widely noticed in the daily press and the week-end literary reviews. Some critics repeated the parrot cry, that Lucien was a humble follower of his father, not so Frank Rutter in the *Sunday Times*: "It is tremendously interesting to see side by side in this exhibition the work of Lucien Pissarro and his father Camille Pissarro. The contrast, while taking nothing from the glory of the father, must surely increase our respect for the work of the son. Compare Camille's *Coin de Pré* with Lucien's *All Saints' Church, Hastings*, and it must be acknowledged that the latter has a greater vivacity and brilliance of colour. If we look at Lucien's other paintings here, his *Sea Mist, Coney Castle*, or *The Postesses*,* *East Knoyle*, it is incontestable that they display qualities of design which we do not find in anything like so high a degree in the work of Camille Pissarro. Great as the qualities of the first impressionists were, I think it must be conceded that the work of the second generation is closer knit in structure, firmer and stronger in design, and it gains accordingly." Sir Claude Phillips wrote in the *Daily Telegraph*: "M. Lucien Pissarro has painted much and with great charm . . . but with a reticence, a fineness of balance, that causes his work to look very unlike the coarse, unmeaning impressionism of most foreign and British contemporaries." The *Arts Gazette* commented: "In this collection were pictures by Camille Pissarro and his son Lucien hanging side by side, so it was possible to recognise the full value of the latter's work. Great artist as Camille Pissarro was, there are points in which Lucien Pissarro is even greater." "Lucien Pissarro," wrote the critic of *The Times*, "paints things as if he loved them: he is not only a sun worshipper." The critic of the *Evening Standard* found the exhibition "exceptionally interesting. As the son of Camille Pissarro, Lucien Pissarro has had to struggle for years before his independent achievement was generally recognised. To be the son of a famous father is a handicap. There is a decorative triptych of tigers and snakes by Orovida, full of life and colour, but hardly impressionistic". It was not meant to be.

1920

Julie was now eighty-two. Very conscious of her age, she stumped about with the help of two sticks. At Eragny, in January, the weather was bad; there were storms and the roof leaked. "You tell me you are sending a cheque for five thousand francs (£200). I thank you for this

---

* Lucien inquired his way at East Knoyle. "It's up by the postesses"—the posts. So when he painted the posts, Lucien called the picture *The Postesses*.

but you can keep it. I don't need the money." On Lucien's birthday, 20th February, Manson and his wife were at The Brook for dinner. "Jolly evening with the Mansons," Lucien recorded in his diary. "Mrs. Manson sang lovely Scotch folk songs." Lucien was engaged on the preparations for the Camille exhibition at the Leicester Galleries, but Julie was not encouraging. "Do not think it is any pleasure for me to see my pictures being sold. It is a mourning, a second funeral. One there is I do not want to sell, *The Harvest Women*, because I posed for them. I am quite *alone, alone*. But the garden is so beautiful, the trees are full of blossom. Poor dear father, how pleased he would be to admire his meadow." She sent twenty-seven of her pictures to the exhibition. Esther went to Eragny to escort her to London, but their journey was delayed by a strike on the French railways, so there were no trains, and they missed the opening day. Julie did not enjoy her visit, Esther wearying her with discussions on money, but she was appreciative that Esther had fetched her and would take her back. They arrived at Eragny to find the girl left in charge had neglected everything; there was not even anything to eat. Julie, ashamed and angry, insisted on doing the cooking, as she would not trust Esther. "You know your wife is unable to do anything," she wrote to Lucien. Soon the two women joined battle with their tongues. "Esther," Julie told Lucien, "worried me so much that I spoke all kinds of nonsense. But I am not sorry for it. She deserved it. Not to listen to her, I left the house." Esther wanted to look at the studio. The old lady refused, she said it made her cry to go there. The exhibition had upset her. She was very emotional. Months went by before she again ventured into the studio. Paul came to unpack the twenty-two pictures which had been returned to Eragny. Five had been sold. "My poor pictures," exclaimed Julie, "they change places and travel here and there."

"The exhibition has been a great success," so Lucien wrote to Lecomte. "For the first time in England the art of my father meets with triumph. Orovida has grown into a woman, she is immersed in art. It was stronger than anything, she had a vocation and could not choose anything else, it was in her blood. Her etching has met with success and gets to be known."

The exhibition had indeed been a triumph. Lucien received a cheque, "on account", fifty-five thousand nine hundred francs* (£2,236)

---

* Payment was made in francs to make easier the sharing of the money among the family.

from the Leicester Galleries. He informed Julie he would send her the money by registered post, and had written to Paul to go to Eragny to show her how to discharge the receipt and endorse the cheque. He hoped she would put the money in a safe place, "you can't leave such a big amount anywhere". But Julie did not want the money. She said she would divide it into five parts and give ten thousand francs (£400) to each of her children.

"You are really too generous," Lucien replied. "Would it not be better for you to keep at least part of the money in order to be more comfortable? Well, if you think you can afford this, I am most grateful, but I repeat I would not like you to squeeze yourself, as you have done all your life, and it is time for you to have some comfort. In any case wait a little while until I discover the best way to send."

CHAPTER XVI

Sophie Breszka

IN THE AUTUMN OF 1920, SOPHIE BRESZKA, LIVING IN A COTTAGE AT Wotton-under-Edge in Gloucestershire, had to come to London on business. Mrs. Robert Bevan asked Esther if she could put her up for a day or so. Sophie was greatly taken with Lucien and Esther. When she returned home she wrote and suggested that Lucien should come and stay with her. "For an artist I am a fairly good chef, tho' a wretched butler. I would, of course, attend to Mr. Pissarro's material requirements, helping as well in searching for beauty. The people here being too curious about all my doings, etc., having even recourse to reading my letters, I shall be pleased if you would simply answer 'very well for October'. I am asking for this secrecy, for if you were to come and not come again, they are laughing and saying that the blooming foreigners don't know themselves what they want. I do not reckon with them at all, and you will find them quite trained now (by me) to leave artists to do as they please. But it is irritating that they should find out what I intend to do." This was not to be a business arrangement, Miss Breszka said. She did not do business with fellow artists, but if Lucien cared to give her a picture it would be valued as a memento of his visit.

Lucien, in doubt as to where to paint for the next month or so, thought Wotton-under-Edge sounded attractive—at least worth the journey to see what it was like. His journey there was wearisome and tedious. "The silly man at Paddington directed me badly." He travelled in slow trains that stopped at every station, and had many changes and long waits on deserted country platforms.

"I met Miss Breszka. She would not hear of me staying anywhere but in the cottage. It is all right. It is most primitive, I do not think you would like it. Lack of things necessary. As for coming with Emma [Ruddick], that is quite impossible. She would be shocked! It is a small place in a row of labourers' cottages," but there was a view at the back and the country lovely. "It is my customary luck that the weather should suddenly change. I arrived with the rain and it has rained ever since. My barometer is at 'set rain.' Miss B. seems delighted to have me staying with her. We have been talking all the time, she says she was starved of intellectual intercourse. The lavatory arrangements are shocking." Nor were the sleeping arrangements better. There was a single, rusty, iron bed with the thinnest of mattresses and a motheaten, broken-down couch. Miss Breszka said: "If your daughter wants to create and live in the manner of Henri Gaudier she must not be too particular about comfort."

None of the Pissarros did want to live in the manner of Henri Gaudier, and various excuses for not accepting Miss Breszka's hospitality were made, but she was persistent. Now at Margate, she admitted that living at the cottage would perhaps be primitive, but a new bed could be acquired. "Here the cliffs are very imposing, the sea magnificent, but such a crowd, so stupid, so vulgar, it is difficult to keep from insulting them." It was arranged that, on her way home, she should break her journey and stay at The Brook for a few days. Sophie appeared at The Brook looking like a Daumier caricature: dressed in a nondescript coat and skirt shapeless on her gaunt, flat-chested figure, something resembling a night-cap pulled tight over her close-cropped hair, and bare feet showing through shoes which had been hacked to resemble sandals. She was hysterical when she arrived and complained of the rudeness of the people in the streets who had turned and stared at her as if she was a freak. As lunch was being placed on the table, Sophie was animatedly talking with Esther, and when Esther laughed at something she said, Sophie thought she was making fun of her, picked up her bag and ran out of the house. Uncaring of where she was going, she hurried along the streets, and walked all that afternoon round and round the Serpentine in Hyde Park, talking loudly to herself and making vague gestures with her hands. Esther, anxious as time passed and Sophie did not return, telephoned those friends Sophie might have gone to, but they had no news of her. Finally Esther telephoned the police. It was not until the next morning that she was found in a restaurant in Praed Street drinking coffee. She was taken first to the police station and from there to Paddington Infirmary. Mrs. Robert Bevan's address was in her bag, so she was telephoned to and immediately came to the infirmary. Here she was told that Sophie was considered well enough to travel alone to her home. Her possessions, taken away from her at the police station, were returned to her with the exception of four gold sovereigns. In their place she was handed four one-pound treasury notes. The value was the same but it was not the same to Sophie.

Those sovereigns had been given to her by Henri Gaudier in 1912, and cherished ever since—a souvenir of happy-sad years when they had lived together, years when Henri had been the unwilling and complaining partner of her obsession with her so-called platonic love, carried to such an excess that at one time, while she slept in the bed, he slept, or rather did not sleep, in a hammock chair. For three hours Sophie pleaded with the police for the return of her precious gold, but was told that it was against the law to do so. She had been wrong in not surrendering this gold long before. She returned to her cottage without them, and their loss preyed on a mind already near insanity, and she drifted into a state of unrelieved melancholia. Soon afterwards she died in a mental asylum, having no longer any desire to live.

1921

In January, Lucien was in rooms at The Mill, Blackpool Vale, near Dartmouth, and remained there for three months, but weather and health retarded painting. Indeed his health worried him for most of the year, and at The Mill his output was only a few pictures. He wrote to Esther that he was comfortable and when at work felt happy and could forget their troubles. "This afternoon I went to the hill and stopped in the little nook where you used to rest after your illness, and it did bring back to me my anxiety for my poor little woman: how I did love you then!! You can't realise how worried I was." He told Julie: "I have come here to pass the months of January and February, and hope to paint. I have lost so much time the last two years that I have nothing to show and I must have something new for my exhibition in March." The weather defeated him. "It has been a mistake coming here," he wrote to Esther. "I will have spent my money and have nothing to show for it. It has rained steadily since I arrived, and if it does not rain, my *motifs* are limited to those I can paint from the side of the road, as since the snow the fields are bogged with mud and it is impossible to climb the hillside." When it was fine the wind whistled and caused him to work under a strain; every minute he expected his canvas to be blown away. All the same he was grateful in such weather to have a good bed, good food, a fire, and much amiability. But he had to have his shoes resoled at a cost of five and six, —"that is how the money fly away". He said it was funny, "the more people like my things, the more I feel what a humbug I am".

Rodo visited Julie at Eragny. He said her health was not good, and her temper dreadful. He had difficulty in persuading her to pay her bills. She said she had no money, that all she had she had given to her children. "It is impossible to manage her. I cannot make her talk sense, and she is surrounded by people trying to cheat her." Lucien, back at The Brook, painted at Hammersmith and Kew, and Orovida shared an exhibition with Marie Laurencin at the Weyhe Gallery in New York, and showed etchings, lithographs and drawings.

The New English Art Club held its annual exhibition and Manson told Esther: "Lucien's little blossom picture at the Unmentionable English is beautiful, so exquisite in colour. It was wonderful to come across it in that extraordinary *mélange*. Have you seen *The Studio*? The frontispiece is Strang's portrait of Lucien." Manson, as ever, was trying to sell for Lucien: "I took two of your pictures to Sir James Murray. He liked them, but didn't buy. He said they were out of harmony with his collection. He said your pictures would kill his others."

Lucien had to go yet again to Paris to deal with his business affairs. On 21st May, he wrote to Esther from Blackpool Vale: "Where will the money come from, and how shall we manage to pass through the summer?" he fretted. The thought of "the battle" before him at Eragny in September when Julie's pictures were to be shared among the family, distracted him. He anticipated difficulties and dissensions. Meanwhile the pictures were on exhibition and when he arrived in Paris in June, he went to see them. "The show looks awfully nice, the pictures are shown in nice old frames. There were a lot of offers but it is thought that my mother has exaggerated the prices. She asks twice what the dealers ask. Nevertheless she sticks to her prices and won't let the pictures go." He met Georges, who was amiable about the *partage*, and visited Cocotte and her children. At Eragny, Julie, pleased with the presents Esther had sent her, said she was very good not to be angry against her after the way she had treated her. But Lucien offended the susceptible Esther by writing an affectionate message on a postcard. It was too public, she said: the postman could have read it. Lucien replied on the 1st July that his outburst was very subdued and showed no signs of "uncontrollable passion. So I don't see what you are ashamed of. Well, I won't kiss you again on a p.c. but you will know that it is only a concession to your modesty and that no kisses really mean terrific ones! As this letter is closed and safe I let myself go to the extent to give you *par la pensée* the most daring kiss you can imagine in the most sweet part of your dear person. You know where I mean."

He went the round of the art dealers and was astonished at the number of doubtful Camille's he saw—"quite extraordinary", he commented. He called on Guillaumin and reported to Esther that they had had a wonderful talk. In another letter he discussed Orovida's painting: "I am not sure that much drawing from nature will help her. I realise more and more that this habit of drawing from nature stultifies the imagination. Each of us must create our own method of work; interference is useless. She will come to the right conclusion in time if she really has something to say. I believe she has." Again at Eragny, on the 21st July, an outbreak of fire occasioned anxiety for the safety of the pictures. Fortunately it was confined to the outbuildings and no harm was done. But the alarm reacted on Julie. Four days later, she wept and begged Lucien to go with her to Camille's grave: here she stayed a long time, putting flowers about the plot. Lucien lamented that she was too lavish, "the way she gives things away, as the poor father did in his lifetime. She does not realise that now it is different, and that her generosity diminishes the stock of pictures". Soon he was at Les Andelys where he planned to spend August painting for his exhibition in the autumn. But rain came; he had no umbrella, no raincoat, and was obliged to remain indoors. Manson arrived for a short stay. It continued to rain, but, said Manson, the village was lovely : "I have done a few water-colours but the weather makes it difficult. Last Sunday the rain fell in torrents—it was tropical. Last night it poured; today it still pours. We have been to Paul Emile's for dinner, he lives a mile away in the little village of Vézillon. He has a charming house, once a peasant's cottage, and a nice garden which goes down nearly to the river." Many artists were painting at Les Andelys, and a rich *amateur* gave a house, the *Foyer des Artistes*, for them to meet and exhibit their pictures, and it was here one night that Lucien and Manson attended a celebration and a dinner. Lucien told Esther it was very gay and amusing.

"We have had a visit of Signac, Madame Signac number two, and the little girl. Madame is a nice and fascinating woman: she paints and plays the piano. But it is sad for Berthe Signac, the first wife." Signac had parted from her but they had remained friendly. On the 19th August Lucien and Manson visited Monet, now threatened with cataract in both eyes. "He was, as usual, charming, and working hard. He showed us his recent work,* a privilege, for I know others who went to see him and were not taken to his studio. After lunch, he went to his *séance*; later his car took us to Bonnard who lives near Vernon.

* Probably the *Les Nymphéas* decorations.

Here we saw Berthe Signac, staying there to look after Madame Bonnard who is consumptive and in a bad state. This Berthe is truly a good angel, always ready to go to friends when they are in need of help. For instance, when de Luce's nephew's wife was having her baby she volunteered to look after her, and took the opportunity to clean the place, which, given the Luce family, was in a state you can imagine. The poor Berthe does all this while her husband is living at Les Andelys with his other wife and the little girl. We went back in Bonnard's car to Vézillon with a quantity of vegetables that Berthe asked us to give to Signac. He has difficulty to find them at Les Andelys, and he has to follow a *régime*. Yes, that woman is an angel."

Lucien painted when it did not rain, sometimes with Signac, sometimes with Manson. There was distraction on the day of the *fête des Andelys*, a display of fireworks on the Seine. Lucien was fascinated by the aspect of the *Château Gaillard* seen through a mist of *feu de Bengal*. But on the 30th August a letter from Esther brought a douche of cold water. Angered to hear of the celebration at the *Foyer des Artistes*, she said it was the wine which made the evening gay for Lucien. Lucien was ruffled at this perversion. "I had your nasty letter this morning which made me quite blue. I was expecting a nice one and waited anxiously for the postman before going to my *motif*, and . . . ! Well, I can assure you I have not been drunk a single time, even at the banquet. I cannot drink the water here. It is not safe, nobody drinks it, and Paul Signac, who is unable to drink wine, is obliged to take Vichy water for his treatment. I only take one glass of wine with my meals and I feel no ill effects."

In September all the family were at Eragny for the *tirage*. It went smoothly, everybody on their best behaviour. There was no argument: good temper and politeness prevailed. It was not until after, when the mother's oil paintings and water-colours had been divided, that there was the rumble of storm. Lucien wrote: "Rodo, who is not a saint, puts his foot into it so very clumsily, and manages to upset the mother's temper." Lucien's share of the *tirage* was twenty-five oils and thirty-three water-colours. Some of the collection remained unapportioned—a few pictures which Julie wished to keep. Rodo, the historian of the family, now began his long labour of making a catalogue of his father's works which would occupy him for nearly twenty years, involving correspondence with owners of the pictures all over the world. Eventually, with the collaboration of Venturi, it was published in 1939.

Rodo's health was precarious; when not well he was inclined to be irritable and disagreeable, but notwithstanding his bark, he was kind-hearted and anxious to put the interests of others before his own. He was known as *le bourru-bienfaisant*, the grumbler who does good. James Brown called him the unsocial socialist. Strangers interrupted him in his work, bringing him pictures for *expertise*. He gave freely of his time and advice and refused a fee. He had a great gift for caricature and humorous wood engravings. An enthusiastic collector of stamps, his humour here was expressed in inventing and printing comic and bogus stamps for the amusement of other collectors. Many of these stamps, and a collection of his engravings, can be seen at the Ashmolean Museum, part of the Orovida Pissarro Bequest. He was the only one of the family who managed to keep clear of the embarrassments caused by lack of money. He had a head for business. When he came to England in 1914 he bought a house at Ashford, Middlesex. Selling this at a profit, he acquired another in Bedford Park. Again selling this to advantage, he invested the proceeds in a block of flats in the rue Girardon, just below the *Moulin de la Galette* in Montmartre. Here he and his wife, Rodette, lived in a studio at the top of six flights of stairs. From their windows could be seen a fascinating panorama of the boulevards and streets of Paris intersected by the Seine. Here Rodo worked until a year or so before his death, when Rodette, now elderly, could no longer manage the steep flights of stairs burdened with her shopping. A move was then made to a studio near the Avenue Junot, and here Rodo died in 1952.

At Eragny, on the 15th September, the family dispersed, only the two young girls, Yaya and Kikite, Georges' children, whose ages were eighteen and twenty-one, remained with Julie and Lucien. Lucien said that Yaya was a beauty, flaxen hair, dark eyebrows, and grey eyes devoid of any blue, but he had a poor opinion of the two girls. "They don't do anything all day except powder their faces. When people come, they go to sleep." Lucien took the pictures, his share of the *partage*, out of their frames, rolled the canvases, made these and the stretchers into parcels, and returned with them to England. He visited Manson at the Tate, who said he had met with no luck on his behalf, invariably getting the same depressing answer: "I'm not buying pictures at the moment." No one was. Money was said to be "tight." There was a slump.

CHAPTER XVII

Eragny and La Frette. 1922–1924

THE NEW YEAR CAME WITH LUCIEN IN BED, ILL WITH INFLUENZA, AND Manson trying to sell for him a Camille picture to Croal Thomson, but it was no good. He, like everybody else, Manson said, was hard up. No sooner was Lucien about again than Paul Emile wrote that Julie was ill. "I wish you would come, you have more influence with her and might convince her that she has to obey orders from the doctor." She was a bad patient. Monet, concerned about her, asked his own doctor, Rebiere, to visit her at Eragny. Lucien packed a bag and crossed to France. Met at the Gare St. Lazare by Rodo, he stayed the night in the rue Girardon. During the evening Paul called. Julie, he said, had engaged a Madame Delbomar as housekeeper, but it made no difference. The "poor old mother" would not let anyone else manage. When a tradesman came to the door Madame Delbomar had to go to her for money which she kept in her bag under her pillow. The next morning, the 25th January, Lucien, at Eragny, was shocked at Julie's appearance. She seemed suddenly aged, and suffered from *mal de coeur*. Yaya was also ill, and in a bed which had been made up for her in the mother's room. Lucien was astonished that Kikite had gone to Paris. "God knows why!" he exclaimed. Another patient was upstairs: Rodette was also in bed with influenza. Rodo, Lucien told Esther, was unbearable.

The next morning Monet's doctor came and made a further examination of Julie. He told Lucien her lungs were congested, and she had heart and kidney trouble. She must drink copiously, and he proscribed salt. But although feeble, Julie retained her characteristic obstinacy. She refused to drink and would not eat food unless it was well salted. Lucien and Rodo passed the nights "in relay to guard the two invalids". Lucien was not a good nurse, although he was able, he said, "to put the poor old thing on a chamber". Rodo was good and gentle "in spite of his bluntness", but Lucien was quite unable to please Julie. When he put a log of wood on the fire she scrambled out of bed to show him how it should be done. Two days later she had deliriums, talked incoherently, and screamed at visions. Lucien was warned by the doctor that her condition was grave, that the end was in sight, and that relatives should be summoned to the bedside. Kikite was now transformed. She became a devoted nurse and exhausted herself with running here and there, and coaxing her grandmother to eat and drink. The doctor lost his patience and told Julie that if she did not follow his instructions he would not come again. This had an effect: Julie became more tractable. She rallied, and in a fortnight was on the way to recovery. Lucien continued to pass the nights "watching the poor lady", but she was not grateful. She grumbled she had nothing to drink. When he offered her the glass, she turned her head away. "The other night I slept a moment in my chair, she said I snored, kept her awake, and she had to get up to get something to drink—which is a pure lie. I am surrounded by people who cannot say a single word true. It seems so strange to me! Well, I do not pay any attention." This was a much used expression of Lucien's. "I do not pay any attention," he replied when Esther made remarks disagreeable to him. His letter ends exhorting Esther "to spend only for the bare necessities as for some time we must give up luxuries, such as tea and dinner parties and theatres".

On the 20th February Georges came and immediately created a terrible disturbance. Rodo had told Julie that Kikite's fiancé was a married man who had turned away his wife. Julie asked Georges if this was true and was he satisfied that this young man was a suitable husband for Kikite? Georges bluntly snapped: "*Qu'est ce que tu veux que j'y fasse*". Lucien was shocked that Kikite "has already been with him", but, after all, "the mother went with the father, but in the most honest way, and she was unjustly kept aside from marriage by father's family, only on account of their bourgeois narrowness". Julie said nothing more to Georges but afterwards had a *crise de nerfs*. "In her weak state she can't stand that sort of thing," Lucien told Esther.

He could not find his nice green hat. He was certain he had brought it with him to Eragny, but would Esther look and make sure it was not left behind? Before she could reply, Paul told him where it had got to. The bedroom of Kikite and Yaya was at the top of the house. At night they dropped a rope from their window; up this climbed a young village ostler, within his pockets a bottle of wine and bags of sweet things to feast on. Kikite had given the boy the hat as a present. "Fancy," wrote Lucien, "the poor old woman being exposed to such things. But she believes nothing she is told; all the neighbours know what goes on but think it useless to tell her, because she exclaims that it is all just village nastiness!"

By the beginning of March, Julie was convalescent, and Paul urged her to go home with him and rest, but Berthe, his wife, said nothing. When she was a young girl she had come to Eragny as a servant. Julie was unable to forget this, and although Berthe was now her son's wife, her manner to her remained that of mistress to maid. "The poor old mother is really terrible," commented Lucien. "She treats people as if they were her slaves!" Julie had no opinion of Berthe: she thought her like Esther, a bad wife and a sluggard. On the contrary, she was an excellent housekeeper. Her antique furniture shone with polish, her house was spotlessly clean, she was a wonderful cook, but she was too good-natured to defend herself and risk a quarrel. All the same she dreaded Julie being in her home and making mischief between herself and Paul.

Julie was alarmed to hear that Lucien considered selling Camille's *Mère Presle*. Manson had written that Walter Taylor offered £100 for it. It was not a purchase, but a loan over two years with the picture as security. Yet Julie would not understand: she said it made her angry —it was no price. Rather than let the picture go for such a ridiculous sum she would lend him the money; Lucien must give her "a paper" in acknowledgement. Lucien was deep in debt again, £100 was not enough to pay his bills, and he returned to England with increasing anxiety. During his absence in France, Manson had talked with Oliver Brown of the Leicester Galleries of Lucien's difficulties. Brown was sympathetic but said: "Why on earth doesn't he sell one of his father's pictures when he has so many?" Actually Manson's visit to Brown had been highly successful, Brown promising an exhibition of Lucien's pictures in the autumn. This was excellent for Lucien, for Brown would do it well. Manson reiterated Brown's advice to Lucien: "Sell one of your C.P.s and then go away and paint hard for your exhibition." But Lucien replied he could not hawk his father's pictures about for sale at such a bad time. It would mean all the prices coming down, and that would affect the family. "If I could sell one of my own pictures, that would save the situation." A day or so later Lucien went to Channel View, Dartmouth, to paint. Manson, assiduous as ever on his behalf, reported that Lord Henry Bentinck was considering buying one of Lucien's pictures painted at Hastings, but the transaction dragged. Manson hoped to catch him at a Trustees' Meeting at the Tate, but Lord Henry came late and went early, giving Manson no

XIIIa. Portrait of Orovida by Lucien Pissarro, 1913

XIIIb. Portrait of his mother by Lucien Pissarro, 1923

XIVa. Lucien painting at Richmond, 1935

XIVb. Houses of Parliament from Lambeth Bridge, Lucien Pissarro, 1914

opportunity to speak to him. It was not until July that Lord Henry again saw the picture at the Tate. He would like to buy it, but said that times were bad with him: his income greatly reduced because many of his investments yielded no dividends. He asked Manson to make Lucien an offer of £45 as he did not like to do so himself. Manson advised, take it. "I feel you must get some money to tide over a difficult period and it is better to make one or two sacrifices, than to live in a state of perpetual worry and anxiety." Lucien replied: "It is a terrible reduction. If he had said £65 it would have been more reasonable. I have £75 to pay out and that does not include the frames I shall have to get for my exhibition."

Lucien also worried about his mother. The family felt it was unsafe for her to be left alone; but whatever companion she had was wrong, and the companion soon went. Rodo wrote: "She doesn't want an elderly companion. She now has as her victim a young maid, fourteen years old, whom she scolds from morn to night. It is a great pleasure to her, and the little maid is sufficient for her requirements."

Oliver Brown, no doubt prompted by Manson, now came to Lucien's aid and sent him an advance of £100 on future sales of his pictures. Brown also wrote to Esther, who was furtively trying to sell one of the Camille pictures: "We have not succeeded in selling any of the C.P.s. The season may be brilliant as you say, but nobody thinks of buying pictures, only of motoring, tennis and polo. The heat is excessive." On 6th July Kikite was married. Julie wrote: "She is very pleased. So am I."

Lucien painted at Dartmouth until the end of September. Despite the persistent mental nag of how to manage with too little money, he had a splendid working summer. The weather was gloriously fine, and he finished twenty-one canvases. His exhibition was a success; collectors were impressed with the luminous beauty of his landscapes. From the opening day it was soon apparent that the exhibition would bring him money. Day after day more red labels were stuck on the pictures, signifying a sale. The tide had turned, Esther beamed with delight, and her faith in Lucien was realised. When the exhibition closed Brown sent Lucien a cheque for £742 and indicated that there might be more to come.

Lucien had repeatedly been advised by his doctor, in view of his weak chest, to winter in the South of France. The money from the exhibition made this possible, and Esther arranged to rent a cottage in the *midi* at Le Lavandou. Julie was invited to join them. The letter reached her when she was in the middle of picking her apples and making cider (the old lady still clambered about the branches of her apple trees). When she had finished, she said, she would be ready. The party arrived at Le Lavandou in December and stayed there for six months.

1923

Le Lavandou began an important period of Lucien's work. His health good, free from niggling money anxieties and worries, every landscape he painted there was eventually sold. He worked with confidence and assurance—the result, seventeen exquisite landscapes and a portrait of Julie. But Manson wrote sadly that their old group of friends had faded away, no longer held together, as it was in the old days, by Spencer Gore who had died in 1914. "Since then we have been gradually drifting apart and now we never meet unless it is by chance."

Manson, generous, reckless, a prodigious entertainer, never counting his money, told Lucien, when he was in London in May, that he had got himself into a frightful mess and wanted money urgently. Lucien was glad to be able to help. Money with him, he told Manson, was plentiful. Manson must not hesitate to accept what he wanted. Besides the cheque he had received the previous year from the Leicester Galleries, he had sold his Camille *Paris Street Scene* for £150. Manson was in a bad way. More than ever he found his work at the Tate boring and monotonous, his days filled with routine and official functions, giving him no time to paint during the day. But lately, he told Lucien, he had been working at a portrait of Elizabeth M . . . . . by artificial light in the little room he rented in Soho, and used as a studio. Often he continued to paint until two in the morning. He wanted to attempt some flower pieces, but it was no good, the flowers faded between one *séance* and another. The day after this meeting, Lucien picked a bunch of flowers from The Brook garden and took them to Hampstead, but Manson was out. Manson wrote and thanked him. He was rarely at home now, he said. "Passing 122 Harley Street this morning the window of the front room was open: on the wall facing the street was one of your lovely Dartmouth pictures."

1924

In January, Lucien, in Paris, exhibited forty-five of his pictures at the *Galérie Marcel Bernheim,* rue Caumartin. He invited Monet to the preview, but Blanche Monet wrote Monet was working hard at his

Nymphéas decorations for the Musée de l'Orangerie. "He was very touched to get your affectionate letter but he no longer wishes to be away from Giverny, not even to go to Paris. He must be ready by a certain date for his Orangerie exhibition. His eyes are in good condition, but I fear that all the time he overworks. He doesn't wish to see or to write to anyone." That summer Lucien intended to spend in Normandy painting for his autumn exhibition at the Leicester Galleries, and he was attracted by the small village of La Frette, on the Pontoise line, its hills covered with lilac cultivated for the Paris flower market. A Madame Docquer, with rooms to let, was recommended. Lucien and Esther visited her and was shown them. The two women understood each other and came to terms. Food was to be provided, Madame Docquer undertook to wash and mend for Lucien, to wax and polish the floor of Lucien's sitting-room, and to provide a picture rail and a more comfortable armchair. Esther returned to England and Lucien remained at La Frette. On the 9th April, Manson came to stay for two or three weeks, Lucien meeting him in Paris. When they arrived at La Frette Madame Docquer had a splendid dinner awaiting them, the "Docquers like him very much and Manson likes them". So Lucien's daily letters to Esther were resumed.

After a day or so of sunshine, the weather became frightful: wind, rain and hail. Painting was impossible. Confined to the house, the monotony was broken with a walk to Confleurs—a charming spot, Lucien wrote, better than La Frette, the river and its banks beautiful. No ugly modern villas lined the streets and he and Manson were enraptured with an effect of sun glancing through storm-wracked clouds, and lighting, in the foreground, an enchanting wood with purple tree-tops, the dark blue distances dotted with white villas. But it could not be painted. The wind was such that the two friends had difficulty in keeping to their feet, easels and canvases would have been blown away. The bad weather persisted. Lucien tried some water-colours, but said they did not "seem to come". Manson on the 17th April described their days in a letter to his daughter, Mary "It has rained nearly every day and sometimes we have had hail-storms. The cold has been very bitter—a nuisance, because there are no fireplaces in our rooms or means of heating them. We have to go out to keep warm, although sometimes madame lets us sit in her kitchen. We have our meals with them, they are working-class people, very amiable, and she is an excellent cook. La Frette is a lovely place, it rambles along the river-bank and the old houses are picturesque and full of colour."

The villagers liked Manson. His bird imitations started all the cocks of the village crowing to the joy of Madame Docquer who laughed so much "that she rolls on her feet". This cockcrow of his was to have sad consequences.

Lucien, in Paris for a day, called on his old friend, Félix Fénéon. Fénéon complained that the size of his Seurat picture, *La Baignade*, overwhelmed the room in which it was hung; he felt the time had come to part with it. But, he said, it was a museum-piece, much too important for a private collection. Manson was thrilled when, on his return, Lucien told him this, for here was an unexpected opportunity to acquire this now historic painting for the Tate. He wrote to the Trustees recommending its purchase, and it was bought from the Courtauld Fund.

Still unable to paint because of the bad weather Lucien and Manson on the 19th April went to visit Dr. Gachet and his son Paul at Auvers-sur-l'Oise. Paul was now fifty-one. He and Lucien recalled their first meeting in Madame Ravoux's café at Van Gogh's funeral, when Paul was a boy of seventeen. Paul had watched by the dying painter's bedside throughout his last night, Van Gogh smoking pipe after pipe, his eyes fixed unwaveringly on the ceiling, but never speaking. Dr. Gachet had painted with Camille at Auvers; he was the friend of all the impressionists and exhibited every year with the *Indépendants*, singing his canvases P. van Ryssel. He showed his fine collection of paintings to the two visitors. Lucien had often seen them before, this time he found the paintings "still more beautiful."

At La Frette it continued to rain, but when the weather turned sunny Lucien complained that in a few days it would be Easter, the village full of holiday-makers and children, and it would not be possible to work quietly and in peace. In Manson's company, he painted many water-colours and began an oil of plum blossom. No, he wrote to Esther, he could not be bothered to boil water and squeeze a lemon in it to drink at meals. The glass of wine he took was better than water. He was well, so why worry for the sake of a theory? He recalled the tone of contempt with which his father spat out the words "Theory! Theory!"

On the 24th April, Manson left. Lucien missed his company and was lonely. They "have had such a lovely time together". Manson had been a great success, everybody in love with him from Madame Docquer and the little girl to the cocks and pigeons. Lucien worked day after day in the open air, catching the effect of the fruit blossom. But he fretted: "If we do not let the house we shall be in a queer hole.

Funds are getting low at the bank." Julie wanted to come and stay with him and afterwards return with him to London, she said that Esther was the only one who could *soigner* her. In a day or so, the wind and the rain returned, the weather became wretched, and he could only sketch. The wind blew the blossom from the trees and his blossom pictures had not been finished. He was bothered with an income tax return: "I cannot remember figures of any kind," he wrote to Esther on the last day of April, "it is enough to have to count the change of a few sous." He lamented, "we may pass again through one of those terrible penniless summers, and that in a foreign place where it is difficult to borrow". Esther should not make him feel miserable, that made it impossible for him to work; the result: fiasco of his next show—then everything would go to the devil! He was disappointed he could not be in London for Orovida's first one-man show, for "the *effet d'ensemble* will be an indication of the tendencies of her art, it will make one realise the direction she is taking". He considered asking two prices of dealers, one for cash, and one where the dealer kept him waiting until the customer paid.

On 12th May he visited his mother at Eragny. He said she was well but too much alone. "The poor old thing is really very sad and says that no one wants her." On the 16th, after his morning *séance*, he went to Paris to see Rodo's private view. "His water-colours really look very fine, all his London work is splendid, full of a special character, well drawn and powerful in colour, it is far superior to the ordinary run of painting one sees in Paris." Would Esther go to the corner shop in the Goldhawk Road and buy him some tobacco? Esther sent it, but said he smoked far too much. "How fussy you are," he retaliated. "Yes, fussy is the right word. I must smoke, it is my only distraction." What else could he do when the weather will not decide to be either grey or sunny? "For the sun comes out when I am working on a *temps gris* and clouds appear when I am finishing a sunny effect." A fortnight later he wrote that he had managed to finish five pictures including one of plum blossom, but La Frette was not so beautiful in its summer dress. Esther kept the cheques. Lucien said it would be nice if she sent him a little one. "How stubborn you are!" he began his next letter dated 24th May. "Letter after letter I tell you that I do not think I had better come to London. All my arguments you do not take into account—you go on as if I had said nothing. You are really terrible! And it is unkind too, for you are tempting me to do something that I consider unwise. I am here to work—there is a great deal of responsibility attached to it—and if, as it happens so often, my work is sacrificed to other worldly things, I would be the one blamed, even by yourself—you would tell me I don't work. Remember I have lost all last year and I am getting on in years; probably I have not many in front of me in which I can produce good work. Really you do not use your brain or you have no imagination, thinking only of the immediate present! There, you succeed in making me angry and you madden me to tell you things in a rough way, simply because if one does not speak brutally, you do not take any notice. It is unkind too, because you know I would like to see Orovida's show—but is pleasure to come before one's duty?"

The weather settled into sunny days. Lucien recovered his tranquillity. He progressed with his work, as usual leaving his business affairs to Esther to manage, and asking where he should send his pictures and how much to ask. Delighted to hear that Orovida's exhibition was a success, he hoped it would not turn her head. Now she would realise the necessity to work harder to keep what she had gained. But he had confidence in her. "How wonderful," he wrote on the 12th June, "to find an *amateur* to buy three pictures at one gulp!" He has never had any luck like that.

On the 13th June he went to Paris to see the exhibition at the *Salon d'Automne*. His pictures looked well and were nicely hung, but, notwithstanding, he said, nobody paid any attention to them and most of the visitors passed without a look! From Paris he went to Eragny, since Julie had asked him to take her some money. She was pleased to see him, but did not need "the cash. So her asking for it was one of her tricks to make me come". Georges was now living at Vézillon, the brothers were to meet there to discuss the sale of some of Camille's etchings. Paul came in his car to fetch Lucien. "I passed the village where we had the delicious melon, and I had the vision of the darling which was not yet mine and that I did desire so much." Georges and Rodo were waiting at Vézillon, where Lucien met Madame Manzana (Georges' wife): "she is rather nice, getting grey, and resembles Berthe Signac, a pleasant person. F. was there, eyes twinkling, he introduced us to a delicious American not dry drink composed of *crème de cacao* mixed with fresh cream. Delicious! We even had a glass of champagne. Georges was most amiable and Rodo as silent as a prison door."

Back at La Frette, on the 28th June, he protested that an air-mail letter sent by Esther had taken longer than the ordinary post: "All these wonderful new inventions are only tricks to catch more of one's pennies!" The weather was again changeable, he worked under difficulties. One morning a gust of wind upset his easel and the T.15 canvas on which he was working fell on a pointed stick which pierced the canvas. Esther was trying to let The Brook. A young man presented himself as a tenant, but this came to nothing. "It is as well that the young man did not take the house. Imagine the bother in the end for the broken things, and how terrible, if father's pictures had been kept hanging, if anything had happened to them." All the same if the house was not let he did not know how they would manage for cash. Things were so terribly expensive in France. Even with the exchange at eighty, he spent two pounds a week, much more than he did at Dartmouth.

By the middle of July the weather was "gloriously hot", and Lucien dressed in white for a fortnight "without bringing any storm". Every day he was in the fields painting, but pessimistically fearing that he made his pictures "too pretty." This, he said, was the pernicious English influence, also he was astonished at his own slowness. He sent Esther many kisses of which some were of a "refined kind". His next letter reverted to gloom and chiding: "It is all very well to say don't worry, it can't be helped. I must worry, or rather, I can't help it. You won't be satisfied until you have driven me to a catastrophe. Any amount of experience does not seem to serve, you always do it again, therefore I cannot have any confidence in your wild combinations. You have a wonderful capacity to take your dreams as if they were realities. I see that you are going to raise my prices again and that may compromise the success of my show. I know it is no good my talking, you don't listen and go your own way, but you take a terrific responsibility."

He sent Esther £40 and she was to join him at La Frette: "If you intend to come you had better do it before you have succeeded in spending the £40." He took a small Camille picture to Fénéon who thought it charming. "He put it at once in a better frame and thinks he can sell it. So I ask twelve thousand francs (£150)." Esther, in a letter, enclosed an account of her July expenses. Lucien, appalled, replied: "A quiet mind about money matters does not remain more than twenty-four hours." She had not even the money left to pay for her ticket and travelling expenses. Lucien feared "we shall be here penniless with people who have such respect for money, and we will have a hell of a time. I have not much the sense of figures, but I come to the conclusion that you are worse! You believe living in France is cheap, but no cash buys nothing. I am so disappointed to be hard up when you come. I have worked hard and hoped to have a little relaxation and go about. I fear it will be impossible. Good-bye dearest, much love from your disappointed old man." Letter followed letter.

"Alas! What I feared seems to be happening. As usual you have been spending, repairing, etc., without taking the trouble to count if you have enough cash to see it through. As usual, I expect a letter, telling me, my darling, so sorry, I have only ten shillings in the bank. Well, if there is not a fair balance, you must not come over—this is the result. You have a beautiful house, clean and charming, and you must remain there!"

"I must finish my pictures, and there is only just enough money for that. I saw it coming for a long while, those wonderful repairs were frightening me but only lately I realised what a serious business it is. Six months' spring-cleaning in preparation for three months of winter!"

"No more of grumblings and miseries. I am sorry you are also blue, but dearest, it is your own fault. You go on spending and spending without counting. You draw on the bank day after day, without knowing how things are, keeping the attitude of the ostrich putting its head under its wing."

Lucien's reproaches were justified. The year had started with a handsome balance at the bank. The money dazzled Esther; it could not come to an end, and she recklessly indulged in grandiose projects for making her house still more lovely with alterations here and there, new paint and repairs. If the money was not spent on drains, much of it found its way to them. Hardly a penny did she spend on herself, nearly all had gone on refurbishings.

At the moment when Esther had miserably resigned herself to the reality that there was no money to take her to France and join Lucien, Orovida, who had made good sales at her exhibition, wrote: "I am so sorry funds are low. I am sending you £50 to put in the bank for comfort sake. You will owe me £40. Go to France as soon as you can, you spend so much less there." An unintentional riposte.

As soon as Esther arrived at La Frette she saw Madame Docquer had not waxed and polished the floor, neither had she fulfilled her promise to provide a picture rail and a more comfortable armchair. Lucien mollified her. The floor was in the same state because his boots got dirty in the fields and he brought mud into the house, and Madame Docquer had been so kind to him that he did not like to put her to the expense of the rail and the chair.

CHAPTER XVIII

Death of Julie. 1926

IN THE EARLY AUTUMN LUCIEN RETURNED TO LONDON TO PREPARE FOR his exhibition. This, like the first, was a success. There were many sales, and he received a cheque for upwards of £500. Oliver Brown was pleased, and after this Lucien had an exhibition every two years at the Leicester Galleries. Even the water-colours which had not seemed "to come" sold well. Despite his frets and anxieties, and despite the weather, he had had a successful season. Never before had he painted with such assurance; his canvases glowed with the beauty of La Frette. Their charm and poesy were praised by the critics.

Lucien had seen for sale at Durand-Ruel's a charming pastel by Mary Cassatt, and as usual, he promptly advised Manson and enclosed a photograph. But the Tate Trustees dillied and dallied, delaying a decision to purchase from one meeting to another. Manson wrote to Lucien: "I am very anxious to have the Mary Cassatt as I told Aitken," but two days later: "I have just heard from Durand-Ruel that the *Sortie du Bain* by Mary Cassatt has been sold to America. I am very sorry that we have lost it, particularly as it is our own fault. Do you think Miss Cassatt would give us anything if she heard we had tried to buy the other? I should like to find some way of getting that lovely oil painting in her room of a child in a white cape and bonnet. I wonder if it could be managed?" It couldn't. Lucien tried but without success. The Tate Gallery is still without a Mary Cassatt, a sad gap in its collection of the Impressionists.

1925

At the beginning of the year Julie escaped the cold and isolation at Eragny and stayed for a few weeks with Rodo and Rodette in Montmartre. Before this visit she had not liked Rodette any more than her other daughters-in-law. Now she told her: "You are nice." A pause then the sting: "But you are lazy. That is because you have no children." Back again at Eragny the old lady, troubled with her age, unable to look after herself, had to depend on a new companion, Madame

Voury. To her she dictated a letter to Lucien explaining she was no longer able to write herself as she could no longer see. Madame Voury said Julie behaved "strangely". Julie's friend, *la mère* Bertine, still survived in the village; she was so old that she walked doubled-up, her nose beaked over a pointed chin. She had lost her teeth, her mouth was sunk in, and when she came to visit and gossip with Julie, she tied a coloured handkerchief over her head. Occasionally Hyacinthe Pozier, the local painter, called. He had been at Eragny before Camille; he also was old. He liked laughter and wrote humorous verse to read aloud at the dinners of the *Indépendants*. Another visitor was the doctor from Gisors, invariably greeted with Julie's blunt peasant humour: "What do you know about medicine?" or "How can you tell what is wrong with me?" "I am blind," she complained to Madame Voury. "Read me the newspaper." Madame Voury read, while Julie fidgeted and looked out of the window. "Gracious!" she exclaimed. "There goes the Jesseaux woman in a new bonnet!"

Lucien and Esther were at Bandol, Var. In quest of new painting locations for Lucien they made excursions to Macon, Avignon, Tarascon, Nimes, Arles and Marseilles. When they returned to Bandon, Lucien wrote to Manson: "Here we are back again. I am going to start working." He painted five pictures, and then he and Esther moved to Le Brusq where they stayed until June, and Lucien completed sixteen further landscapes. Here he helped his landlord to learn English and made friends with the local *curé*, M. Stanislas Vache, who had a wonderful cellar, the neighbouring *vignerons* presenting him without stint of their best vintages. *M. le curé* also appreciated good food: his housekeeper coddled him, an excellent cook who well understood his tastes. He was interested in the arts and painted watercolours, but much of his energy was spent in warfare against those museums attempting to pilfer the treasures of the village churches. He and Lucien enjoyed each other's company. The *curé* tried to express himself in English, and when Lucien went, he continued his efforts in letters: "How much we are sorry since you left us, we had become accustomed to your gentle company. You and Mrs. Pissarro had become such good friends. And now all day long methinks I am wanting to learn some English lessons and behold landscape paintings in your room. But there is nobody any longer. The windows are shut and no coffee or tea is prepared for *M. le curé qui va venir*. You arrived safely in Paris. But you are in a very noisy and troublesome town. How nice and lovely is Le Brusq with its quiet sweetness and peaceful

seashore, silent pine trees, blue skies and sunsets, when M. Mistral does
not blow too strongly. M. Charbonneau will write to you in English
also. He got out all his English books. Beware!"

In August Lucien sold one of his father's treasured pictures, *Le Pont
Royal et le Pavillon de Flore*,* for £600, and in November the Tate
bought another, *Boulevard des Italiens. Effet de Nuit*,† for 1,500
guineas. With the money the mortgage on The Brook was repaid.
Now, said Esther, the lovely house was really hers.

1926

Good fortune continued. Early in the year Courtauld bought three
of Lucien's landscapes for £275. The Brook was let, and a house
rented at Bormes les Mimosa. Situated on the hill over Lavandou, it
had a view of the sea. Emma Ruddick went with Lucien and Esther,
Orovida being left behind. The journey south was broken at Paris and
a visit made to Eragny. Lucien thought his mother looked the picture
of health, but was frightened by the way the "cash vanishes". He had
to see many people and was distracted. "I do not know where I am.
The business side of things really drives me crazy and bores me. How
I long to be quiet and to be able to think of my work!" He called on
Vollard, his mother warning him he was touchy but could be generous,
and was shown a dozen landscapes by Cézanne: "Very nice, but always
the incomplete kind, things evidently left unfinished." It was getting
dark when he saw a T.30, a woman's portrait, "most beautiful in texture, drawing, composition and colour". Enchanted, but unable to
examine it very carefully in the bad light, he wrote that evening to
Manson that it would be a wonderful acquisition for the Tate. But
afterwards he reflected that perhaps it was not a Cézanne, the balance
of the drawing suggesting it might be a Gauguin influenced by
Cézanne.

There was a suggestion that Julie should lend Camille's *La Causette*
to the Tate for exhibition, and it is typical of the niggardly means at the
disposal of the Tate in those years, so different now, that Manson had to
reply: "I am afraid we cannot have the *Causette* on loan even if the
family will lend it. We have hardly any funds to pay for carriage and
insurance so that we could not afford to get it over from France. It is a

* One of Camille's last pictures painted in 1903. Listed in Rodo's catalogue
(No. 1288) as *Pavillon de Flore et Pont Royal.*

† Painted 1897. Rodo's catalogue No. 994. Rodo's title is *Boulevard Montmartre. Effet de Nuit.* This painting is now at the National Gallery.

pity. The powers that be only reluctantly let us have very small sums for expenses."

Soon after Lucien and Esther had settled in at Bormes Emma received a letter from an old friend, a young man from her village. They had been at school together, but Emma had not seen him since she was fourteen. He had emigrated to Canada. Now in London on a visit, he was anxious to meet her again. He had never forgotten her. "Will you marry me?" he asked. "What shall I do?" Emma asked Esther. It was obvious what she intended to do. "You had better buy your trousseau here," Esther said. "Much cheaper than in England." Emma returned to London, being met in Paris by Rodo who escorted her from one station to the other. She met her young man in Orovida's flat, and Orovida wrote to Esther: "Emma looks most blooming, and the young man is quite nice, steady, sensible, clean-looking sort of man. I am clearing out today and tomorrow in order that they may have a chance of being alone together." The young couple, delighted with each other, were married in their native Suffolk village. Esther sent orange blossom, Orovida said the wedding "went off all right and the house was full".

The young man had a farm in Canada. Here he and Emma settled and had children, but in a few years Emma was a widow. She took over the running of the farm, made it a success, and became a grand-mother. She wrote to Orovida in 1959: "I remember staying at Eragny in Madame Pissarro's house, it was so interesting, then we went to Paris for a short time before going south. What a lovely country with its flowers all the winter and the blue sea. I've always been so glad I had that trip. Your mother was a second mother to me after my own died, and a fairy godmother to my children. They still have some of the lovely books she sent. It was at The Brook I learnt to love good pictures and music."

At Eragny, Julie's health began to fail. She coughed incessantly and lived on fluids. Madame Voury wrote daily to Lucien. "She keeps such a fresh complexion that it is hard to believe she is an old woman, she looks so young and good-looking." But it was trying to be in her company, one had to be very patient, "she is so outspoken". On 5th May, Paul Emile wrote: "If you wish to see *maman*, come at once." Lucien and Esther hurried to Eragny. Julie did not survive their arrival long. She died on 16th May at the age of eighty-seven.

She had been a remarkable woman. Beautiful as a young girl with a most sweet expression; child bearing and the hardships of her life had erased beauty and scored her face with anxieties. Her temper was soured by adversity but sweetness persisted and made her lovable. With her children she was like an angry hen, clucking and pecking, trying to drive them to her way of thinking, scared at their inclination for the precarious lives of artists, urging them to trades for their material comfort and a safeguard against want. She had known the lack of money too well; she dreaded her sons would endure what she had endured. Despite her tantrums, her nagging, her desire to dominate, she was beloved by them. Always, when they were in need, she had contrived to come to their assistance. She did not know when she died that she had fulfilled her ambition. None of her children was to want in the future. She was buried by the side of Camille in *Père Lachaise*.

It was a sad year. Esther's mother also died. Esther, hurrying from Julie's deathbed, reached home too late to see her alive. Grievous news came of Mary Cassatt: she was blind, and a letter from her was unreadable. Mathilde Valet wrote a postscript to it that Miss Cassatt grew weaker and weaker in mind and body, and, in June, she wrote to say Mary Cassatt had died on the 14th. Blanche Monet had written, on behalf of Monet, a letter of condolence to Lucien. She said Monet was very unhappy, in pain, unable to go out, unable to do anything. But they were pleased to hear of Orovida's success. On 5th August she had no good news of Monet. He went on suffering, getting thinner and thinner, weaker and weaker. "We are all very sad to see him in this condition, and he himself is miserable because he cannot work, and his work has been his only interest throughout his life." Monet lingered until December when he died on the 6th.

"We had an awful day yesterday with the succession business," Lucien wrote to Esther. "They have started the inventory." But all went well, the atmosphere was subdued. The brothers felt Julie's influence still about the house, and difficulties were smoothed over. When all was done, and the house sealed, Lucien returned to Bormes.

In November, Esther was in Paris learning to drive a motor. "I am afraid she has not the sort of capacity for that sort of thing," Lucien wrote to Orovida. He considered this acquisition a terrible mistake, he did not think Esther would make a safe driver, "you must be quick in decision, methodic, orderly, all qualities she particularly lacks. It is a dangerous undertaking. We may be robbed of our belongings and left wounded or killed on a lonely road." "Poor mother," he wrote on the last day of the year, "has little time to attend to Lizzie which is passing her time in the garage out of mischief."

Lizzie was the name given to the car, an ancient Ford with spokes like those on bicycle wheels—the first of a succession of second-hand cars that Esther was to drive recklessly over the roads of France and England. They were all referred to as "Lizzie" or "The Old Lady". Lucien's forebodings were almost justified. Esther was a bad driver, but she miraculously escaped accidents except when a London bus collided with Lizzie and smashed her bonnet, but as Esther's claim for repairs was paid by the bus company, this accident could not be said to be due to her bad driving. Perhaps this would be more accurately described as eccentric rather than reckless, although it was said that in later years villagers and children in Somerset and Devon villages scattered for safety when they heard the cry: "Here comes Mrs. Pissarro in her car." The cars were always going wrong. Esther knew nothing about their mechanism, and there were many long waits on country roads until help arrived and the car towed to a garage. One car stalled on hills—for this emergency two large stones were carried in the boot. Once, when this happened, Lucien was sitting in a back-seat deep asleep. Manson, in front with Esther, got out, opened the boot and lodged the stones against the rear wheels. Esther started up and drove off, Manson forgotten. He had to trudge three miles with the stones in his arms. He did not dare leave them behind.

"I looked out of my window at the Tate," Manson once said, "and there was Esther, whirling along in her car. What a car it was! Open to the elements, there was no cover of any description, even in those days it was a vintage."

Esther inherited over £2,000 from her mother's estate. She told Lucien she proposed to let him have the use of this money during his lifetime, the residue then to go in trust to Orovida until she attained the age of fifty. Lucien did not agree, he thought a trustee for Orovida unnecessary. "Orovida has more head on her shoulders than any of us. If it was a question of small babies after her it would be different. If she spends all the inheritance and has some good out of it, I am quite satisfied. Don't be afraid. She is quite capable of adding to her capital instead of losing it." At Bormes, Lucien met a Madame Pit-Vermorel, an artist, who had converted the old *Moulin de la Verne* into a studio. Picturesquely situated, with a terraced garden of orange and lemon trees, Lucien took a liking to it and agreed to rent it for the winter. Esther now joined him at Chaumont and proposed that the two of them journeyed south in Lizzie. The discomfort of such a trip in cold weather and snow terrified Lucien, but he hoped his fears would come to nothing as Esther would not get her driving licence in time. Nevertheless the journey was made, but it was a hired chauffeur who drove. Esther believed it was cheaper to travel by car than by train. No doubt it would have been if her various cars had behaved and had not involved her in costly bills for repairs and replacements.

1927–1928

Lucien stayed at Bormes for six months and painted thirteen important pictures. *M. le curé* Vache visited him and Esther and was delighted to meet Miss Orovida, Lucien's "good and very artistic daughter". Janine Pit-Vermorel introduced the Pissarros to her friend the Countess Leuterem, a Russian *émigrée* living on the chemin de l'Hubac above the village of Dardennes outside Toulon. The Countess dressed in shabby clothes, kept goats, and managed to exist on their produce. She suggested that the Pissarros should rent her bungalow when their tenancy of the mill expired, but Esther said there was no garage for Lizzie. The Countess, who said of herself that she had the soul of a hermit, replied that that was nothing, she would sell one of her jewels and have one built.

From November, 1927, until April of the next year Lucien was in Paris, embroiled in the complications and entanglements of his mother's succession, his days spent going from one notary to another, testifying at courts of law and listening to judicial arguments. Clerks wrote, typed, copied and duplicated an accumulating mass of dispositions; an inventory was prepared which ran to hundreds of pages. One impasse followed another. The inheritors disagreed; one demanded a *partage judiciaire* against the others who favoured a *partage à l'amiable*; another disputed Lucien's right to the pictures given him by Julie before her death; these should be returned and added to the *tirage*. Lucien was called to a magistrate's office to establish his identity, and the court argued interminably as to whether his nationality was English or French until his exasperated notary, M. Guillon, rose to his feet, banged his fist on a table and thundered: "What does it matter?"

Lucien became disgruntled. The disagreements, he said, were made by the lawyers, not by the family—disagreements were to the lawyers' interest, so settlement was delayed, the weeks went by, nothing was done, costs mounted and mounted, "and", wrote Lucien, "I run about from morning to night, doing nothing, and nothing accomplished.

I am sick of the law, lawyers, tribunals, judges." Patience finally gone, the family decided to ignore the lawyers, to divide the pictures into lots, and draw for choice. No sooner had this been agreed when Rosenberg, the art dealer, offered to buy the entire collection, the pictures to be estimated by an independent expert whose valuation Rosenberg would increase by ten per cent. "It is in this way," Lucien explained to Esther, "that Rosenberg bought the *succession* Renoir, and that explains the high prices the pictures afterwards fetched". Paul sat in the studio at Eragny listing the pictures in the *tirage*, noting each one with the current price. He estimated the total value was over three million francs. When Esther heard this her imagination as usual took wings, she speculated on how she would spend all this wealth about to drop into her lap. Lucien gently curbed her. Their share would not be such an enormous sum, when it came to spending, as she seemed to think. "Nowadays," he wrote, "a rich speculator of my acquaintance places three million to gain double or more. He says when he refrains from going to the *bourse* he makes a million." The logic of this, if any, suggests that even Lucien was indulging in day-dreams and already making a fortune on the stock exchange. It all came to nothing. An appointment was made for Rosenberg to meet the brothers when the offer would be accepted and the matter clinched. Rodo, Paul and Lucien gathered in Rosenberg's office, but Georges did not appear, and without him, nothing could be done. Georges afterwards explained that he made a mistake in the date and went to Rosenberg's on Monday to be told that he had been expected on the previous Saturday. "Rosenberg is disgusted," wrote Lucien. "He says it is all too complicated. No one talks any more of Rosenberg. I suppose it is all over." It was. The pictures were divided by the drawing of lots. Lucien took his to Chaumont where they were packed in boxes and sent to England.

Julie's investments were realised. Lucien's share was £2,000. The house and furniture, including easels and frames, were sold at auction.

CHAPTER XIX

Disaster at the Tate. Campagne Orovida. 1928–1929

WHILST LUCIEN WAS THUS ENGAGED IN FRANCE, DISASTER BEFELL THE Tate. At Christmas, falls of snow outside London and in the Cotswolds, followed by sudden thaw, doubled the daily flow of water down the Thames. On Friday evening, the 6th January, 1928, a south-westerly wind stiffened and, blowing with the ferocity of a gale, met the tide as it turned. The flood heaved between wind and tide, barges and boats were tossed about as if in a storm at sea. In the early hours of the 7th, the waters burst the embankment wall near Lambeth Bridge and then the wall opposite the Tate Gallery. Surging across the road, the flood unhinged doors, pushed aside masonry, and roared into the lower galleries. In the vicinity, streets were flooded. Many people living in basements had to swim for their lives, and over 4,000 homes were temporarily abandoned. Aitken, awakened from sleep at 5 a.m., sent a warning to Manson before making his way to the Tate. He had to wade through flooded streets on the final stage of his journey. The damage at first sight seemed appalling, the pictures, in the lower galleries, including a collection of Turner water-colours, were submerged in the water. However, pumps were set to work, the sodden pictures were retrieved, taken out of their frames and carried to dry in the upper galleries. Water-colours and the separated leaves of sketch-books were placed between sheets of blotting paper, and as was expected the colours of the water-colours did not run but remained firm.

Manson had undertaken the care of an important part of Lucien's collection of his father's work—paintings, water-colours and pastels—and these had been stored in wooden boxes in Manson's office in the basement. When Manson reached the Tate his room was flooded, the water reaching nearly to the ceiling. Cupboards had been wrenched away from walls and smashed. A treasured possession, a portfolio of drawings by Dunoyer de Segonzac, a gift from the artist to Manson, had been reduced to pulp, as also was the manuscript of the book *Hours at the Tate Gallery*, which he had just completed. Nothing could be done with it, Manson had to face the job of entirely rewriting. One personal belonging was undamaged: the box containing his ceremonial top hat floated on the water, inside the hat was in immaculate condition.

"I was glad to have your wire," Lucien wrote to Esther on 9th January, "as I saw in the paper the tragedy of the Tate Gallery." But on the 5th Esther had written a letter which must have been delayed: "You can't tell what we have felt since Manson phoned to me on Saturday afternoon to tell me of the awful calamity . . . Manson's and Aitken's rooms were smashed up, the furniture looks like broken matchboxes. How they have saved all they have is marvellous. We had a hellish night of anxiety. I rang up Manson this morning and asked if I should go with the keys and try and find our boxes and arranged to get there just after him."

The boxes had been salvaged, and Esther opened them. Some of the pictures were covered with a mud-deposit, others fairly dry. "The portfolio was soaked. I put the pastels and drawings between sheets of blotting paper and brought them home, where they are drying in the studio." Esther and Orovida returned to the Tate and assisted in the drying of the water-colours. Orovida wrote to Lucien on the 8th: "Just a line to reassure you that the pictures are all safe. Dirty but not seriously hurt. Poor Manson and Aitken have been working night and day to save the things. We have been very lucky that we did not lose everything." Incredibly, after the water-colours and pastels had been thoroughly dried, and the oils cleaned, not one picture showed any sign of damage.

Lucien returned from Paris in June. During his absence Esther had again indulged her passion for structural alterations and was in the midst of a vast project to metamorphose the printing-room into a studio. Lucien went to paint at Youlgreave, near Bakewell, Derbyshire. He said the problems arising from his mother's death had nearly exhausted his capacity for work. His landlady, Miss Hayes, was "nice and obliging, she cooks well and everything is clean", and he lived like a fighting cock. "For the last two days it has not been raining, and I have two water-colours done."

His luggage arrived, eight shillings to pay, his trunk in a terrible state. It was a fine morning, and he began another water-colour, but the best *motifs* were at the other end of the village, with a tiring climb back to the lodgings at the end of a *séance*. This corner was the meeting place of the village women, who congregated there, hands on hips, and gossiped all day long in the midst of their "dirty bawling youngsters. Just opposite where we saw the nice view is the very centre of it." But he hoped to find undisturbed places with *motifs* as good. He smoked excessively to smooth his nerves, but was worried that the nicotine would harm him, so he tried herbs, but they were "beastly. It is like the stuff people put in bags and hang in a wardrobe to keep the moth away. It is an impossible kind of smoke to enjoy after a good dinner." The weather turned hot and sunny, but he worked with difficulty. He thought he had lost the habit of standing while painting, and in the heat his Norfolk suit made him perspire and tire quickly. Esther sent him his white trousers to wear, but when they arrived the weather changed, the sun disappeared, and the days became cold.

Meanwhile Esther continued with her wonderful plans to improve The Brook. Lucien read her letters with alarm. He hoped she would not be too extravagant with her building plans, "that studio has already cost as much as a decent little freehold property in the country. Now fencing! How shall we pay for all that? Cash doesn't seem to be pouring in."

Before Lucien had gone to Youlgreave, hospitality had been given to a nephew, Frank McEwen, whose father had shocked his family by marrying a young woman of the chorus. Frank wished to become an artist. Young, good-looking, charming and romantic, he had made an immediate appeal to Esther who tucked him under her wing. She now suggested to Lucien that it would help the boy's painting if he came and stayed with him at Youlgreave. Lucien was not at all enraptured with this. His own painting took all his energy, he did not want to be distracted with another's problems, and he replied: "No, I don't think I would like him with me. I am too struggling. I feel I want to learn, not to teach." But of course Esther had her way and Frank arrived. He was not the nuisance Lucien had feared, and Lucien continued to fight his solitary battles against changing weather and man. "I am hoping," he wrote, "that in the coming week I will be able to finish my famous T.15, as I fear the magnificent hay in the foreground may tempt the farmer to cut it down. It would be disastrous; that is the part of the picture I am so anxious to work over. It has remained only roughly coloured from the start."

Another link with the past was broken: Esther sold the printing press on which she and Lucien had laboured to produce their exquisite books. "The poor old press!" Lucien said, when he heard of this. "It is really the end of a period of our lives, and perhaps the one in which we did the work which will count. The true collaboration, the expression of our mutual love." But this was followed by an angry letter: he was "most upset" to hear that the builder was still owed £400. "That studio," he exclaimed, "will have absorbed nearly all my share of the inheritance. Do stop short of any more fancy."

The sun restored his good humour. Day after day he was able to work at a new *motif*, stopping when the sun disappeared behind a cloud to light his pipe and smoke. Every day he was silently watched by a small girl who arrived when he did and remained as long as he painted. One morning she broke her silence and made a grave statement. She declared, Lucien said, "that she did like me". But onlookers were too often a nuisance. On one occasion two boys greatly flustered Lucien: they made bets on the colour he would use next. "Bet yer it's a blue," one would state, and the other would reply, "I bet on a red." Lucien, exasperated by this inanity, and to confound their predictions, would use any colour than the ones named. It didn't help his painting.

It was a good year. In November the Leicester Galleries reported the sale of a Camille picture for £1,400, and in December Lucien's picture, "Elmbridge, Devon", on show at the Venice Exhibition, was sold for 90 guineas. He had also received £600 from the sales of others of his pictures, and there was a further £190 to come.

In December Lucien was in Paris for the sales of the family collection of Camille's own paintings, and of the collection made by him from such artists as Mary Cassatt, Cézanne, Dufeu, Delacroix, Guillaumin, Blanche Hoschedé, Jongkind, Le Bail, Luce, Manet, Monet, Piette, Seurat, Signac, Sisley and Van Rysselberghe. The Gauguins, the van Goghs and many Monets had already been sold. The auctions were held at the *Galérie Georges Petit* on the 3rd December, and at the *Hôtel Drouot* on the 7th and 8th December. There were further sales at the *Hôtel Drouot* the next year, on the 12th and 13th April, the ultimate result to Lucien was that he was enabled to repay a bank loan of £1,150 and enclose a further cheque for £1,250 in addition.

1929

Frank McEwen had gone with Lucien to Paris. In January they were staying at Chaumont-en-Vexin. The Brook had been let, and Lucien hoped the young couple who had rented it were steady and not the type to give dancing parties in his studio. Money continued to jingle pleasantly in Esther's purse, and she contemplated buying another car. The prudent Lucien wrote to say they could not afford two cars, one for England and one for France. "Be careful! I know already the beautiful arguments you will put forward. Don't I know them all!" But Esther was not deterred. Her brother, Sam, had an old car, a Fiat, in which his wife drove him about. He had written a book on his travels in it, now he wanted to be rid of it, and Esther bought it. It had been called "The Tramp", now it became another Lizzie. As Lucien so often said, nothing would stop Esther from an extravagance once she had made up her mind.

Frank had a driving licence, and Lucien wrote that Esther would be happy to hear they had used her Lizzie and she had behaved splendidly. "In the morning we went to Gisors and were coming back at a good pace when she stopped on a hill. No petrol! We had miscalculated her appetite. We had to leave her on the road and walk two kilometres to get some." Meanwhile, the Countess Leuterem had contrived to sell one of her jewels. With the money she had a rough shed knocked together to house Lizzie, and Esther now agreed to rent her bungalow for the next few months. She planned to cross to Dieppe at the end of the month with the luggage. There Lucien and Frank were to await her, and then they would make the journey south together in Lizzie. Lucien protested. How could the enormous amount of luggage which Esther wanted to bring be packed on poor Lizzie? "The vast green trunk won't be able to stand on the weak luggage rack, and the picture box, and Frank's trunk, and also probably the blessed tea basket. It seems I will have to be jammed behind among the overflow. I must say that if it is so, I won't go. I shall take the train. I have been too miserable on the first voyage. It is really wonderful that Esther so complicates things in order to simplify." But Esther's arrangements miscarried. She was delayed in London, and Lucien and Frank drove to Toulon without her. On the 15th February, Lucien wrote to Esther: "The cold continues, the fire is frostbitten, the taps frozen. I am in perfectly good health for the time being, my nose, despite the cold, allows me to breathe freely." He hoped Orovida would have a success with her exhibition, but warned her it took a lifetime to be recognised. His impression of the neighbourhood was that it was very grand, but had not got the kind of intimate things he liked to paint: "Enormous mountains too near look nothing on canvas." He took Frank to see *M. le curé* Vache. The *curé* was delighted and provided a delicious lunch. But all did not go well with Lizzie. "We went yesterday to

Toulon with Lizzie to fetch the luggage. Tho' she was full of petrol she failed to negotiate the hill. As she was dripping water on the ground we looked inside and saw that the envelope of the engine was cracked, and had been cracked a long time, as there were rust marks around the damage. She will be out of action for some time."

No sooner did Esther arrive than she was excited to hear of a furnished old Provençal farmhouse for sale, owned by a Mr. Bruce, and acquired as a home for his aged mother, but the steep climb up the hill to the house had proved to be beyond the old lady's strength. Esther saw the house and was immediately obsessed with a desire to own it. Always worried over Lucien's health, there was an excuse. Here was a house in the South of France where Lucien could shelter every winter away from the damp English climate. Already her mind was busy visualising the wonderful improvements she could make; her genius for alteration would have full scope. There was neither lavatory nor bathroom, good English lavatories could be installed, a bathroom, modern in design, perhaps the addition of a studio, and, of course, a garage for Lizzie. She saw it as charming as her adorable London house. The purchase was made, Lucien in the background muttering how the cash vanished, and the farmhouse was named Campagne Orovida. It had eleven acres of land, large rooms with circular windows were furnished in the Provençal style with chairs resembling those which van Gogh painted, and it was situated half-way up the hill in the Quartier des Moulins on the chemin de l'Hubac, the main route from Toulon, five miles away, to La Garde. Below it straggled the little village of Dardennes. The road uphill degenerated into a mule track strewn with boulders: downhill it was not much better, a cart track with rough stones and a ditch on either side. When she drove Lizzie into Toulon, Esther, black hat with ribbons tied under her chin, sat upright at the steering wheel, her eyes glinting through her *pincenez*. Other drivers, coming uphill as fast as they dared go, afraid of losing pace on the incline and abrupt bends, forced her to the extreme side of the road, but somehow she prevented Lizzie from falling into the ditch. Coming back, Lizzie would stall and her passengers patiently wait while Esther cranked and cranked until Lizzie decided to re-start.

The outlook from the terrace in front of the house, perched on the side of the cone-shaped Mt. Faron, across the valley to the small mountain town of Le Revest les Eaux, was magnificent. The house was supplied with water from a rain cistern on the roof. This fed an underground tank from which the water was pumped, but the pump did not work and water had to be hauled up in pails. In the cellar was an old wine press, but the vines outside had been neglected. Their grapes were small and sour, but there was the green-silver smoke of olive trees, and an abundance of quinces, apricots, figs, almonds, and black cherries. Outside the back entrance to the house flourished a mulberry tree. A devoted friend was found in Maria Agraz who came daily from Toulon to housekeep. When Lucien and Esther were in England she looked after the house. Every year she and her husband picked the olives and took them to a mill to be ground and sold, she and Esther dividing the money.

Esther delighted in her collection of friends and lame ducks. Besides Janine Pit-Vermorel and the Countess Leuterem, they now included Miss Russell, known as "Mademoiselle Miss" by the locals, whom she vainly tried to persuade not to shoot thrushes for their tables. Miss Russell, a would-be composer, lived at the top of a ruined mill at Cotinac. Another newcomer was Madame Nicholaeff, a charming Russian *émigrée*. She, her grandmother, her mother, her husband, and three children, herded together in squalor in a small, stone farmhouse. She kept chickens, the family lived on their produce. Their living conditions, compared with those of the Nicholaeffs, were palatial, their runs having been built by Madame's husband in accordance with modern and sanitary methods. Madame sold her eggs and chickens in Toulon market. At first she stood there with a basket, later she acquired a mule, and finally a van. Somehow she found the money to support a daughter studying at the Sorbonne. Campagne Orovida had been bought in Orovida's name, and when war broke out, Orovida gave Madame Nicholaeff a power of attorney so that she could look after her interests. Madame found it difficult. In good faith she let the garden to a syndicate of gardeners who broke into the house and then petitioned for its requisition. Esther, after the war, encountered considerable trouble in regaining possession. After Esther's death, Orovida placed it at the disposal of artist friends who went there to paint and for holidays. The rates were excessively high and Orovida, realising she would never go there again, in 1954, finally sold it.

Lucien had a wonderful season. Every picture he painted he sold. In October, Esther returned to England, leaving him behind with Frank. Mrs. Voynich was at The Brook, and Esther must have upset her, for she left and wrote from Chalfont St. Giles: "I had a very comfortable trip and arrived to find a warm sitting-room, a good dinner and a smiling landlady. So I am lucky and am looking forward to my bed with a single mind. After two or three days in this good air, I shall be another person. But *you won't*, unless you amend your ways. Having already reduced Lucien to a jelly, me to a file, and Orovida to a buzz-saw, you will reduce yourself to a really sick woman if you go on tearing up and down with bare feet, standing in draughts, and generally behaving like Beelzebub's maiden aunt. Will you, won't you, will you, won't you be a little reasonable for once? Ethel. PS. You do exasperate me, but you are also a dear. Love to everybody; and I am very sorry to have been such a damnable nuisance. But I couldn't help it."

CHAPTER XX

Two Johns. 1930–1937

LUCIEN WAS IN PARIS FOR THE CENTENARY OF THE BIRTH OF HIS FATHER: IT was officially celebrated by a double exhibition of his works at the Musée de l'Orangerie, an annex of the Louvre, and at the Luxembourg. Camille's work was exhibited in two sections, pictures and engravings, and his *chefs d'œuvre* from public and private collections were included. Visited by upwards of 20,000 people, the exhibition was a great attraction. As the public interest seemed unabated, and also in view of the many letters received from French and foreign *amateurs* asking what time they had left to study Camille's work, the closing date originally announced was extended by a fortnight.

In June of 1931, Lucien was in London. He painted a few pictures in The Brook studio, but his prostate gave trouble, and he was often in pain and discomfort. Finally in September he underwent an operation in University College Hospital. He recovered slowly, but Esther fretted, and she wished him back at The Brook, where there were no visiting hours. But it was not until January, 1932, that he was home again. At last the slow and protracted affair of the *partage* came to an end, Lucien's final share being £360. Still shaky from the shock of his operation, he painted with difficulty. Nevertheless, in August, he went to Leintwardine in Salop, and completed four pictures, one, *Trippleton Farm*, was sold to the Belfast Art Gallery.

His health did not improve, and 1933 was again a bad year in which he painted only four pictures, three of these at Reynoldstone, near Swansea, and one at Pennard, *Cefn Bryn*, sold to the Swansea Art Gallery. The operation had not been altogether successful. Lucien stood and walked with difficulty, and needed Esther's help and ministrations during both the day and at night. Now disconcerting news came of the Campagne Orovida, left in charge of Madame L. Esther had let it for a few weeks to some friends, and they arrived to find a stone-cold house without coal, and were told it was impossible to have hot water or to cook a meal. The bedroom was dirty, damp sheets were feared, the lavatory in disuse, the cistern broken, and the door was hanging by its hinges, blown in by the mistral. Madame L. excused herself: she said she had been ill with influenza and indeed still looked ill. The visitors stayed one night, sleeping in their own travelling rugs, and departed the next morning. Orovida's friend, Margaret Anderson, went there for a holiday. She was met by Madame L. with the keys and a meal was cooked for her. Margaret noticed traces of mice, but as it was now late at night nothing could be done until the next morning, then it was discovered they had overrun the house and caused much destruction. Upstairs they had been in the beds among the blankets, in cupboards and on shelves, and downstairs into every nook and corner. Margaret swept up shovelfuls of their droppings. Shelf-linings had been nibbled into minute fragments, chewed lumps of fur dropped out of skin rugs, rolled up by the side of the stairs. But it was not only mice; Campagne Orovida was in a mess. Saucepans, with remains of food congealed into a green mould, had been pushed out of sight in the kitchen; dirty cups and saucers, with the lees of tea and coffee, and littered with ash and cigarette-ends were strewn in every room on tables, beds and floors. Windows had broken panes and the garden outside the studio was neglected and overgrown with coarse grass. Margaret's holiday was spent in restoring cleanliness and order.

In November, the Trustees of the Tate Gallery "accepted with grateful thanks" Lucien's offer of his father's *Cardeuse de Laine*, painted in 1880 on cement. Heavy and brittle, it had been twice broken. After the first breakage and restoration, Julie gave it to Lucien; then a workman in his studio had knocked it over, and again it had had to be repaired. The restorations are now beginning to discolour and there are several other diagonal breaks extending from the top left to the right-hand side. In this same month Lucien presented to the Victoria and Albert Museum six books of the Eragny Press, together with fourteen original drawings of the illustrations, and twenty-two proofs of the woodcuts.

1934–1936

The year began auspiciously. The President and Council of the Royal Academy purchased under the terms of the Chantrey Bequest two of Lucien's oil paintings, *All Saints' Church, Hastings* (painted in 1918), and *April, Epping* (painted in 1893), at 125 and 150 guineas respectively. In March, Lucien, at Campagne Orovida, wrote to Orovida: "I am not surprised that the fresh colours of your pictures don't look as if they had changed. Those colours were used by your grandfather all his life, and you know that his pictures have not lost their freshness." Soon he was at Cotignac where he painted during the months of April, May and June. He said how extraordinary was the evolution which took place in him even when he was not working. He had frequently noticed this, it seemed that the subconscious mind was never really at rest. Wet weather and his health interrupted his work, one *séance* a day exhausted his strength. His legs troubled him. He was accustomed to paint standing, but this became so great a strain that he had to sit and rest. Cotignac, he said, was a curious place, almost too picturesque. Back in England, he worked during August and September in Essex, first at Langham, then at Stratford St. Mary. He wrote to Manson: "The weather is fine indeed, the changes between morning, noon, and evening are really too much for an old man like me. So I caught a cold and am in bed today. I also feel disappointed with my work. My method is too slow to be able to complete quickly enough the beautiful fugitive effects at this season. People like the old impressionists managed to do it, but they were so extraordinarily skilful. This is one of the reasons why I wanted so much to show you my work, especially as I am getting slower and slower, probably I am more difficult to satisfy than in the old time. Given the little time you have to work it seems to me that you get results much quicker; in harmony, light and texture. I suppose I am getting old." Lucien was seventy-one that September evening.

In December there was an impressive exhibition at the *Marcel Bernheim Galérie* in Paris, *Pissarro et ses Fils*, where works by Camille, Lucien, Manzana, Rodo and Paulémile were shown. Fénéon wrote to Esther that he had hoped to have seen Lucien there "where I have been able to admire his masterly pictures, full of his personality. The exhibition is important, a beautiful show where one is able to meet the sons of the great Camille, all different from him, and each different from the other." One of the pictures Lucien showed, *The Garden at Dartmouth*, painted in 1922, was acquired by the French State for seven thousand francs (£87. 10s.) for the Luxembourg. Lucien had not been able to go to Paris: he was again in hospital. His prostate trouble had recurred due to lack of medical care after his first operation, and, in consequence, a stricture had formed caused by a gradual growth of fibrous scar tissue. This time the operation was successful, but it was again many weeks before he was able to leave his bed. When he was well enough to go home, it was impossible to do so, since workmen occupied the new studio, and all day long there was the clamour of hammers. The Brook was no place for an invalid. Esther had indulged her craving for alterations and improvements while he was in hospital and was supervising a plan to make the studio into a separate flat. A sleeping gallery and a bathroom were being added, and a lavatory converted into a kitchen. This involved the demolition and rebuilding of an outside wall, and trouble with the conduit in which, under the side of the house, flowed the waters of the Brook. Lucien went to stay in rooms at an hotel in Richmond (Surrey) for three months. Here, as he recovered his health, he painted a series of river-side pictures.

For six weeks in June and July of 1935, there was an important exhibition of Lucien's work at the Manchester City Art Gallery. Sixty-six oils and twenty-seven drawings were perfectly hung in two large rooms under the supervision of the curator, Lawrence Haward. Margaret Pilkington, a wood engraver, who served on the Arts Committee, invited Lucien, Esther and Orovida to be her guests for the opening week-end. Unable to have them at her home, as her father was ill, she engaged rooms for them at the Midland Hotel. When he arrived in Manchester, Lucien was made much of by civic dignitaries and art lovers. He was fêted and honoured, dined and wined, and the week-end was a great occasion, one long to be remembered—the best exhibition, he said, he had ever had.

1937

Lucien once more fled from the treacherous English winter. In March, he and Esther were at the *Hôtel du Cours*, Cotignac, where the town clock strikes twice for those who do not hear it the first time. Their nephew, John Bensusan-Butt, and Sam, Esther's brother, were also living at the hotel: John painting, and Sam writing his daily quota of 1,500 words, either of a story or an essay. His first Essex book, *A Countryside Chronicle,** had been published in 1907. He was then a young and pompous London journalist with a shoot in Essex, then quite the "doggish" thing to have, where he entertained Gaiety girls. On these occasions Ruth was shoo'ed away. But as he gradually got more interested in his neighbours, he sat and chatted for hours in stuffy cottages, and so began the stories and sketches of Essex life which made him widely known, both through his books and the radio. John was Lucien's favourite nephew: "I have a great affection for the boy and think a lot of his talent," he wrote to Manson, asking him to write a

* *A Countryside Chronicle: Leaves from the Diary of an Idle Year.* In 4 seasons. Illustrated. Heinemann. 1907.

foreword to the catalogue of John's first exhibition at the Goupil Gallery. He had first begun to draw when a small boy, Ruth ingeniously encouraging her three children to use chalks by installing a nine-foot long blackboard in their playroom.

In 1935, Lucien staying at the Minories, wrote to John: "I have seen your latest and I am very pleased with it: I see that you have applied what I tried to explain to you. There is one or two things I must explain to you next time we meet and then the next step would be only for you to work and work till you develop your own style, for after all what is teachable in art is so very little that it is not worth while passing years in an art school! To put things in a simple formula, it means putting in the close relation one's own feeling and nature: how to do it, everyone has to find out for himself. The master can only tell you how he does it himself, that is provided he has some feelings of his own." And in May of 1937, he wrote from Cotignac, when John had gone: "If you aren't a Pissarro you are certainly 'School of Eragny', and the school is glad to have you as a disciple. I am sure my father would have liked your work and would have encouraged you just as much as I have tried to do." A few days later: "Have you begun your campaign to paint in oils? (John invariably painted in water-colour). Do not forget, if you get into difficulties, you can always ask me what you want to know. Separate your touches, put them side by side. First, the light, second, the shadow, third, the local colour of objects: naturally every touch must be in value. Work in dots to begin with, reserving the right to develop a freer handling when you are used to analysing the elements which make up the colour of things." When John tried oils he told him he was painting far too flatly. Much of his preparatory painting Lucien called *engraisser la toile*, fattening the canvas. He warned John that oil was a medium not to be mastered quickly!

Lucien and Esther had arrived at Cotignac in Lizzie, a few minutes ahead of the bus which brought their luggage. Madame Luche, the former proprietress, darted forward to kiss Esther on both cheeks which made John comment that Esther had mastered the art of being both a nuisance and beloved. "We are being very firm with Esther," he wrote to his mother, "and between us should manage to sit on her effectively when necessary. Her first meeting with Sam was extraordinarily funny, a series of declarations by Sam that he was not interested in this, didn't want to hear that, and he'd leave by the seven o'clock bus if she dared insist about the other." In July, Lucien was back at The Brook and glad to have his studio again as a working place instead of, as he said, a kitchen, drawing-room and only sometimes studio—a disastrous state of affairs, "for it makes one take the habit of not working". In October a second visit was made to Cotignac, John planning to arrive late, to avoid Esther persuading him to paint her favourite *motifs*. This worked well, but one day Esther insisted on a drive in Lizzie while Lucien remained indoors. It was beating with rain, a drifting mist covered the landscape. They roared up hills slowly in first gear so as to not miss anything, but nothing could be seen. "Oh," exclaimed Esther, "if only it had been different weather. There's such a lovely view from here. And in February there are the smallest pimpernels I've ever seen under that rock."

On his way to Cotignac, Lucien had been held up in the Grand Hotel, Toulon, with a *forte bronchite*. He wrote to Rodo: "Ruth's eldest son, John Bensusan-Butt, who had been bitten by the daemon of art and, by Jove, has quite a marked talent, is staying in Paris for a few days. I tell you in case he calls on you, so that you can make him welcome. He's an intelligent lad, well educated, who understands artistic matters. I have guided his studies a little." In Paris, John made himself known to Rodo who introduced him to John Rewald.

In 1932, John Rewald had gone to Paris for a year to study the history of art, but when Hitler came to leadership he did not return to Germany, the more so as his father Dr. Bruno Rewald, a bio-chemist, and his Russian wife had immediately migrated to England. While preparing his Sorbonne thesis on Cézanne, young Rewald met Rodo, they became warm friends and Rewald lunched or dined with Rodo at least once a week, stayed repeatedly at his country house, and went with him to Dieppe to explore the places where Camille had painted. Rodo suggested that on one of Rewald's frequent visits to his parents in London, he should make himself known to Lucien. With a letter of introduction from him, Rewald called at The Brook and was cordially received by Lucien, Esther and Orovida. He asked if Lucien had any Cézanne material, to which Lucien replied that he had not, but pulled out a drawer and added: "But here I have several hundred letters from my father which might interest you." It was agreed then and during numerous subsequent visits that Rewald would edit these letters for publication when he had finished his thesis, and the publication of Cézanne's correspondence. In 1937, when work had begun on the letters, Lucien wrote to Rodo about the project and sent him a batch of Camille's letters to read. Rodo raised objections. He thought it

would be stupid to publish the letters. "The private lives of artists have
nothing to do with art, also writers are very fond of anecdotes." The
reading of the letters saddened him. "This perpetual struggle to find
money is terrible enough, but it is more awful to hear about those fits
of depression, the lamentations and disappointments. It is a long nightmare." But, persuaded of the importance of the letters, he became as
unremitting as Lucien in helping Rewald, indeed he became so interested as to plan, when the letters were published, to collaborate with
Rewald in a life of Camille. It was never written. Rodo is dead, and an
authentic life of Camille has yet to appear.

The letters were copied in England under the supervision of Esther.
Rodo corrected the many mistakes made by the typist, Rewald edited
and prepared footnotes. A French publisher was found, and advance
excerpts appeared in periodicals, but when war came the printing had
to be postponed. Rewald by this time had become a *Docteur ès-lettres*
and had published several books. Although influential friends had
assured him that in the event of war he would be automatically
naturalised, in the ensuing panic bred of spy mania he was interned as
an enemy alien at Vierzon, Cher. Friends, in France and in London,
did all they could to obtain his release, and finally they succeeded.
When France fell, Rewald and his young wife, despite dangers and
difficulties, managed to reach America. He was able to take his material
with him. His flight to New York explains why the first edition of
Camille Pissarro: Letters to his Son Lucien was published in an English
translation, and not, as first intended, in the original French of the
letters. A French edition, issued in Paris after the war, included selected
letters from Lucien to his father.

Lucien had a warm affection for Rewald; he was regarded at The
Brook as one of the family. Rewald never failed to visit the Pissarros
when he was in London, and corresponded regularly when he was not.
The correspondence continued between London and New York during the war, but as Lucien aged Rewald found it increasingly difficult
to obtain information and details concerning his father's letters which
he required for footnotes in the book. But by this time forty years had
elapsed since Lucien had received them.

After the Pissarro letters had been published (a source of happiness to
Rewald that this was while Lucien was still alive), Rewald embarked on
a detailed history of Impressionism, rendered possible by Alfred H.
Barr, Jr., Director of the Museum of Modern Art, who arranged for
him to be financed by the Museum, which subsequently issued the

book, the first publication not directly connected with its activities, and covering a period preceding the one in which it was primarily interested. The success of the book, now among the required reading for many university courses on modern art, prompted the Museum to commission a sequel on Post-Impressionism.

Rewald's intimate knowledge of Camille Pissarro (Rewald said he felt closer to him than to any other of the Impressionists), his friendship with Lucien and Rodo, and his familiarity with Camille's private papers, enabled him to make Camille the key figure of his *History of Impressionism*. He had conceived this book, despite its scholarly approach, as not unlike a novel, involving as it did people whom he had to bring alive. Camille provided the most opportune central figure from whom to branch out. He is also the only old-guard Impressionist prominently cast in Rewald's first Post-Impressionist book. This was demanded by Camille's friendship with Seurat and Signac, his participation in the Neo-Impressionist movement, and his friendship with Gauguin, and he will appear again in Rewald's next Post-Impressionist book as a defender of Cézanne and an early admirer of such artists as the *Douanier* Rousseau.

XVa. Portrait of Lucien by J. B. Manson, 1940

XVb. J. B. Manson with his portrait of his daughter

(*Collection Orovida Pissarro*)

XVI Ryland's Copse (Devon). Lucien Pissarro, 1913. Oil on canvas,
$25\frac{1}{2} \times 21\frac{1}{4}$.

CHAPTER XXI

English Law. Manson's Cockcrow. 1938–1939

RODO CONTINUED TO WORK ASSIDUOUSLY ON THE CATALOGUE OF Camille's paintings, and there was a constant exchange of letters between him and Lucien. Pictures were traced, owners corresponded with, a photograph obtained here, and the particulars noted. Lucien, at home at The Brook, was told by John's brother, David, that a painting by Camille was being shown for sale in the shop window of an art dealer in Shaftesbury Avenue. The description of the subject puzzled him; he could not remember such a picture, and it certainly was not listed in the catalogue. He went to the shop to see if he could identify it. A glance was enough. The picture was one painted by himself in 1896 at Epping, titled *Les Prairies* and sold for a trifling sum. In December, 1936, it had reappeared at a sale at Sotheby's and had been knocked down for £22. But the picture Lucien saw was not quite the same. The signature had been altered: the L had become a C. Lucien, angered, returned home, and consulted Esther. What could he do? David Bensusan-Butt called at the shop, professed interest in the picture and was assured by the dealer that he could gurantee it as a genuine Camille Pissarro. The next move, Lucien was advised, was to establish that the dealer was the purchaser of the Lucien picture at Sotheby's. Esther went to the shop accompanied by a photographer who kept in the background. As Esther talked to the dealer at the shop door, the photographer, unnoticed, managed to take his photograph. The picture was now no longer in the window and the dealer boasted he had recently sold a Camille Pissarro for £450. From the photograph, he was identified at Sotheby's as the buyer of the picture sold by them in December, 1936, described in the catalogue as an oil painting by Lucien Pissarro. With this evidence Lucien asked the Imperial Arts League to take legal action for him. Their reply was disconcerting. Their solicitors advised that forgery of this description was not considered a criminal action under English law. Lucien's only action could be for damages, but it would be a bad case, as his reputation could not be said to have suffered because one of his pictures had been attributed to his famous father! Lucien, not satisfied, attended at Bow Street, but here the magistrate rejected his application for a prosecution, on the grounds that there could be no case unless the picture was produced in court. As the present owner of the picture was not known, this was impossible. Lucien, strong in faith in English justice, and convinced that the law must be on his side in such an obvious case of forgery, and false pretences, now appealed to St. John Hutchinson, K.C. He told him he was unable to pay him the fee his standing required, but if he would undertake the case he offered him the choice of any one of his pictures. St. John Hutchinson accepted, and the case was heard at the Old Bailey. A letter which Lucien wrote to *The New Statesman* records the result and his reactions:

"Sir—I am not a lawyer and do not claim to appreciate all the subtleties of our legal system. An episode that has occurred to me recently makes me think that my profession at least cannot easily protect its honour and interests.

"I was recently told that a picture by my father Camille Pissarro was exhibited in a dealer's shop window. My informant not having succeeded in getting details about it for the catalogue of my father's works which is in preparation, I went to the shop myself and recognised it immediately as one of my own. My signature had been effaced and C. Pissarro painted in. For the sake of my father and myself, I put the matter in the hands of my solicitor. But five visits to court, first about the copyright and then about false pretences, failed to secure the erasure of the false signature, and the picture is now apparently sold. I am therefore in the position of knowing that someone—I do not know who—possesses a picture I painted, and in all probability believes that the picture is my father's; and I cannot but fear that some day the owner of the picture will suspect me of having had a hand in a very despicable act.

"Now there is, of course, no doubt that the case was tried perfectly fairly, and that the result was in accordance with the law. May one not suspect, however, that if a grocer had offered for sale margarine as fresh butter the result would have been different?

"If things like this happen to artists—I see nothing to prevent it—surely some tightening up of the relevant parts of the law is necessary?

Lucien Pissarro."

There is little doubt that the dealer was unscrupulous. He tried to persuade Clifford Hall to alter the costumes and hair styles of pictures from one century to another, a common trick of fakers. Hall did not respond. While painting his picture of *The Caledonian Market* (now in the London Museum) Hall had met and become friendly with the dealer's assistant, who sold antiques and china from a stall in the market. Hall, having only recently left the Royal Academy schools, was then unknown and was trying to interest West-End dealers in his work. After a weary day of walking from one to another laden with heavy portfolios he was glad to rest in the shop and for his "Caledonian Market" friend to make him a cup of tea. Curious as to the pictures displayed for sale, particularly those purporting to be by artists then fetching high prices in the auction-rooms, he suggested that they were fakes. "All of them!" the naïve old fellow laconically replied. "Who painted those Birket Fosters?" "Somebody up in Manchester. Thirty bob a time." "Does that include the signature?" "Gracious no. The boss does that." Sometimes, said the assistant, a customer would return and say he had failed to authenticate the picture he had bought. "The boss never argues. He says he sold it in good faith, believing it to be genuine. 'If you are not satisfied, you can have your money back' he tells them."

The dealer was not an expert, he could sell fakes but not judge them. Once a runner came into the shop and offered him a chalk drawing in red and black for thirty shillings. Hall looked at it: it was a Watteau. "Oh, no," said the dealer. "It's a fake," he told the runner. "I don't want it." It came up at Sotheby's soon after and fetched £250. There were two genuine pictures in the shop. Whistler nocturnes. They were kept locked up in a safe.

Fourteen years after Lucien's death a strange postscript was added to the episode. In 1958, Orovida's telephone bell rang. The call came from an unknown young man. On holiday for a few days in London he said he would like to show Orovida a picture which his mother so valued that when she had been forced to abandon her home in Czechoslovakia, she would not leave it behind. Rolling the canvas, she had taken it with her on a terrible journey with other refugees to Palestine.

The signature on the picture was indistinct, the young man thought it might be Pissarro, could he bring it to Orovida for identification? Orovida identified it at once. It was *Les Prairies*.

In April came disconcerting news of Manson who had gone to Paris on an official duty as Director of the Tate to attend the opening ceremony of an exhibition of British Painting at the Louvre. In a letter to Elizabeth Manson, Manson wrote: "Out early in top-hat for the opening, followed by an official lunch. Afterwards, when I went to the flat to change, I passed out and slept for five hours."

Something more than that had happened. After the lunch there had been some more than usually dull speeches and Manson exhausted from a long journey, and feeling desperately ill, became bored. In the middle of one oration, he suddenly stood up, cried *"vive la France"*, and crowed like a cock. Although his ribald comment had passed almost unnoticed, except for subdued laughter from French friends, it was not so in London, where one or two of the English guests indignantly complained of unseemly conduct to the Trustees of the Tate. French official circles, they said, had been outraged by the incident. The miserable result of this was that Manson was retired on medical grounds. Nearing the age of sixty, he was within a few months of the time when civil servants then had no option but to retire. So it did not much matter. It did however matter to Manson. Convinced that he was the victim of an intrigue, he felt himself humiliated and disgraced. "Yesterday," he remarked, "I had five hundred friends. Now today I doubt if I have five." In one way the calamity appeared as a relief. For many years he had longed for freedom from official duties to give him time to paint, not only at week-ends and holidays, but every day. Now he planned to rent a studio and spend the rest of his life doing the one thing he wanted to do. But it was not be. The war came, and with it, illness, and once more he was only able to paint at intervals. His resignation led to a further convulsion. He left the wife he had lived with for thirty-six years, and from then until his death he shared his existence with the woman he had loved since 1920. Whilst this did not effect the friendship between him and Lucien, it created difficulties with Esther. Loyal to Lilian, Manson's wife, whom she had known for many years, she could not bring herself to recognise Elizabeth. The two women did not speak until the day of Lucien's funeral.

Meanwhile domestic peace was threatened. Over Europe the shadow of Hitler stretched more and more menacingly. Fear grew.

The Swastika had become the symbol of cruelty, persecution, ruthlessness and war. Trenches were dug in England, air-raid shelters constructed, gas-masks issued, the Navy mobilised. The gullible Chamberlain had been to Berchtesgaden (strange stories were told of the Führer rolling in a frenzy on the floor and biting the carpet), and now he tried Munich, returning in triumph, waving a piece of paper, signed by Hitler, a solemn undertaking that their two countries would never resort to war. "Peace in our time." Lord Beaverbrook continued pontificating that there would be no war: spend your money, kiss your sweethearts. Winston Churchill, one among few, remained unconvinced. He declared: "The German dictator, instead of snatching his victuals from the table, has been content to have them served to him course by course", and he warned his hearers in the House "that his demands at the pistol-point would not cease". Lucien also had no faith in appeasement or the magic preventive of Chamberlain's impeccably rolled silk umbrella, which did not seem quite adequate should rough weather come. The French blood in Lucien with good cause distrusted the Germans: they had destroyed Camille's pictures in 1870, the pictures had suffered a narrow escape in the Kaiser war, and now he again feared for their safety as well as for those of his own. The most important Camille pictures in his collection were taken off the walls of The Brook and packed into the travelling picture boxes which had been made and slotted when his father was alive by the village carpenter at Eragny. The rest of the Camille's were already in a safe deposit in Chancery Lane: it was decided to leave them there. Lucien divided his own pictures into two categories, the less important ones being left in the picture rack in the new studio. The important pictures, together with a trunk of water-colours and, drawings, were carted by road to Orovida's friends, the Bekassys, to their farm near Bury St. Edmunds, and the boxes containing the Camille pictures went to Esther's brother, Sam, to his house at Langham, near Colchester.

CHAPTER XXII

Flight from London. 1939–1941

WHEN WAR CAME, LUCIEN AND ESTHER RESOLVED TO GO TO THE WEST country. It was Lucien's farewell to The Brook; he was never to see it again. They set off in Lizzie, burdened to her capacity. Already the country was crowded with evacuated children and mothers, rooms were difficult to find, and for a time a stay was made in Lymington, but in November they were at Axminster. Esther wrote that Lymington was a lovely place with hundreds of *motifs* for Lucien, but the landlady was horrid, a virago. She told Lucien that her house was not a nursing home, not a place for invalids, and that they had come under false pretences. There was nothing for it but to go. Esther drove to Axminster, where rooms had been promised, through torrential rain and a howling cold wind. Three miles from Winterbourne Abbas the over-weighted Lizzie broke down, the accelerator spring and the big end had gone. Lizzie gave no shelter, and in the rain and wind, soaked to the skin, Lucien and Esther had to sit patiently and wait for help and a tow to a garage, the rest of the journey being accomplished in a taxi-cab, "Fortunately," Esther wrote to Manson, "we got no harm, although I was scared for Lucien. We had an awful week at Lymington and Lucien is very depressed, wonders if he will ever see his pictures again. You know, if only he could work in London, and if it was warm enough, I feel sure he would be best at home. I went all over a glorious little village near here, Wilmington, on the Honiton road, and there was not a place to be had, but the country was wonderful. Not having the car, Lucien can get out so little, and it rains every day. The place is full of soldiers and evacuees. We are longing to get settled. Poor John Rewald is not free yet. Some weeks ago his wife wrote that she had had a charming letter from the Director of the *Musées de France* who said he had given in the 'dossier' himself! I heard from her yesterday and she said she had no news of his release. They have been married six months and so soon separated."

Lucien wrote to Orovida from Axminster that they were staying with a nice woman who looked after him and Esther "very motherly".

The food was good, but the beds hard and English-like. "But she cannot keep us, we have to leave this afternoon." That same day Lucien had a letter from Manson whom he had invited for a visit: "Things could not be worse than they are at the moment. In fact I could not pay for a ticket to Axminster." On the 17th November Lucien and Esther were in a boarding house at Lyme Regis. Lucien had a beautiful view from his window, but it was, he said, the coldest place he had been in this winter. It was so cold that he was unable to leave the fireside to stand and paint at the closed window.

Rodo's catalogue was at last published in Paris. Paul Rosenberg wrote to his secretary, Winifred Easton, in London, "it is really a marvel", and asked her to get in touch with Lucien and tell him he would like to buy some of his father's pictures. Esther answered that they had several pictures which they would be willing to sell. Rosenberg, through Miss Easton, promptly replied he would like the three pictures: *La Route de Versailles, Louveciennes, La mi-carême sur les Boulevards,* and *Le Terre-plein du Pont Neuf.** He offered £2,000 for the three, "immediate and for cash". Lucien thought the price too low and Esther replied they would accept £3,000. It was a courageous gesture. In the last two years Lucien had sold two pictures, buyers had been scared by the menace of war, no one was buying pictures, and Lucien, living on the small capital he had left, was overdrawn at the bank. His friends in London, particularly Manson, concerned at his lack of money, were trying to obtain a Civil List pension for him.

He and Esther were now at Coney Cottage, Fishpond, Dorset, and Lucien wrote to Orivida that the days were sunny but cold. "I have not started work yet, but pass the whole day at the corner of the chimney near the fire."

Rosenberg cabled: "Unable to accept offer stop will you accept", and there was nothing for it but for Esther to reply "yes". Money had become all-important again. But now the Germans were in the Low Countries and the French Government refused Rosenberg's application to send the purchase money. "They won't let any money go abroad until they can be certain that its equivalent in goods will arrive in France." As the traffic service between England and France had been suspended, there was little hope of the pictures reaching Paris.

One door closed, another opened. Lucien had two pictures on show with the Travelling Exhibition of the Artists' International Society.

* Numbers 77, 996 and 1226 in Rodo's catalogue.

The curator of the Hereford Art Gallery wrote to the organisers that he had received a gift of £100 for the purchase of one picture, and that with this he would like to buy *Mist, Sun, and Smoke, Hastings* (painted 1918), but the picture was catalogued at 130 guineas. Would Lucien accept the £100? The offer, coming at this anxious time, was accepted. Only a week or so later for the curator to write that his committee refused to authorise the purchase. Miss Easton hoped that, somehow or other, the Rosenberg offer would still be practical, but on the 23rd May she reported that he had disappeared. There was no news of him at all, she was anxious for his safety and feared he had been arrested by the Gestapo. With him disappeared the stock of Rodo's catalogue, never distributed. Later copies came to be on sale in Switzerland at the price of fifty to sixty pounds each. In 1944, Miss Easton wrote to Esther, and quoted from a letter from Rosenberg, who said that when he left France, practically all the copies were left behind in Paris, "most probably the Germans got hold of them and sold them. There is no manuscript in existence and the catalogue could only be reprinted by using one of the orginal copies". Orovida had a set of the page proofs, and these she had lent to the Leicester Galleries who returned them bound into a book. It is now almost impossible to get a copy of the catalogue. Rodo had worked on it for twenty years, the correspondence alone that was involved was enormous, but, his task completed, he did not receive a penny. He did not mind. He had regarded the compiling of the catalogue not only as a labour of love, which, as it turned out, it was, but as a duty which he owed to his father.

At the beginning of July, Miss Easton wrote that she had received a telegram from Rosenberg: he had escaped from France and was at Caldas da Rainha in Portugal.

Lizzie again broke down on the road, Esther being rescued by Mr. Perrott, a haulage contractor, who towed Lizzie to a garage. Esther told Perrott that she was looking for a small furnished house but it seemed hopeless. On the contrary, said Perrott, there was one to let near here at Hewood. Hill Cottage. A letter was written to the owner, terms were arranged, and the cottage was rented. But no sooner had they moved in than the landlady, a prickly and difficult spinster, the daughter of a country clergyman, began to be troublesome. She heard that Lucien was almost an invalid, and for some reason this disturbed her. She wished to get rid of her new tenants, and suggested they would be more comfortable elsewhere: in her letter she enclosed particulars of a "lady's" cottage near Exeter to be let "privately". As this failed to elicit a reply from Esther, weary of searching for some haven for Lucien, and content to come to rest, the landlady now sent a formidable list of stipulations and restrictions. The house must be kept as it was, no alterations, no additional furniture moved in. This she felt strongly about as "this is no time for spending money as we are on the verge of a siege". Esther had written that the sitting-room would make a nice studio for Lucien: this could not be allowed, and it should have been mentioned before the cottage was rented. Hanging on the walls were some wishy-washy water-colours by the landlady's aunt. These, under no circumstances, were to be moved. They were best there, and there would come to no harm. Her wishes were respected. The pictures in Essex had been moved again, first to Mrs. Clark's house at Fishpond, now they were at Hill Cottage. The Camilles were hung unframed over the dismal insipid water-colours. It is difficult to surmise the root of the landlady's objections to Lucien and Esther, for they gave no real cause of complaint. Perhaps she had in her mind a mental picture of them as ungodly bohemians who, with their wild parties and way of life, would wreck her home. She made one more attempt to get rid of them, and sent Esther a month's notice to vacate the premises. There was no written agreement and Esther was advised to ignore the letter. She did, and remained in possession. But indignant letters of protest still arrived from time to time.

The ground rose from the village to the house which had a view of the small cluster of cottages and of the surrounding gentle contour of hills. Immediately in front of the house a common, which became a bog in winter, sloped up to Muddy Lane. In their early days at Hewood, and in the sunny weeks of the 1940 spring and summer, Lucien's easel and painting stool were perched on the common. With the help of Esther's arm, he was able to stumble there from the house and sit and paint. A visitor asked a farmhand where he could find Mr. Pissarro. "Why there be 'e sitting up there with his blackboard," was the reply. Lucien did not paint on Sundays out of respect for the prejudices of the villagers. Hewood was crowded with evacuated children from London; one East-Ender locked his teacher in the school coalshed and threw the key away! They were a rough lot, but did not interfere with Lucien. Occasionally they would stand, finger in mouth, watching with wonder the picture on his canvas grow with touches of a brush.

Lucien was now seventy-seven, enfeebled, unable to walk without assistance, his hearing nearly gone, more and more withdrawn into himself. Sometimes Perrott took him about in a wheeled chair. He felt himself isolated from all those things he had loved, particularly the talk of his friends. In early days at Hewood the weather had been bad. Lucien wrote to Manson: "I have not been well during these east winds. I managed to paint (?) two pictures from the windows. I have no idea what they are like, having felt all the time that I did not know how to paint. I am longing to see them later, they will probably be quite bad and clumsy. I put the colours on at hazard, not knowing what I was doing. A very queer experience. Come and help me."

But he continued to write letters of advice to John: "I am delighted you have done a still life and I advise you to do some more . . . so that you can develop your own technique. I could have told you how I should go about it, but I wanted you to find out for yourself how to use this damnable medium (*sacrée matière*) which is terribly difficult. Even if I could tell you something you could or should have done, like this you will progress in your own way, which is important. Art schools which teach technique don't turn out artists unless they are so very talented that they can afford to waste several years shedding what they have been taught." Here followed some remarks on politics. "Enough of that! Let's work. It's the only happiness!"

There was a farm next to the cottage; in a field a lambing shed stood on wheels, now never used, as there were no sheep any longer. Esther thought how well it could serve Lucien to sit in and, sheltered from the weather, he would be able to paint out of doors. She asked Retter, the farmer, if it could be rented. He was helpful. He did not want rent, he would have it moved to the side of the house, make a break in the wooden fence which ran along the garden, and put in a gate, this, with a rail fixed along the hedge would make it easy for Lucien to get from the house to the shed. Esther wrote to tell the landlady of this and said the fence would be restored when the cottage was vacated. A furious letter resulted. How dare Esther interfere with her property!

Esther was also getting old, but more than ever convinced that her way was the right way, and intolerant of criticism. She could get little help in the house from the village, and Lucien demanded much care and time. Orovida, disturbed at the difficulties these two old people had to contend with, and the strain on her mother, felt it her duty to give up her painting and go and give them what help she could. Esther was not grateful. She became a second Julie, hard to please and exacting. Orovida undertook the cooking, worked about the house, dug and sowed vegetables in the field outside the cottage. It was not enough; Esther nagged her to fresh tasks. Orovida was patient, but occasionally there were fierce quarrels.

Early in October an incendiary bomb penetrated the roof of The Brook and burned a hole on the main water-pipe where it had lodged: the escaping water extinguished the flames. Later, two incendiaries dropped into the garden, but as they did not explode, no harm was done. On the night of the 15th October a rain of incendiaries descended on the studios in Gilston Road including the one lived in by Manson. His furniture, clothes, personal belongings, all were destroyed by fire and water, but he saved his pictures. "Got out with overcoat over pyjamas and felt slippers on feet," he wrote to Lucien. "My dear Old Boy," Lucien replied. "How dreadful, what luck you were not badly hurt. I wonder how you managed to get to Esher in your pyjamas and slippers.* All the same it was lucky your pictures were not destroyed. I really wish you could come to this nice little village where you could work. The weather has been fine. The trees are turning of a lovely colour. Do try to come and have a rest. It would be like the lovely old times when we were working together at Fishpond, which is quite near this place. Much love from your old friend, Lucien Pissarro."

Rosenberg arrived in New York and now offered 10,000 dollars for the three Camille pictures "payable arrival subject you paying war insurance sixty shillings per cent sterling". The dollar was then 4.02 to the £. The offer was accepted. "When, at long last," Miss Easton wrote, "the licences are in order, the pictures can be packed," but it was not until the end of November that Orovida finally completed her struggles with a Bank of England C.D.3. form, and forms required to be filled up in triplicate, applying for permission to the Board of Trade to send the pictures out of England. "Explain," advised Miss Easton, "that the pictures are classed under works of art." Esther wrote to Manson: "We have had rather an agitated time and I am ashamed we did not thank you for all the trouble you have taken about the Civil List pension. It has been a dreadful wrench to let those three pictures go and so far. They looked so lovely. We had to accept Rosenberg's offer. Well they've gone and we only trust that no U-boat will get near." The pictures safely reached New York, but it was not until early in the New Year that Rosenberg's money was received, and a bank overdraft of £150 repaid.

Now there was a new alarm bringing anxiety and worry, Lucien being notified that the Safe Deposit in Chancery Lane had been burnt

* He went in borrowed clothes.

to the ground by the action of oil bombs. The Camille pictures there had been stored in safes in the cellars, so it was not possible to say what had happened to them for a week or so, until an entrance into the cellars could be made. This was terrible blow to Lucien; his agitation was intense. It seemed, recalling 1871, that the Germans had a special hate for his father's work. It being impossible for him, in his state of health, to travel to London, and Esther not caring to leave him, Orovida undertook the journey and camped at The Brook. She sought out Manson and enlisted his aid. For days he gave all his time to her, comforting, consoling, and helping with decisions. They went together to Chancery Lane. The devastation appalled them. The building was gone, workmen with dippers and cranes were clearing the ground where it had once stood of a wilderness of débris. The cellars were under a crater: a workman said they could get into what was left of them "if they cared to chance it". There was a ladder they could use, "over there, against the girders". Or there was a staircase. "Whichever way you go, it isn't safe!" Manson and Orovida gingerly descended the stairs and, after searching, found the safe and unlocked it. The boxes containing the pictures were opened; at a first glance they seemed undamaged, but at the bottom of the safe was stagnant water, and as the pictures were examined, the paint began to lift.

A fortnight later it was possible to move them, the boxes being hoisted by a muddy crane and dropped into a van. Messrs. Stiles of Hammersmith put a workshop at Orovida's disposal, and here the pictures were taken and the water-colours and etchings laid out to dry. The oils were filthy, and it was first thought that the chill of the atmosphere to which they had been exposed, and the smears of chemicals on the canvases, had ruined them. Herbert Walker was consulted, and after a year's work he was able, by judicious cleaning, to restore the paintings to their original condition, an extraordinary example of patience and skill. But nothing could be done with the water-colours. They were utterly ruined. As were also three exquisite Camille fans painted on silk.

1941

When Lucien received payment from Rosenberg he wrote to Manson. He has had a bit of luck, he said, and enclosed a cheque for £50. Soon Lucien wrote again: "Dear Old Boy, I am so anxious to see you for a very selfish reason. Since my last illness I am only beginning to work a little. I can do no more than one sitting a day. At first I did seem to have lost all power of painting, and I had to try learning how to do it. I did things which appear very bad, and it is only my last picture which seems a little better. I am anxious to show them you to have your advice. You are the only painter friendly enough to me for me to have any confidence to ask advice. When you are free again I hope you will be able to help your old friend. I am sending you a small cheque to help you not to be too much out of pocket when you come. Much love from your old friend Lucien." Manson replied that he would come soon, but remonstrated at the cheque. Lucien replied: "Thinking you were having difficulties and my getting a fair amount of cash I thought I would do something (for once that I could) to help a dear friend. Far from me the idea of paying you for any service. Also I thought that to come to Hewood would be an expensive journey and that it would help you to undertake it.

"You have no idea of the kind of old helpless man I have become! I get up very late and pass my day (or what remains of it) sitting near the fire in the rainy or cold weather. I painted only five pictures in 1940. None yet in 1941. We shall be glad to have you with us for as long as you can. Do come soon. It is dreadful to think that your studio might have been saved."

It was not until March that Manson came for a few days to visit his old friend. It was a joy for Lucien to show him his paintings and to sit and talk of happier days, such as, now so far away, the jolly Saturday afternoon gatherings at 19 Fitzroy Street. War-time travelling was never comfortable in overcrowded and delayed trains. Manson on his journey back to London had to stand in a van among insecurely fastened milk churns. Shaken about and exposed to a bitter draught, the result was one of his devastating migraines. Esther was sorry to hear this, and Lucien added a postscript to her letter: "I never realised the drawback of my deafness until you came and it makes me so miserable. I continue to think of the happy time we had together. Well I do hope we shall see you again soon. Much love."

In this month, a Civil List pension of £130 was granted to Lucien for services to art. Lucien wrote to the Prime Minister asking him to accept for the Nation his father's painting: *Anse des Pilotes, Le Hâvre,** which he had already lent to the National Gallery. Winston Churchill replied: "I thank you most warmly for the generous gift of your

---

* Number 1309 in Rodo's catalogue. Camille had lettered on the stretcher: *Anse des pilotes Hâvre matin temps gris brumeux.* Orovida watched Camille painting this picture, she remembers he had difficulty in making the mast appear upright, he considered the use of a plumb line, finally he got it right by eye.

father's picture *Anse des Pilotes, Le Havre*, to the Nation. The circumstances of the gift touch me and I accept it with gratitude. It will be presented to the National Gallery where it will be a treasured possession." He ended the typed letter in his own handwriting: "Your generosity to the Nation will not be forgotten." This letter became a cherished possession, Lucien always carried it about with him in his pocket-book, where it was found after his death.

In May, Esther wrote to Manson: "Lucien is beginning to be a bit more vigorous I think and hope! He has had five *séances* on his second picture and when it is sunny sits in the garden most of the afternoons. I wish you could come again without any work to do, only your own sketching or painting. Now we are beginning to feel that as the disaster (the fire at the safe deposit) happened more than six months ago we ought to make our claim (for compensation under war damage) very soon. Would you be very kind and get in touch with Herbert Walker, and with the help of your notes (made here) make out the claim for us and include your good (well paid) fee as an expert. Do forgive my continual worrying about our business. I do not know what we should do without your help. About thirty-five bombs fell around Fishpond and Marshwood on Tuesday, and one plane was brought down on Lambert Castle. What place is safe, I wonder, for the pictures? No one was hurt."

In a letter from New York (30th September) John Rewald said: "At an exhibition of English wood engravings at the Public Library in N.Y. I saw an etching done by Orovida and that touched me as greetings from far away. I hope your lives so quiet and far away from London will spare you all the emotions of this dreadful war."

One morning, strangers, man and wife, knocked at the door. They said they wished to buy a Camille. Invited in and shown the pictures, they bought a C.P., two Luciens and an Orovida. "Of course they cut down our prices," Lucien told Manson, "but we were glad to have the £1,000 they gave for the C.P. and eighty-four for mine." There was an awkwardness over the payment, the Margulies, the name of the strangers, opening a suitcase full of one-pound notes. Lucien said so much money would be unsafe in a cottage, so Mr. Margulies wrote a cheque. It was a happy morning, for the Margulies now took Lucien and Esther to Yeovil in their small car and gave them a good lunch.*

* The Margulies formed an extraordinary collection, the majority of their pictures being abstract. Their eighty-three pictures were exhibited at the Towner Art Gallery, Eastbourne, in December, 1960.

They were the first of many visitors who now began to call at Hill Cottage and continued to do so until Lucien's death. Some came to buy, journeying from London; others to gaze at the pictures and say how nice they were. The villagers came and even the headmistress of a school, followed into the house by a crocodile of small girls. It pleased and diverted Lucien.

Esther, irked with the difficulties she encountered in a small village of adequately feeding her household, thought egg rationing the last straw. She sent a telegram to Lord Woolton, the Minister of Food: "Impossible to register for eggs in this village nearest town five miles away eggs necessary daily food for delicate husband of seventy-eight elderly vegetarian friend in neighbouring village faces starvation." There was no response. Orovida exchanged two of her own paintings for a weekly supply of eggs, and, when this source was exhausted, she bought some hens.

Before the year was out with characteristic honesty, Lucien wrote to the authorities that he was no longer in need of a Civil List pension. Manson had luck: he sold his portrait of Lucien to the Manchester Art Gallery for £200. Lucien wrote to him in December: "Orovida tells me that you will probably come to see me before Christmas. Please do not leave it too near the holidays as the Government will stop people travelling. I am so anxious to see you as I feel so isolated, never seeing anyone to speak to about art. True I am getting so frightfully deaf that I am unable to follow a conversation, and the result is I feel so out of touch with the outside world. But all the same I should so enjoy having you near. I had a present of some French wine and I am waiting to your visit to drink them. So do come." But Manson was unable to make the journey.

CHAPTER XXIII

Mostly Sad Days. 1942–1951

"COME FOR MY BIRTHDAY PARTY ON 20TH FEBRUARY," LUCIEN AGAIN wrote to Manson early in the New Year. "I was pleased to hear my pictures looked well in the Academy. I have no idea how my work looks among others. It is now such a long time since I have seen an exhibition!—but I am afraid your friendship makes you exaggerate their quality. I heard The Brook has been visited by burglars." Soon, in a further letter: "No wonder you seem so depressed under such conditions (Manson was living in a bungalow. There was snow on the ground and he had no fire and could not get coal). We must be lucky as we had no snow to speak of, and I am writing in a warm room with a lovely log fire. There is nothing like a wood fire to make one cheerful and comfortable. On the other hand, when sunny outside, as it is sometimes, I am ordered by the doctor not to go out, so I pass my days sitting to such an extent that I wonder if I will ever be able to walk again." Later: "My old paint box has become so rickety and shabby that I would like to buy another. I wonder if you could do that for me? I am most happy to think my dear old friend will come for my birthday." Manson did not fail him; when he came for the celebration he brought with him a new paint box. When he had gone, Lucien wrote, in a letter headed *Sunday Night. 12 o'clock*: "It is quite true it made me quite happy to have you though my deafness did prevent me to talk and tell you all I would have liked to explain what I think about Cézanne, and the curious 'incomprehensible' influence he had over the young generation of painters. His motto was 'I will make impressionism an art of museum'. As he worked entirely from nature it is difficult to understand what made his so-called disciples turn away from it. I would understand better if they followed his example of analysing colours and richness of pigments to find patterns based on natural objects without representing a view or panorama of any existing place."

Lucien commented on the Pre-Raphaelites in a letter to John: "Their return to nature had nothing to do with nature for its own sake, but was only a means to collect information to use in their illustrations of literary subjects: besides it was a rotten *milieu*. We, in France, when we decided to return to nature, did it with a blank mind, receiving direct feelings without preconceived ideas, and so got a more healthy result and discovered the poetry of light and sunshine. Of course, you had here great ancestors in the painters like Turner, Constable, Bonington, but extraordinary, they had no *suite* so to speak, except on the continent."

"Although it is so beautiful and hot I have not yet started work. Imagine my dear that I cannot stand nor sit without great pain; my sitting place is all bruises and gives me great pain, and I am so weak on my legs that I can't stand, and in order to paint one's mind must be completely free of everything else."

Sam Bensusan visited Hill Cottage, and on his return to Colchester he told Ruth that Esther treated Orovida wickedly. Ruth wrote and reminded her sister that Orovida had sacrificed herself and her painting to go and live at Hill Cottage to try and help, but Esther was not at all grateful, only grumbled at her. Ruth thought it was as well that Lucien was deaf. Dr. Bruno Rewald wrote and reflected what a curious world it was. "At first the French intern him [his son, John] in a camp, then he has to leave the country, and then, during the occupation, the *Académie Française* award him the *Prix Charles Blance* for his book *Cézanne et Zola*."

Manson had a bad fall. He wrote on 30th June: "I took a header down some stairs with a fifteen-stone friend on top of me. They took me unconscious to St. George's. I had a miserable time lying flat on my back, but I did not break my neck or anything else, so they eventually let me out." "How unfortunate falling on the stairs with a fat man on top of you," Lucien replied. "You are lucky not to have broken any limbs. I wish you could see the way to come to us again. Orovida is very proud of the results of her gardening and of her poultry undertaking. I had started to paint a morning sunny effect, but every morning lately seems to make up its mind to turn grey. That is the drawback of the country: the wretched weather changes from day to day! Well, good-bye, my dear boy. Hoping to be soon delivered of this war, and to be able to come back to London and see some friends. I feel so isolated now, with my deafness. It is a very sad condition."

There was a party at Hill Cottage on the 11th August. On that day Lucien and Esther had been married fifty years. A few friends came and Orovida killed one of her hens. On 17th October, Manson wrote that Lucien's pictures looked very distinguished in the New English Art Club exhibition. "The smaller one, your newer one, has a marvellous light. It was difficult to hang for that reason as it made most of the other things look so dull. They are both beautiful pictures." The letter did not cheer Lucien. "*Hélas*," he wrote. "I am becoming too old to work any more. I cannot go about freely enough, I cannot stand. Having stopped working so long I seem to have lost my technique. Do come for a few more days here." But at least he was no longer troubled with lack of money. There had been many sales this year, and the wealthy artist, Edward Le-Bas, had bought Camille's *Esquisse de la Batterie à Montfoucault,*★ paying £750, and Lucien's *Muddy Lane* was sold to the Rochdale Art Gallery for 80 guineas.

1943–1944

After a visit to Hewood in January, 1943, John wrote to Diana White: "I got to Chard at seven and had a lovely walk up the hill in moonlight. Men and women on bikes came charging down on me, saying good morning as they passed. At the cottage I left my case in the woodshed, and then stood on the lawn waiting for signs of life in the house. A blackbird sang with great variety near by. Then inside the house, a voice: 'Mother! News!' and I knocked, and there were Esther and Orovida down in their dressing-gowns for the eight o'clock (B.B.C. news). The rest is mainly meals, very good (including some of Miss Kyd's Canadian noodle soup very much appreciated by L.P.) but I got O.C.P. out for two short walks. They are very pleased, having got a girl from the village to help in the house, and I hope they won't drive her out, overworking her. Lucien looks very well, much better than last winter, but is very deaf and not working. He sits in the sitting-room and reads: he could work I think if they could make it a studio, but they live round keeping the furniture in order. Lucien longs to be back at The Brook, and talks of trying something quite new."

"I have to ask myself," Lucien wrote to John in February, "if I shall ever really paint again. I am so weak on my legs, I have lost the ability to walk, though perhaps I could teach myself again if the ground here was level. Imagine it, I can hardly keep my balance and I am always nearly falling over. What would happen to me in a London street if I fell against a jeweller's window! Tableau. It's a drunk. Crowd. Policeman. He takes my name, magistrate, etc. etc. No, it's too annoy-

★ No. 368 in Rodo's catalogue.

ing even to think of. With a little work, determination and time, you will regain your confidence. But I, alas, shall never regain mine."

American soldiers came and were billeted in the neighbourhood. One, a Lieutenant J. D. Walp, interested in painting, asked a newsagent in Chard if he knew of any artists living in the district. Lucien's name and address was given him, and he called at Hill Cottage, was asked inside, and met Lucien. Walp said he painted, and that he was an amateur. Lucien thought him a nice boy and, taken with his naïve enthusiasm, showed him his pictures. Walp said they were wonderful, very lovely, and that he would like to buy one, but his face fell when told the prices. Embarrassed, he explained they were beyond his means. Invited to call again, he was unable to do so; a few days after his visit he was in North Africa. He had particularly liked a painting of an Essex landscape, and Lucien wrote and said that if he cared to donate what he could comfortably afford to some society that provided comforts for the Free French, or, if Walp thought their need greater, American soldiers, he could have the picture. Walp was greatly pleased and asked that it be sent to his mother in Ohio. He wrote frequently. He said he kept up his pencil sketching, but some water-colours he tried were failures. In Italy he visited Pompeii, "it must have been a beautiful city in its time. It was a real pleasure and privilege to get a glimpse of the old ruins". He wrote again to say: "I am one of the happiest men in the war today. I have received news that your picture has reached my mother safely. You will never know what a thrill that was. You are two of the most wonderful people alive." In France, he met Rodo and Paul Emile, and through his mother he sent them and Lucien food parcels from America. It was quite an occasion when the first one arrived at Hill Cottage containing almost forgotten luxuries.

An exhibition, "Three Generations of Pissarros", had been held in Lewes; in June, it was transferred to the Leicester Galleries. The three generations were Camille, Lucien and Orovida, and seventy-six oils, water-colours, drawings and etchings were shown.

It was suggested that Lucien might go. The prospect of this jaunt delighted him. He had not seen London for five years. His doctor did not think the journey would result in any harm; on the contrary it might do him a lot of good. Esther and Orovida were to go with him, leaving the cottage and pictures in the care of village friends. Perrott drove the family to Chard, here Lucien's wheeled chair was put into the guard's van, and the family into a reserved compartment. At

Paddington, he was wheeled to a taxi-cab and taken to the Berner's Hotel where he stayed for eight days, Esther and Orivida agreeing that he would be sad and upset to see the neglected Brook.

At the private view at the Leicester Galleries Lucien sat on a chair and held court to the many friends who came to see him. Happy and excited, he shook their hands and tried to hear what they said. It did not much matter that he could not, it was such a joy to see them again. Taken to lunch at the Garrick Hotel, there was a small disappointment. The waiter who had served him in pre-war days had gone. He had appreciated that Lucien was a slow eater, and when, as usual, Lucien ordered two cutlets, he only brought one, keeping the other hot in the kitchen until Lucien was ready for it. This day Lucien spurned cutlets. He ordered smoked salmon, a delicacy to him after his restricted diet at Hill Cottage. The next day Orivida took him in a taxi-cab on a tour of the bombed sites. Wistfully he said he was now content to live in the country until this destruction had ended. Another red letter day was a visit to the Academy. Here he refused to be pushed around in his chair, but insisted on walking through the rooms, missing nothing, taking great delight in seeing again the paintings of other artists. Everything was lovely, and he extolled the merits of the pictures. On another day, on his way in a taxi-cab with Orovida to see friends, he caught sight of pictures in a shop in King Charles the Second Street. He must get out and look at them, and the taxi-cab was stopped. The dealer, eccentrically dressed and adorned with much jewellery, was Jack Bilbo, the painter and sculptor. Flattered that his visitor was Lucien, he made a fuss of him, and showed him Picasso's *La Belle Hollandaise*, then in his possession, which Lucien admired. Bilbo called to his wife who came into the gallery and made a ceremonial pot of tea.

Sir William Rothenstein was invited to the private view of the exhibition, He wrote to Lucien: "*Far Oakridge, Stroud, Glos. 10.6.43.* My dear old friend, I wish I could see your exhibition, the work of three generations of your family—if I get a chance of coming up to town I shall give myself that pleasure. Your father has during recent years had the place given him which he has always shown to be his right, though the poetic side of his genius, which it is unfashionable today to recognise, places him, to my mind, above that of either Monet or Sisley. But what especially pleases me is the position you yourself have slowly won through your own beautiful paintings, long admired by myself, and by the resolute integrity with which you have pursued your quest throughout life as an artist. Do you remember coming to a little show at le Père Thomas of the first works of Conder and myself with your father, now fifty-two years ago!* Maybe not, but to me it was a memorable day when I had gentle words of encouragement from that great man and august painter. It must be a source of pride to you to have your daughter associated with parent and grandparent. I send you all my warm good wishes and am ever yours affectionately, William Rothenstein."

"Dear Rothenstein," Lucien replied, "I was greatly touched by your kind letter. I have been three years now buried in this tiny village far from any of my friends and living, so to speak, outside the art world. I can do little work now for the doctor makes me keep in when it is at all cold or windy, and we seem to get no really fine weather. Well I remember the day when I introduced my father to you in Paris. Yes, he was a charming old man and delighted to encourage all serious artists. I remember many occasions when he has helped artists, not to follow him but to find themselves, among the best known ones were Cézanne, Van Gogh and Gauguin. The immense influence he had on his time begins at last to be recognised. Well, my dear friend, I hope you will see our exhibition and that this frightful war will soon be over and that we may all meet at The Brook. Believe me always your sincere friend, Lucien Pissarro."

Lucien returned to Hewood from London cheerful and lively; and he began a new picture, his last. *The Yellow Farm, Hewood*, occupied him for three months. He had difficulties with it, but he grappled with them with patience. He deplored to Manson that he had to paint sitting, he had done so for some time, but could not get used to it. "It upsets me very much. I can't see the whole of my canvas and am obliged to work each part without seeing it in its relationship to the whole." "*Enfin on fait ce qu'on peut,*" his letter sadly concluded.

In September in a letter to John he wrote: "I must tell you of the success of our 'Three Generations of Pissarros'. For the first time in my long career we have had a success, which I didn't expect in wartime. Not only a *succés d'estime* but of money. The show brought us £1,876!!! If because of Hitler you hadn't lost all these years, you could have been with us and have made your name, and we could have

---

* Père Thomas had a small gallery in the rue Malesherbes. The exhibition referred to is of March, 1891, when Conder showed paintings, and Rothenstein pastels, mostly portraits.

gone on to form a group of some importance in this time of pictorial decadence. We must talk of this."

When winter came, his occupation gone, he relapsed, and became bored and apathetic. The weather was biting cold; it rained, and so he could not go out. He sat by the fire, isolated from conversation by his deafness and, now his vision was failing, and he found it difficult to read—his one solace was gone. Even his father's pictures on the walls were now blurred to his sight, but he knew these old friends so well that he did not need to see them. They were there and that was comfort. So he sat through the grey light of day and the lamp-lit evenings with his memories.

He enjoyed food, but it was impossible, with rationing restrictions, to give him the food he liked. He did not understand rationing and thought it unkind of Orovida, who cooked the meals, that the dishes set before him seemed always of a monotonous sameness. It was all Orovida could manage to provide for the small household. Hill Cottage was the last call of the butcher's round, Orovida had to take what was left. There was no choice. Often it was three chops in a fortnight for three people. The tails of the chops Orovida cut off and made into a stew, Lucien had the chops. Sometimes a chicken was killed and cooked, sometimes Retter, the farmer, shot a couple of rabbits and gave them to Orovida.

Some days before his eighty-first birthday he wrote, as always on this occasion, asking Manson to come. "Remember," he said, "I won't have many more opportunities to see my friends."

After John was called up for the Hitler war, he was rarely able to draw. On sending to Hewood a water-colour he had painted at York, his aunt (Esther) wrote gently: "Even your uncle works badly after a long pause." John spent part of three leaves at Hewood, his last sight of Lucien was his head and shoulders in tweed hat and overcoat, waving his thick stick in farewell as he watched him go down the hill to Chard Junction.

Spring and summer came, with Lucien's health slowly failing. The day before he died, Eardley Knollys, who represented the Society for the Preservation of Ancient Monuments in the west country, a collector of paintings, called, bringing a bottle of wine for him. The doctor that morning had warned Lucien not to attempt to climb the stairs and this had fussed him. Knollys offered to bring a carrying chair to get him up and down, but it arrived after Lucien had died. He died the next day, the 10th of July, Camille's birthday. For a while he had wavered between consciousness and oblivion, then had come a last whisper: "*A quoi bon!*"

Esther, Orovida and Mrs. Perrott were at his bedside. As soon as the villagers came to know he was dead, they called and showed great kindness, doing what they could. One went to make arrangements with an undertaker, another to the doctor. Mrs. Perrott and her sister washed Lucien and did those other services which are done for the dead. It rained throughout the day of the funeral. The only road to the cottage was by way of the farmyard, and it was said that if the hearse was allowed to pass through, a right of way would be established. So the coffin was carried out of the house, down the sloping, boggy common and across a marshy trickle at the bottom to the waiting hearse. When all was ready, the hearse began its melancholy journey, followed by a hired car in which sat Esther, Orovida and Mrs. Clark from Fishpond. Lucien was cremated at Weymouth, as he had desired. There were no flowers. Manson, with Elizabeth, had arrived at Weymouth the previous night, Manson ill, and Elizabeth not caring for him to make the long journey alone. Now they waited at a cottage, where they had been given shelter from the rain, opposite the chapel on the hill, for the hearse to arrive. Manson went out to meet Esther. He told her that Elizabeth was with him—she was at a window. Esther saw her and beckoned her to join them. "You must come into the chapel," she said. They had been at the same social functions, but this was the first time Esther had spoken to her.

There was no service. Atheist to the end, Lucien had wished it so. The living and dead were together in the silent chapel, the dead unseen in his wooden box, only from outside the drip, drip, drip, of the rain, soon, inside, a faint stir as the coffin slowly slid from sight.

Esther said Manson and Elizabeth must return with her to Hewood, and they could not refuse. There was no room for Manson in the hired car, so he sat with the driver on the hearse. When they came into the cottage, emotions were overstrained. Manson was near to crying, upset when Esther made him sit in Lucien's chair; it had a queer effect on him. He felt it was the last place where he should have sat. At the back door the butcher had left some kidneys. This upset Orovida; she exclaimed that Lucien had loved kidneys, but they had not had them for months, and why should they be left on this day of all days? Hardly knowing what she was doing she went out to the garden and picked a lily which she placed in an empty chianti bottle on the lintel of the boxed window near the urn containing Lucien's ashes. Someone made tea, a meal was prepared and eaten, and Esther found relief in a flood of talk. Meanwhile Elizabeth watched Manson's face become greyer and greyer. She and Manson slept that night in a room in the village, and the next morning they returned to London, Manson still overwhelmed by the shock of his friend's death and the funeral.

Esther and Orovida stayed on at the cottage until probate of the will was completed. John Rothenstein came to value the pictures on behalf of the Estate Duty Office. A postcard arrived from Rodo: he had heard of Lucien's death from the radio and had read an obituary notice in the newspaper *Paris-Soir*. Happily all was now well with him and Rodette. They were at Les Andelys, no trains or cars to Paris, but he managed to get there and had seen Veber, the bookseller, who had just bought for three hundred and fifty thousand francs "a curious album of drawings of political and social subjects, under each drawing a short text in Camille's handwriting, mostly extracts from Jean Grave's* paper. They are drawn in a manner so far from his usual way, that the experts in Paris thought they were forgeries. The cover is designed by Lucien in gold on brown paper. Paul's house has been entirely demolished by bombing: the S.S. ransacked and plundered all the village. He has lost everything."

When Esther returned to The Brook, the cantankerous landlady resumed possession of her cottage. Now believing she had entertained angels unaware, and that there were better paintings than her aunt's water-colours, she wrote she had so wanted to see Mr. Pissarro's pictures "that he did here, and I wondered if there was anything *small* that might be within my means of purchase?"

Esther found The Brook in a bad state, damp and unscrubbed, in need of soap, paint and repair. Soon the house echoed with the sound of hammering. Workmen came and went, plastering ceilings, painting and repapering, with Esther camping where she could in the prevailing muddle. But the confusion, the plans she made, the concentration on once more getting her beautiful house in order, did not free her from brooding. Lucien haunted her, she could not get over his death; the bottom had gone out of her world. When the workmen came no more her mind became set on perpetuating his memory. She organised memorial exhibitions, and so as to have material to show the work of the Eragny Press, she printed what was left of Lucien's black

---

* Friend of the Pissarros: both Camille and Lucien gave him drawings for his weekly, *Père Peinard*. He was an anarchist, "the sweetest old man possible" Orovida commented. "Incapable of hurting a fly."

and white engravings. Old Mr. Taylor, now seventy-six, Lucien's printer in early days, emerged from retirement and came to assist. Day after day the two worked together, Taylor recalling old times and looking forward with increasing excitement to the first Memorial Exhibition at the Leicester Galleries; it was to be a great day for him. He was expected there on the morning before the opening, but did not arrive. He had died on his way.

The first Memorial Exhibition at the Leicester Galleries was a success. Divided into two parts, one of Lucien's paintings, water-colours and drawings, the other of his wood engravings, drawings and books for the Eragny Press. They were held in January, 1946, and December, 1947, respectively. There was a further Exhibition at the same gallery in 1950, and the Arts Council sponsored a travelling exhibition of "Designs and Engravings for the Eragny Press". After Esther's death and in 1954 a further exhibition, "Three Generations of Pissarros" was staged at the O'Hana Galleries, where the work of Camille, Lucien, Manzana (Georges), Félix, Rodo, Paul Emile, Orovida and examples of the Eragny Press books were represented.

After the first Memorial Exhibition, Esther began to visualise The Brook as a State Museum, its walls hung with Camille's and Lucien's paintings, and with Lucien's books and engravings displayed in glass-covered show-cases. With this purpose in mind she commenced a catalogue of the collection. A young Turkish girl, Lulie Abul-Huda, studying at the Courtauld Institute, was allowed to choose this catalogue as her thesis for her doctorate, and for over a year was daily at The Brook to help Esther with its preparation. It was a fantastic time when housekeepers came and went, and meals were served as their whim dictated. Esther, in her strained and emotional state was not an easy mistress, her behaviour indeed was often eccentric. Fortunately Lulie Abul-Huda was of an equable temperament, and she and Esther got on well together. Lulie had a happy and calming influence on Esther. Finally Esther was convinced that The Brook was too small to display the pictures adequately. It was also pointed out to her that if she persisted with her intention of presenting all the pictures to the Nation, this would leave no provision for Orovida. That Orovida would have been left penniless did not seem to have occurred to her. She was now persuaded to divide the collection with Orovida. History repeated itself, and, as at Eragny, the pictures were drawn for by lot. After mother and daughter had returned to London, Orovida had rented rooms in Chelsea, at last free to resume her painting and live her own life. When she had possession of her share of the pictures, she sold some of the smaller and less valuable ones and, for the first time in her life, had money.

Esther presented her half of the collection to the University of Oxford Ashmolean Museum, where it is now housed in a special room. The gift represented the work of all the family; it has since been considerably added to by gifts from Orovida. Among these is a portrait of herself by Carel Weight.

Manson did not long survive Lucien. He died at Carlyle Studios, Chelsea, a week short of a year after his friend. On that morning of the 3rd July, 1945, he was painting a still life of roses. Elizabeth remonstrated: "I wish you would spend less time at that easel and rest." "The roses are dying and so am I," Manson replied.

In September, 1947, Esther went with John to the south of France. It was on this crossing that the Brook fount was thrown into the sea. A car was hired, and a hired *chauffeuse* drove them through Eragny on the way to Paris, where Esther made a round of visits to all the relatives, then visited Mlle Herchin in Chaumont, Mme Blanche Hoschedé at Giverny, Leboeuf in Pontoise, Mlle Moreau-Vauthier in Fontainebleau, Chantel Queenneville in Burgogne, went into ecstasy over the church at Tournus, and finally reached Toulon. Here, with the aid of Mme Nicholaeff, she went thoroughly into the affairs of the Campagne Orovida which she had in mind to sell. She saw a lawyer about the market gardeners who had taken possession of the grounds, interviewed those responsible for the supply of electricity and water, builders about repairs, Marie Agraz about the olives, went over the insurances, questioned the neighbours about a cable, and a *garagiste* about the car. Lizzie was still safe in the garage with all its narrow tyres unstolen throughout the war. She also found time for excursions to Bormes and Cotignac, John, now a little bewildered by this maze of activities, being left behind in Toulon to cope with difficulties arising there. When Esther returned, there was a dramatic interview with the committee of the *jardins ouvriers* in an underground café near the port. They consented to leave the Campagne Orovida on being forgiven their arrears of rent and on being allowed to take their crops, but not the olives. Esther's lawyer, who had hoped for protracted litigation, was taken aback when told of this and was somewhat shaky. Esther had suspected him of collaboration with the market gardeners, and he no doubt wondered what Esther had learnt.

Thus, Esther, after Lucien's death, had set herself innumerable tasks to complete, and now completed they were. There remained one last objective. She had a great longing to go to America and see her old friend, Ethel Voynich. Her doctor warned her of a possible stroke if she flew. She told Lulie Abul-Huda this and smiled as she said: "As if it matters when I die now." Nevertheless, she asked Orovida's opinion, and Orovida, well aware that once her mother had made up her mind to do anything she would do it, replied: "Do what you want to do." Esther went, accompanied by Mrs. Voynich's adopted daughter, Winifred Gay. In America she had an attack of paralysis. She recovered, but was not well enough to travel home by plane, and so she returned on the *Queen Elizabeth*. On board she became so desperately ill that the ship's doctor warned the captain that death could not be long delayed, and Winifred Gay was asked if she could give permission for Esther to be buried at sea. But Esther survived to reach London, where she was hurried to a nursing home; and here she fretted, craving to be home at The Brook. But she told Lulie: "It was worth it." To John, she said: "How Lucien would have loved the view of New York from the sea." "When she was allowed to return home," Orovida said, "she was happy to get back and more peaceful than I have ever known her." She was like that when, soon after, she died. She had kept Lucien's ashes in a box. Hers were now mixed with his and scattered in the garden of her beloved Brook.

Chelsea, 1959-1962.

Index

241

Index

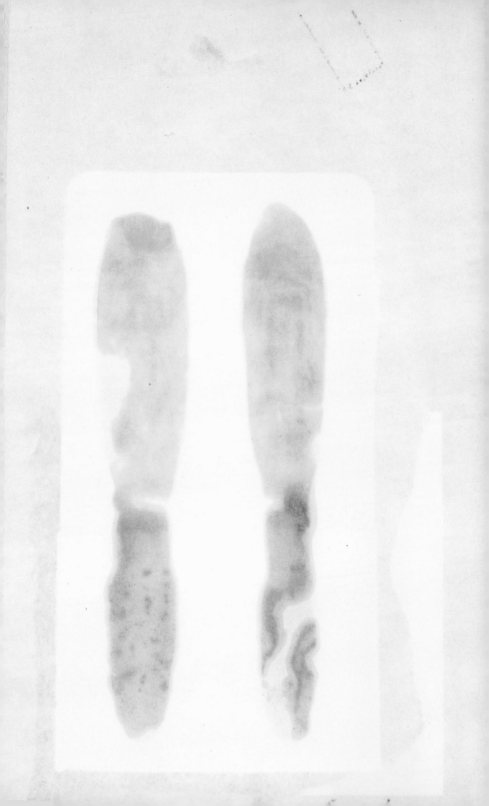

11/15/63

DATE DUE